Gilbert Parker

Round the Compass in Australia

Gilbert Parker

Round the Compass in Australia

ISBN/EAN: 9783337189112

Printed in Europe, USA, Canada, Australia, Japan

Cover: Foto ©Andreas Hilbeck / pixelio.de

More available books at **www.hansebooks.com**

SIR HENRY PARKES, K.C.M.G. [*Frontispiece*
From a Photo by J. H. Newman, Sydney, and engraved in the Studio of "Black and White."

ROUND THE COMPASS

IN AUSTRALIA.

BY

GILBERT PARKER.

LONDON:
HUTCHINSON AND CO.,
25, PATERNOSTER SQUARE.
1892.
[*All Rights Reserved.*]

I Dedicate

THIS BOOK OF TRAVEL AND INQUIRY

TO THOSE WHO WILL READ IT MOST AND THINK BEST OF IT—

TO MY FATHER AND MOTHER.

PREFACE.

THE first part of the book, including chapters I. to IX., appeared in *Harper's Weekly*. A considerable portion of the remainder first saw the light in the *Sydney Morning Herald*; and papers are included which were contributed to the *St. James's Gazette*, *The English Illustrated Magazine*, *Black and White*, and *The Illustrated London News*.—To the proprietors of these journals I am indebted for permission to republish. The first part of the book is a review of Australian affairs brought up to 1891; the second part is an account of my travels and inquiry not carried beyond the time of their occurrence, and a record of impressions received during the period between 1888 and 1891. The chapter on the granting of responsible government to Western Australia may appear to be superfluous, since the new constitution has been launched; but there is information in it which, I believe, is as important to a knowledge of the colony as when the question of the Enabling Bill was before the public. It is possible that this work may not be of less general interest because it is written by one who, through many years of residence, is familiar with the life and political conditions of the great sister colony, the Dominion of Canada. And Australia has been viewed from the standpoint of this knowledge.

G. P.

CONTENTS.

PART I.

CHAP.   PAGE

I. GLIMPSES OF AUSTRALIAN LIFE: THE PROLOGUE . . 3

    GLIMPSES OF AUSTRALIAN LIFE: IN TIME OF FLOOD . 17

III. GLIMPSES OF AUSTRALIAN LIFE: IN TIME OF DROUGHT 35

IV. RURAL AUSTRALIA 53

V. RURAL AUSTRALIA (*continued*) . . 64

VI. RURAL AUSTRALIA (*continued*) . . 76

VII. URBAN AUSTRALIA 98

VIII. URBAN AUSTRALIA (*continued*) . . 120

PART II.

VICTORIA, SOUTH AUSTRALIA, NEW SOUTH WALES, QUEENSLAND, WESTERN AUSTRALIA, AUSTRALIA ALL.

IX. MELBOURNE AND ADELAIDE IN 1888: THE CENTENNIAL EXHIBITION 147

X. SOUTH AUSTRALIA IN 1888: FOREST CONSERVATION . 187

XI. BROKEN HILL IN 1888 . . . 198

CONTENTS.

CHAP.		PAGE
XII.	QUEENSLAND IN 1889.—AT THE CAPITAL	213
XIII.	THE QUEENSLANDER AND HIS HERITAGE	225
XIV.	CAIRNS—THE BARRON FALLS—THE CAIRNS-HERBERTON RAILWAY	250
XV.	THE HINCHINBROOK CHANNEL—TOWNSVILLE—CHARTERS TOWERS	266
XVI.	MACKAY—ROCKHAMPTON—MOUNT MORGAN—MARYBOROUGH—GYMPIE	291
XVII.	THE RAILWAYS—THE PASTORAL INDUSTRY	332
XVIII.	WESTERN AUSTRALIA IN 1889-90.—THE VOYAGE TO ALBANY	345
XIX.	NORTHWARD FROM ALBANY TO PERTH	365
XX.	PERTH, THE CAPITAL—FREEMANTLE—MINERALS AND LANDS	382
XXI.	RESPONSIBLE GOVERNMENT IN 1889-90	405
XXII.	CONFEDERATION IN 1890 AND 1891	417
XXIII.	STRAY PAPERS: ART NOTES—FRONTIER LIFE	428
GLOSSARY		445

Proem.

The Empires of the golden-hearted South
   Rose, sun-swept, when the Earth was in its prime;
Theirs was the vigour of a splendid youth,
   A noontide of great deeds, a gift to Time:
Their poets caught the singing of the stars,—
   We hear the echoes in this later day,—
The chords were struck 'mid majesty of wars,
   And played the prelude to a long decay.

Their sun went down; the North arose to claim
   The heraldry of power, and there fell
The languor of past glory on the name
   Of all the South; and wrapped it in a spell:
Slow-footed, feeble, all her sons grew wan
   With looking backward, and they stretched their hands
Skyward; and so they waited for the dawn
   Of a new sun to shine upon her lands.

Long time they waited, and at last there came
   The crimson streaks; the morning's rosy palm
Was raised in benediction, and a flame
   Of swinging light shot over all the calm;
And then the Old South strove again to rise,
   To breathe full-breasted with her ancient might;
But through her striving came the sick surprise
   That all her strength had vanished in the night.

Yet, as one feels the tramp of armèd men
   Shake the quick world and stir the quiet air,
There came the march of puissance once again,—
   The New South rising with her forehead bare—
Her forehead bare to meet the smiling sun—
   Australia, in her radiant panoply;
And far-off kingdoms see her work begun,
   And her large hope has compassed every sea.

PART I.

CHAPTER I.

GLIMPSES OF AUSTRALIAN LIFE: THE PROLOGUE.

HOW shall one see Australia? That question has been answered often enough by men of culture, observation, and literary skill. But the point of outlook has been, in many cases, a metropolitan city and the cheerful comfort which a club-house affords: a dinner at Government House, if the traveller is well accredited; a run into the country for a couple of hundred miles; an excursion to the famous Gippsland Lakes and Big-tree Valleys; a picnic on the beautiful Hawkesbury River; a look at Broken Hill, perhaps; a glimpse of a sugar-plantation; a trip to the Jenolan Caves; the exploration of Sydney Harbour; and the thing is done. But it has been done on the arc of a circle. One cannot get into a railway train at some city on the eastern coast of Australia and cross the continent as one can in America, touching cities all the way; nor as in Canada, fringing prosperous towns. The population of Australia is massed on the eastern and south-eastern portion of the continent, and the concentration of wealth and commercial force is there. But the source of this wealth and force is not there, the influences really Australian, nor the special characteristics which may be recognised as peculiar to this southern continent. The general wealth has come chiefly from wool-growing. To mining is due a tremendous impetus to settlement, momentary expansions of trade, keenness in exploitation, and some special wealth. There has been taken out of Australia since mining began £73,000,000 worth of minerals, of which half was gold.

Mining was Australia's great advertisement, its radiation of attractiveness. It has proved its special blessing and its accidental curse. Wool-growing and cattle-raising are its staple and reliable resources. But lest what I sketch later may appear a contradiction to this, let it here be stated, that the reliability of the resources is attained by the process of average. One year is not the same as another on this continent, nor one three years the same as another three years. It is, therefore, six years, or five years, at least, on which estimation must be made. In the Land of the Golden Fleece loss and destruction and violent misfortune have success and bountifulness hard at their heels, and in the great average are overtaken by them. The source of the troubles that befall the Australian squatter and ranchman is an uncertain rainfall. So far as settlement goes, one-third of the country at least is a desert, a No Man's Land as yet, and sore perils come as encroachment on that desert proceeds. To see Australia, therefore, one must leave the spots where the clubs and comforts are, and go into the heart of this Greater Britain. It cannot be done in a day. What is written here is the result of nearly four years' travel and responsible inquiry in Australia, as the Special Commissioner of the *Sydney Morning Herald*, the *Times* of that country.

The best of Australia is in the east. The large rivers and the possible and profitable land are there—the land for the many. For there is little profit to a country in the depasturing of 150,000 sheep on 1000 square miles of land. Along 1500 miles of the west half of the southern coast of Australia there is but one harbour, and not one river flowing to the sea. There is no Mississippi, no Missouri, no Hudson, no St. Lawrence, nor any Lake Superior or Lake Michigan; and, far inland from the coast, there is no great watershed. The River Darling, seventy feet deep one year, is a stream on which a skiff could scarcely float the next. The Warrego, the Barcoo, the Mitchell, the Fitzroy, the Ashburton, and many others are of the same fashion. The centre of the continent should be a land of infinite promise, like the heart of the American continent. It is, however, a land of tested and perilous uncertainty. It is a basin, not a plateau, a vast and arid sponge which drinks up moisture at a marvellous rate, and still is thirsty. None of the rivers, save the Darling or Murray, drain any considerable extent of country. So far as the eye of the explorer could see there were no foundations for dominion. How empire is being wrung from nature, like Hercules wrestling with death, is history that is being written on the face of the land with scars and suffering—but written. In Western Australia, where Nature has put her minerals, she has sardonically refused water; where she has given land, pastoral and productive, she has cynically withheld rain; or as often as not, when sending it, has drowned the gaping country, and submerged the town that but yesterday was feverishly praying for moisture. The broad fringe of two-thirds of the continent is bountiful and blessed, though even on this blessed margin tropical floods occur, which overwhelm plantations, wreck villages, and destroy human lives. The casual traveller does not, as a rule, emphasise these things. Perhaps rightly, if he thinks it pleasanter to write praise than history, to speak truly but only of a hospitable and generally prosperous people, of national vigour, of sanguine effort, and of successful squatters and planters. He has been to a station homestead, but not a selector's cabin; he has sojourned at a plantation bungalow, but not in a kangaroo-hunter's humpey;* he has visited the barracks of the station hands, but he has not inquired how many of them had sunk their all in abandoned homestead leases and selections, nor how misfortune battened on them through losses by flood, and drought, and mines, and farming, and wool-growing on a small scale. He does not meet the gentleman kangaroo-hunting and rabbit-killing; he does not set down how many sheep were lost in the last drought, nor what ruin and desolation the rabbits have made; how cattle and sheep, reduced by millions to starvation-point, are kept alive by the leaves of the mulga and edible scrubs. The pictures that he could draw, having known and seen these things, might not be pleasant, but they would be true to the life.

"A wealthy Australian" is, in London, as usual a phrase as "A wealthy American." There are good reasons for this. Rich Australians make London their Mecca, as rich Americans do Paris. One seldom hears of a wealthy Canadian; yet Canada is older than Australia. The difference lies in the fact that Canada has risen from a base of agriculture; Australia from a base of mining, pastoral, and planting life. Canada has more homes, Australia more fortunes. The Canadian farmer, with his hundred acres and a score of cows, lives in comfort; the Australian selector often exists in danger.

---

* There is a glossary of words and phrases, chiefly Australian, at the end of this book. In the body of the text they appear without explanation or quotation marks.

English capital has flowed into Australian cattle runs and sheep-runs, and the banks have stretched antennæ (liable to contract now or hereafter) over parts of the interior.

These statements are broadly put. They have reference to the general lump, not to the special sections. Agriculture is not the plane on which Australian progress moves. It is incidental to the natural wealth, not a radical part of it. Australia has no Minnesota, no Manitoba, Ontario, or Montana. From her foundation of pastoral pursuits and mining, with plenty of capital expended, she has naturally had a powerful and successful development. But it must be remembered that the area from which her wealth has been drawn is a large one, and is occupied by only three millions of people. Her time of trial must come too; and that will be when, her best land taken up, and her coastal population crowding, she has to face the vicissitudes of her unworked and untempting country.

Let us stand now in the centre of Australia, and look forth as if our eyes could scan the continent from rim to rim.

We are at Mount Stuart, where the courageous explorer Stuart himself stood and looked into the unknown lands before him. We are facing the south; we are looking upon the great Australian Bight, where cliffs, six hundred feet high, "beetle o'er their bases to the sea." For a thousand miles along the Bight there is not a population of a thousand. The enthusiastic spectator might be tempted to exclaim upon the time when that vast coast-line should have a wall of masts to front it. But standing here in a waste that no man tills, nor will ever till or feed upon, here are the words of John Forrest,[*] another explorer, coming down an avenue of twenty years: "But

---

[*] Now Sir John Forrest.

for hundreds of miles along the shores of the Bight no vessel could reach or lie safely at anchor." And of the land between us and the Bight, the land where the spinifex waves like ripe corn under the hard monotonous azure, let him again speak : " On our route we passed over many millions of acres of grassy country, but, I am sorry to say, I believe entirely destitute of water." But that is half a generation ago. This is the remark of John Forrest, Commissioner of Lands in Western Australia in 1889 : " From my own observation, I may safely say that the greater portion of the Eastern Division is not likely to be utilised in the near future ; there are no rivers in the division." Again : " With the exception of a small fringe along the coast, the Eucla Division is unoccupied, and, unless water is conserved, must remain so." Yet these two districts represent 635,000 square miles.

Turn now, through this glamorous air, and look towards the west. There nestles a little, but proud capital, Perth, on the banks of the Swan River, one of those short streams found along portions of the Australian coast so often, and of such momentous value. We are 1500 miles from this western capital, and between us and it there lies at least 1300 miles of wanton waste and silence. There are no birds of song; no rippling streams ; no ranging fields of grain; few wandering herds ; sparse settlements of pioneers. In all that 900,000 square miles of country, known as Western Australia, there are but 45,000 people. Turn slowly towards the north-west. We are looking now upon a country tropical, yet not having all the characteristics of a tropical country—that is, superabundance of rain. It is a pastoral country, chiefly in a belt of 150 miles or so. A little further still, and there is the Kimberley pastoral district and the Kimberley goldfields, where an earnest Government is trying, with artesian bore, to induce Nature to render up the fulness of her fountains. But water is hard to get in Western Australia.

Still turn, until you are half way round a circle, and are looking directly north to Port Darwin, just as if, standing in the heart of Kansas, you had begun with the Gulf of Mexico, and turned slowly round to San Diego, to San Francisco, to Portland, to Helena, to Grand Forks. In that half-circle you have seen "the Arizona desert"; but you have seen, outside of it, a watered land, with great rivers, vast mountains, and deep valleys. Through every part of it man, the pioneer, can venture and reap reward. But, standing on Mount Stuart, what do you see? What have you seen? Here is a railway at your feet being driven across the continent from Adelaide to Port Darwin; a railway running through a lonely silent land, with good country at each terminus only. But there are, between you and the sea-wall which makes the bounds of that half-circle to your eye, weary oceans of spinifex desert; endless ridges of scorching sand-hills; desolating expansions of mallee scrub; long samphire flats; chains of salt lakes and thirsty clay-pans; mulga forests; acacia thickets; quartz plains; deceiving water-holes; alkali marshes; solitary hills, rising like islands from a grey and changeless sea; sandstone bluffs and copper cliffs which project in burning menace; and only one indifferent range of mountains which, rising nowhere beyond 4000 feet, is the source of but few rivers. Scores of streams in Australia rise in a lonely plain, no mountain near, and wandering on for a hundred miles perhaps, suddenly sink again into some vast subterranean river or sea; for no heat could so absorb the quantity of water which is drunk up as it flows uncertainly over these plains.

With our faces turned to the west, we see a land of no mountains. The plains in this arid centre are lower than the level of the sea. We have looked upon the scene of the sufferings of the heroic and undying explorer, Eyre; of the devoted Warburton, and of the stalwart and noble Forrest. We have seen the field of the labours of Flinders, Grey, the Gregorys, Gosse, and Giles. And the voice of History from the rugged coast-line says: "It is the country Dirk Hartog discovered in the time of Mary of England, and called 'Land d'Endracht'; the shore that Edel touched in 1619, and called 'Land of Edel'; the territory Viaven visited in 1628, to which he gave the name 'De Witt's Land'; the 'vast and wandering grave' of Pelsart's mutineers of 1629; the scene of Tasman's explorations; a region which Dampier the buccaneer hailed; one of the points in Vancouver's compass; where D'Entrecasteaux raised the standard of his native land: and yet since the fifteenth century there are only 45,000 people here. Here is food for curiosity. Has not, however, the explanation been more than hinted at, after all? . . ." Yet this region is not all barren. On the coast and along these short rivers, there is fine squatting country, and some good agricultural land; and there are minerals also, if they can but be reached and developed. There are men making money too on the coast; but what are a handful of people in that vast region? Even in this tenantless waste on which we have looked there are great stretches of grassy plains and fine areas for sheep and cattle. But turn the medal over and read what is thereon: "No Thoroughfare!" And "No Thoroughfare" means "No water." Here, where millions of sheep might feed, a mighty ban is laid. Stretch out your hand. This is a hot day on Mount Stuart. See the specks of moisture in your palm. That is the proportion of water to this half—this more than

From Harper's Weekly.—Copyright, 1891 by Harper & Brothers.

A Camel Train—The Interior.

half—of the Australian continent. We are dealing with facts now, not with pretty dreams of politicians about "wondrous possibilities," and "unexplored vistas for settlement." For this country which we see has been crossed and recrossed east and west, and north and south, and under what grim trials, and with what unchanging conclusions they of Western Australia at least know. And the rest may learn.

But we have only completed half the circle. We have seen that the course of empire is not always westward. The nomenclature is an evidence of that. Coffin Bay, Anxious Bay, Denial Bay, Cape Arid, Mount Barren, Mount Despair, Doubtful Island—these are the ominous signs that greet us as we note the scene. It is not so in America. Explorers of all that continent breathed an atmosphere of hope, of confidence, of achievement, of prophecy. But see the explorers of Australia: Leichardt, the gallant, the for ever lost like Franklin; Burke and Wills; the unhappy Kennedy; the shattered Stuart; the noble and unfortunate Sturt; the fated Grey; the desperate and long-abandoned Eyre; the heroic Forrest; the disappointed Lindsay. Have their predictions, generally speaking, ever been discounted? They walked through suffering to death all too often; they looked out upon a melancholy horizon; they could not feel the joy of the gallant Champlain, the brave Marquette, the dauntless Joliette, and the resistless La Salle.

But let us now inspect the other half-circle. It is the better half, else the case of Australia would be hard indeed. In it are all the great cities—Adelaide, Melbourne, Sydney, Brisbane; in it is nineteen-twentieths of the population. America was settled first largely on the east, and the march of progress was westward through and to a country of rare possibilities. But that would have been natural under any circumstances, inasmuch as the Atlantic coast was so much nearer the great populations of Europe. Holding to this principle, Western Australia should have been expanded first, since it lies nearer to England by three thousand miles than does New South Wales. Western Australia, from the day that real settlement began in the east, has had directed towards it a great deal of energy and capital. But there she lies with 45,000 people and 1,000,000 square miles of land, of which only 173,000 square miles are under lease for agricultural or pastoral purposes. The fault lies not in its star, but in itself, that it is in such condition. But the view is fairer as we veer round this other and better half, beginning at Port Darwin. Flowing into the Gulf of Carpentaria are longer, deeper, and more frequent rivers than we have seen heretofore. They are not rivers as Europeans and Americans know them, but streams of varying permanency and *débouchement*. And turned to this northeast, we are viewing a colony of striking commercial possibilities. Queensland, like another United States, has within it two fine belts of resources. Gold and silver, timber, pastoral products, sugar, rice, cotton, tobacco, and all tropical fruits are in its northern part; and coal and gold, pastoral land, wheat land, and the agricultural products of the temperate zone in its southern part. The heart of the southern half of Queensland is a high tableland, unlike any other portion of Australia, and one sees millions of sheep grazing upon the famous Darling and Fitzroy Downs—downs, indeed, stretching in waving undulations to that portion of its western and southern border, where its pastoral excellence is merged into the invading barrenness of western New South Wales. But look far out to sea at the east. A long beautiful line of white foam meets the eye. That is the Barrier Reef whose coral bulwarks range the ocean for a thousand miles parallel with the coast. Inside it is one long harbour of peace, one stretch of summer beauty in mountain, valley, and tropical jungle. Out at sea even the mangrove swamp, with its deadly damp, looks cool and beautiful. But greater than the beauty of the colony is its wealth. We are seeing a plane of action 700,000 miles square, and having 400,000 inhabitants, all of whom are working pioneers. The colony began about the same time as Western Australia, but now, besides its sugar plantations and its mineral wealth, it has 13,000,000 sheep, 5,000,000 horses and cattle; and since 1859 there has been taken out of Queensland gold to the value of £21,310,947.

Let us pass on. Turned towards the south-east we see the parent colony of New South Wales, begun by those who laboured at the mouth of guns, and who were always spoken of by those they left behind in the Old Land as having "gone to Botany Bay." But from that beginning there rises a structure of prosperous commercial proportions; a social and national dignity which is only accounted for by the immigration of free, upright, and industrious pioneers. Sydney lies there, with its 360,000 inhabitants, set on the margin of a renowned shore and harbour. Between us and its centralised forces, its fine architecture, and its progress, there stretch ranges of desolation, weariness, and unprofitableness. But again, between this trinity of misfortune and the city is a land of plenty too; a land from which over 225,000,000 pounds of wool were exported in 1890. The River Darling, which drags its tortuous mud-banked length along, the third longest river in the world, is the boundary line of prosperity. Between Mount Stuart, where we stand, and it the earth dips. Still farther south, though, let us look, and there we shall see Mount Kosciusko, with its white head 7,000 feet up in the changeless blue,—Australia's one mountain of prominence. There in the south also we see Victoria, the most compact, the smallest, and the most active, in proportion to its size, of the colonies or states of Australia. Agriculture, pastoral pursuits, mines, and manufacture—these are the sources of Victoria's wealth. And the city of Melbourne, lying on the shores of Port Phillip, with its 360,000 inhabitants, is Sydney's august rival.

About five degrees to east of south of our vantage-ground lies Adelaide, at the foot of Mount Lofty, hot, cleanly, prettily built, and instinct with metropolitan life.

Now we have completed the circle, and from a dreary centre looked out upon a continent of three millions of square miles, where the Anglo-Saxon is working westward towards his Golden Gate, and northwards towards the sun-line. The reader should now be ready to interpret, with a sense of proportion and conception of broad conditions, the scenario of Australian life, which I shall briefly sketch hereafter.

CHAPTER II.

GLIMPSES OF AUSTRALIAN LIFE: IN TIME OF FLOOD.

A FEW months ago word came across the sea that the town of Bourke, among others in Australia, was under water, and that lives and property were being destroyed at war-time rate. On the North Queensland coast, where it rains twelve feet in a year, and sometimes two feet in a day, the flood records are frequent. Plantations float under water, and sheep and cattle are caught in a wide death-trap. On the River Darling, and in the south generally, the floods are not so frequent. When, five years ago, I set out to pierce the heart of the country, and see the stuff of which Australia was made, Bourke was my first objective point. To it one could get by rail. First we cross the Blue Mountains by the famous Zig-Zag, from which, 3,000 feet up, one looks out upon the Nepean valley, sun-swept, green, and luxurious; a region of orange orchards and agriculture. Then we descend upon a tableland, passing such typical Australian towns as Bathurst, and again down, until a plain is reached where the far interior is seen at its best. This had been a flood-year, and the country should be blooming, buoyant. But through long vistas of ring-barked gum-trees we pass; through a brown and silent land, broken only by the sight of towns like Byrock, where corrugated iron, canvas, and iron-bark compose the architecture. This is the first touch of the sadness of Australian scenery; and it was kept up through hot and lengthy hours of travel, broken by a stop at some village or township, sitting gloomily in its red dust. A mounted policeman, a black tracker, a settler on his horse, a shearer knocking down his cheque, or a squatter in his trap, would occasionally give a little life to the scene, but the prevailing feeling was one of melancholy. Yet over this gloomy area hundreds of thousands of sheep were depasturing and doing well.

I had been travelling with a Royal Commission whose duty it was to make inquiry into the question of Water Conservation. It was my good fortune to receive an invitation to travel in their company, since I was going in their direction. Because of this I altered my plans somewhat, and determined to follow where they led. The Royal Commissioners, Mr. J. B. Donkin and Mr. F. B. Gipps, the secretary, two reporters, a photographer, and myself, constituted the party; and we seven looked out upon Bourke, one Sunday evening, as it rose from the scrubby plain, and eyed apprehensively the River Darling, which was aflood, and also debating whether to rise four inches more and cover the streets. Had it done so, portions of Bourke would have been floating down towards the Barrier Ranges, as they did the other day. There would be little use in banking, because the surrounding country is flat, and if the river over-topped its banks at all, there could be no salvation for the town. Fortunately the stream decided otherwise, and its feeder, the Warrego, also stopped its outflow in time. But the journey of The Seven is not begun. They have not done with flood. They embark in a little paddle-wheel steamer called the *Florence Annie*, and a journey of three weeks down the River Darling, towards Adelaide, begins. The *Florence Annie* was a paddle-wheel craft, such as did duty in the early days on the Mississippi ; and she had just such a task before her as the Mississippi steamers. It is no labour of ease to navigate the River Darling, which winds its devious way for 2,000 miles. 'A few miles below Bourke the Darling was no longer the Darling, but the Nile, flooding the country for miles on either side. The channel wound between lines of ragged, gnarled, and almost shadeless gum-trees. It was the custom for the *Florence Annie* to tie up every night, and, if near a station, The Seven would repair to study water conservation and land conditions by taking evidence from the squatters ; and, during the day, it was also the habit to stop at every station with the same end in view. A man with half his sheep-run under flood should be able to speak to some purpose on the conservation of water. His house was banked up to keep back the muddy invading river ; his record may have been 25,000 sheep lost. And yet in two years more his record might be 60,000 lost by drought. Seldom has traveller had such opportunity of studying a country as that afforded the unofficial one of The Seven, who listened for hours daily or nightly to the tale of the squatter and the selector. And when he wearied of the monotonous sameness of the evidence, the plaints against hard land conditions, treacherous climate, and the everlasting iteration, " This country is in the hands of the banks," he would wander out in the silent night to scan a scene of strange pathos. Under a soft and ample moon lay far wastes of water, out of which a ragged forest grew fantastic, ghostly. Taking the boat that trailed after the *Florence Annie*, he would row away into the forest, regardless of river channel, careful only that he had his bearings. A long-necked crane peering out from its place of resort; a pelican with moaning sound beating its way down the river; the whir of wild duck flying upon the flood that had covered their haunts of marsh mallow and reeds; the shrill cry of a cockatoo as it angrily resented the violation of its peace; the languorous sighing of the current; the thud of a platypus: and that was all. No, not all. There, sweeps a selector's home adown the waste; there, floats his waggon; and there, his implements of cultivation; and here, just at your right, a tangle of horns tells of life destroyed. Many a settler has waked up to find his hut a swaying wreck, so sudden has the devastation come,—and without a drop of rain. Rain five hundred miles above him has sent this wide wave; and lucky is it for him and all that are his if they escape with their lives. Sometimes they do not achieve that, and then the scene becomes indeed "a waste of water weltering over graves."

Any one who had seen this could understand better Heffner's picture, *Desolation*, a flood of endless vista washing the feet of the Colossi; and, over all, a glowing amber tone. But this is Australia, and not Egypt; and this is a new country, not an old one. Yet, sitting alone in this groundless grassless forest, he who watches the scene might fancy the Genius of the Land exclaiming upon its deformity:

"Sent before my time
Into this breathing world, scarce half made up."

. . . . Then to return to the *Florence Annie*, and watch from her little deck the lights on shore, the panting machinery in the wool-shed, and the rouseabouts and hands packing the wool, that it might be got down the river while yet it was aflood—this was the custom many a night. But the feeling of it all is hard to put upon paper.

Yet there were days when this region seemed to rejoice exceedingly. The Seven saw occasionally flood and wreckage give place to broad plains carpeted with the gayest flowers, velvety and abundant. Flocks of wild turkeys fed in the grass; masses of wild ducks tempted the rifle from the bow of the *Florence Annie*; congregations of bright-plumaged parrots and cockatoos quarrelled in the trees; those stately birds, the native companions, performed their gay quadrilles upon the flowery track; and an occasional troop of kangaroos galloped from us, tail and hind-legs at work, horizonwards. And not the least interesting thing was the dance of the native companions. They deliberately and with regular form go through a kind of quadrille, or Circassian circle, in a manner that suggests a different origin for man than the ape.

Sometimes the *Florence Annie* would consider it wise policy to leave the regular channel of the Darling, and cut across country to save a horseshoe-bend; and once she did it to get out of the way of a steamer, whose name I have forgotten, but I shall call it the *Eliza Jane*. The history of the *Eliza Jane* was peculiar. Before we left Bourke the proprietor of the hotel said: "You'll very likely meet the *Eliza Jane* coming up the river. I sent by her to Adelaide for a load of lumber three years ago, and she is just bringing it up now. She went down all right, but the river went dry on her way back, and she had to stop short. So the captain turned her nose into the bank, tied her up, and they ran her as a saw-mill for three years." And this historic and adaptable boat we met on our journey. So certain was it of its right of way that it seemed anxious to interfere with the bows of our craft. It was the habit afterwards among The Seven to say that the officers of the *Eliza Jane* had been indulging in Shearer's Joy; but of that I am not certain. The nervous affidavit of the captain of the *Florence Annie* could not be sufficient warrant. He was prejudiced. But the tale of the *Eliza Jane* does not end here. When, with a Damascian sarcasm, our captain asked the other captain what was the matter with him and his floating coffin, he was coarsely bade to wait until he got to Grath. Grath is not the real name of the place, but it protects the inhabitants. We arrived there the following day. The hotel-keeper, the children, and Lukes, a squatter, called the King of Grath, were sober. From the hotel-keeper we learned that Lukes, the King, had sent to Adelaide three years before by the *Eliza Jane* for a granite monument, that Grath should have a piece of architecture, —of which indeed it seemed sorely in need,—and that his two "dear departed wives" might have some visible token of respect to their sacred memory. But we know what chanced to the *Eliza Jane*, and while the people of Grath waited for the monument, which was to be accompanied by a function, the drought went on. Lukes the King married again. But the marriage baked meats were hardly cold when the floods came, and with it the *Eliza Jane* and the monument. Lukes was not dismayed. He had the function. The third wife declared the stone well and truly laid, and in the evening a banquet was held, at which the King toasted "the dear departed" in florid eloquence, coupling with the toast the name of his third wife. And thus Grath got its architecture, and, as Lukes put it, "the bygone partners of his bosom could now rest in pride beneath the sands of Grath." Grotesque as this is, it is true.

It was Lukes who led me to ask, with him, a question which involves a tale of what is grimly grotesque in Australian existence. It is given here, because, more than pages of general description, it suggests life in the back-blocks. And here I ask: Where are those five shillings?

Early in the Eighties a traveller lost his way in the great scrub land beyond the Dunlop Range. He could find no water; he could find no station. Perhaps he wandered round and round a circle, ever coming back with the weird fatality of lost travellers to the same spot again,—returning to his fate, like a murderer to the place of his crime. Far and wide stretched a stricken land. The glare of a hard and pitiless sky overhead, the infinite vista of salt-bush, brigalow, stay-a-while, and mulga, the creeks only stretches of stone, and no shelter from the shadeless gums—these only meeting his eye, his brain reeled to the verge of madness, and to keep starvation back a day, and to quench his thirst, he killed his dying horse and drank its blood. That night, as the sun was setting over the grey bastions of mallee-scrub, a boundary-rider found him. But it was too late; now he was cold, never again to be warm in a land of a thousand furnaces. In his pockets were five shillings. The boundary-rider took them, and at the township to which he was going he gave the five shillings to a sundowner (for bushmen are superstitious, and he would not keep the money or spend it). The sundowner was found on the plains months after, dead, in a clump of yellow wattles, and on him were those five shillings. The two stock-riders that found him came to Grath, passed through it on foot, and struck off to a station where they were to work. They too were found, one hanging to an ironbark tree, the other dead beneath. The man who found them was a rouseabout for Lukes the King of Grath. He became possessed of the five shillings. Lukes advised him to throw them into the river; but he was a new hand, he had no superstitions, and he went off next morning to carry a message to the back-station twenty miles away. But before he got there the floods came and covered the land, and he was never seen again, nor any trace of him. He might be lost for generations in a country where one man leases a thousand square miles of land, and has but one sheep to ten acres. . . . Where are those five shillings?

It is a comedy of peoples. The Darling flows moodily on to the far-off coast in the sensuous gloom of the evening. On its either side fires are flickering in the jarrah and myall trees, and disturbed cockatoos are flitting across the night. Figures pass and repass through the brighter glare of one side; a barge is drawn close into the shade of the trees, and from an open door, where the light is brightest, there comes the sound of machinery. We draw nearer, and see the hydrostatic presses working upon the wool; the busy workmen sewing up sacks, and others bearing them down to the waiting barge. Day and night they are labouring that the plenitude of this fortunate year may come to the getter of wool. The hammer of the commercial Thor beats here, the pulse of success palpitates. In the game with nature man has won this season. The shearers have "knocked off"; they will not work at night; they must preserve the dignity of labour, the renown of the Shearers' Union. The long shearing-shed is empty, where all day three score of shearers have shorn at the rate of a pound a hundred, and where many have earned their pound. They are to be found now in the barracks, where, through the lurid glare of the slush-lamps, there comes the sound of a knuckle struck on a table, and a voice saying, "Count two;" "A royal flush;" "I'll trust to the ace;" "The game!"

From Harper's Weekly.   Copyright, 1891, by Harper & Brothers.

THE ABORIGINAL.

This is life half Arcadian, half barbaric; a touch of Perdita, and more than a touch of Sechet. On this side of the river is the wave of Anglo-Saxon progress that everywhere swells against "the high shores of this world."

But over the river—what of those flickering fires? Let us cross. . . . We are in a land measurelessly far from that in which we stood a moment before. Aboriginal Australia holds here its sorry court. This remnant of a once powerful tribe sit outside their gunyahs, and cower over their handfuls of fire, imperturbable and awfully alone. Once its warriors were the slayers of the white men; once they hurled the spear and the axe, and fought hand to hand with the nulla-nulla, and whirled the demoniacal boomerang. They are victims of a policy of Reprisal; of an unwritten word which went forth from high places: "Disperse the aboriginal." Like dogs they fell everywhere; like dogs and jaguars, as many of the tribes were. To creep on the shepherd or bushman, and drive a spear through his body; to drag him away; to celebrate the hateful thing by a fiercely dramatic scene in which the bloody deed was acted over again with a hideous mirth; to eat the victim, and then to close with a wild corrobboree—this was the life. But it was not altogether the life of these southern tribes, though they suffered with the rest. Destruction came upon the men, and destruction and worse upon the women, and here they are.... "Well, mate, how are you?" said the traveller to a grey-beard.

"Me no mate, me Major," he muttered, poking his fire and not looking up.

"Well, Major, can't we have a corrobboree?"

"No corrobboree; blackfellow gone dead, along-a big God up there. Blackfellow jump up white fellow, long-a God."

"Where is your tucker, Major?"

"O my word, no tucker; fill up bingey all along-a tea!"

"Do you like rum, countryman?"

"Rum, my word! Baal that fellow blackfellow,"

pointing to a motionless figure by a wurley, "fill up bingey long-a rum. That fellow white fellow make blackfellow hell. No more spear, no more boomerang. Come from Albury sit down here, long-a yisteday. Blackfellow gone, my word!" And so he maundered on, and drank his billy of tea with a great content, pausing between the gulps to mutter: "Fill up this fellow blackfellow all along-a tea! No tucker. O my word!"

Beside another handful of fire—they make their fires small so that they can get close to them—sat two old crones, one smoking and caressing her pipe, the other blind and decrepit, throwing bits of leaves upon the fire, her chin between her knees.

"Well, Lubra, where are all the blackfellows?"

"Nobody—nobody; all gone—no tucker—nobody."

"Would you like some tobacco, Lubra?"

The blind hag held out her shrivelled hand, and fondled the bit given as though it were some talisman; then reached over for the hand of her companion, and putting the tobacco into it, turned again to the fire, shaking her grizzled head slowly, and began again gathering leaves and bits of twigs. And rocking to and fro, they gathered their tattered skirts about their emaciated bodies, and wiped their sunken and watery eyes in the half-darkness, and were silent. Near by, another old wayfarer, in a single loose gown, was hanging tattered clothes on the gunyahs in an aimless kind of way, and a young and stalwart fellow was weaving a semicircular wall of sandal twigs, in which were stuck his boomerang and his spear. He would not speak to us. We turned and asked the old fellow who had chatted to us why the other was so silent. "That fellow, blackfellow's lubra gone along-a river a-white fellow." . . . The same bitter story of all conquered and conquering peoples. . . . We left them there with their misery, but not till we had given them some tucker. And one in an undertone said, as he stepped into the punt, "God help them!" And perhaps He did: if not here, then in the great Hereafter.

We found another aboriginal camp after two more weeks of journeying down the river. But during one week's journey between, we had seen King Jemmy of Mara and Queen Polly under the hands of the photographer. King Jemmy and his tribe were in mourning for some of their people. About their heads were twisted white cloths, and some had filled their hair with lime or flour, to express the intensity of their grief. But this new scene before us suggests nothing of the gloomy thought that comes with a view of a fading people, upon whose lands another race have made distraint.

At Ned's Corner, on a point of land where the myall and willows were swaying, an aboriginal camp was set; —low bush houses of woven twigs and bark, with spears and boomerangs stuck here and there in the sides. Fires were burning, on which the Murray cod lay stretched and hissing, while the flesh quivered with the life not yet extinct. Naked, and not ashamed, the old men, grey-bearded and eyes bright, watched the cooking of the fish, and the younger, with the lubras, did the honours of reception. One never saw a more dignified, leonine figure than William, as he moved about with swaying stride, emphasising his great good-humour by long two-octave chuckles, and winding up with the ever-present "O my word!" The photographer had nothing to suggest when it came to posing. The old men drew blankets round their shoulders, William arrayed himself in garments, that they should not be thought out of the fashion when posterity should gaze upon their counterfeit presentiment; and without a word of suggestion these natives arranged themselves in a group, the grace and unique character of which a skilful artist only could show.   And William with spear in hand upon a log, and with eyes upon an imaginary fish, said : " This fellow blackfellow all right."

The *Florence Annie* carries The Seven from Grath still down the river to Wilcannia, from whence we were to go across country to Menindie on the same river, and embark again on another steamer. After my experience of the *Florence Annie* I was willing to place faith in the accuracy of Mark Twain's description of the early steamship days of the Mississippi. Part of the time she had a barge of wool towing after her, and, with a slack rope, it would come gliding down after us. When she made up her mind to visit a station-homestead, as would occur at least once a day, she would swerve to the right or left, and let the barge float into a fork made by the gum-trees; then she would lunge round, and churn herself into the snuggest spot in the bank, with imminent peril to her smoke-stack and pilot-house. Sometimes she would be fractious, and break a chain or rub a limb down with her shoulders ; and again she would become sulky, and stick on a sand-bar for an hour. The captain would let her wheeze and slash the water for a while, then he would run the wheel round a few times ; a couple of sailors, aided by the advice of The Seven, would poke the sand with their sticks, and she would give a snort, and start off again like a French pony. After a while the captain had so coaxed her and petted her, that she grew as obedient and domestic as a kitten. She had on board a dry-goods shop, a fruit stand, a grocery store—an emporium, in fact ; and the owner of the boat, in the interludes of psalms and somnolence, parted with his homely wares for an equivalent in mutton or money, whenever the flag of necessity was hoisted.

It is high noon at Wilcannia. A yellow haze stretches away to the burnished horizon, and on the plains clouds of dust rise, telling of sheep on the march. Making towards the River Darling is a herd of nine hundred cattle. They have come a thousand miles over the plains from Thargomindah and beyond in Queensland. They must cross the river. As the unofficial one of the party rides near, he finds them rounded up a mile from the river. The cattle seemed to know that a stranger was at hand, and began to stamp impatiently. One broke out of the bunch, and came over to inspect the alien. Others moved wildly, and threatened a stampede. But at that moment the horses were sent ahead to lead the cattle to the river, and on they all go. But on the very banks of the stream they begin to ring. There is danger in this. Should they ring in the river hundreds will be drowned. Round and round they go in a painful centripetal motion, a wheel of horns upon a heaving base of brown and red and grey. But the stock-riders force their horses in, and break the ring, with many a sharp call and snap of whip and sudden expletive. Then into the river the cattle plunge, following the horses, first with a tremor and snort of fear, and then with a rush. It was a forest of horns, where shaggy manes tumbled and tossed in the swift current; a *mêlée* of floating heads, warring and wrangling. The current at first carries them down. Then they begin to ring again. The spectator is thrilled by the struggle. The stock-riders thrust in, and the stock-whip cuts the air like a knife. Some steers floated down, but struck out bravely, and were caught in the trees on the bank, where

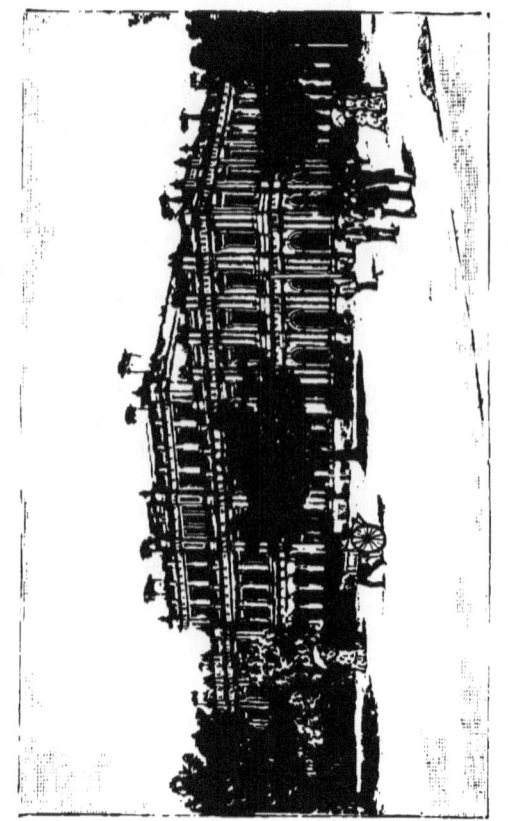

New Government Offices, Adelaide.

they were held fast, for the water was flowing among
the branches of the gums. A forlorn hope at last made
straight after the horses for the shore. They ranged
into line; they swam shoulder to shoulder; their heads
became motionless; they put forth their utmost strength;
they reached the solid ground. And after that, in
phalanxes, the herd fought its way across, and the great
feat of the long travel was over. The Darling was
crossed, and with only a half-dozen cattle lost.

"Thus far into the bowels of the land
Have we marched on without impediment,"

said a lithe-limbed stock-rider, bearded like a pard, as
he lit his pipe—the bushman's only friend. And this
was once a fellow of St. John's, Cambridge. Such are
the fortunes of the gentle as the rude. And there,
beside a clump of sandal trees, they cooked their chops,
and made their damper, and drank their quart-pot tea,
and the world went very well then, whatever its errant
course had been.

At Wilcannia we left the *Florence Annie*, and started
on a journey across the plains towards Menindie. The
plains were gleaming with the Sturt pea—a flaming
plant which, it is said, drives horses and cattle mad.
The Unofficial One sat beside Morrison, the driver, as
we fought our way through dust-storms, or tempted the
depths of some short-lived watercourse. And many an
hour was whiled away in listening to tales of adventure,
of enterprise, and of disaster. A rail-girt grave would
call up an incident; a deserted homestead would bring
out a life-story; a wandering sundowner would suggest
"a chap out here five years ago," and his curious per-
sonality and history. Sometimes an emu crossed our
track, and the three rifles of the party would attempt
to ruffle his feathers; for that indeed was the most that

3

occurred in shooting emus. They were either iron-clad, or the sportsmen were inaccurate. Yet one of these sportsmen was a champion sharpshooter. They were more successful with wild ducks. Perhaps necessity made them more precise, for we had no food, and it was uncertain whether we should make Menindie at all, so desperate was the condition of the roads. On the banks of a lake we cooked and ate our ducks, and plunged again into the night—the Southern Cross dimly glowing, Sirius quivering far above us, and the cry of the laughing-jackass in our ears.

And from Menindie to Adelaide and the sea, and from the sea to Sydney again, we heard a long *Thank God!* for the flood which had come and enriched the land, so that thousands were saved from ruin. The squatters would have two good years, and that would give many of them, who were but as bailiffs for the banks, a chance to get on their feet again. Here and there loss would be occasioned by the flood, but the country would be a paradise for cattle for two seasons, the wool could be got to the coast, and the hearts of the people, as the land itself, would be refreshed.

CHAPTER III.

GLIMPSES OF AUSTRALIAN LIFE: IN TIME OF DROUGHT.

THREE years have gone since The Seven made their journey into this, the Darling country. The curtain again rises. The Unofficial One has now grown more or less official, and on his shoulders are responsibilities. He is to inquire and make record of conditions, which the dwellers in the spaces of long drought declare are growing past endurance. He is to try and see how the land laws are pressing on the protesting people; to draw a picture of the land, that legislators and the people may see, and, it was hoped, be wiser for the seeing. And once again into this country, over which he took you for three thousand miles in the last chapter, he plunged again, but by a different route. This time he went from Adelaide north-east on the path of the explorers, visiting Broken Hill on his way. There was no Broken Hill three years before, so far as the great world knew. Now from vast smelters the glowing slag was pouring down the hillside; in a region of desolation men were becoming rich, and all Australia was marking the smallest fluctuation in Broken Hill shares. From this jagged wall, beneath which a dull red plain stretches away to an unpeopled horizon, let us set forth. Good fortune now be thanked. Here is Hanna, a brave pioneer, who travelled with The Seven hundreds of miles, three years ago, on the box-seat again. What a host of memories a clasp of his hand brings up! Trollope of Wentworth (son of Anthony Trollope), Quin of Tarella, the Kennedys of Nuntherungie and Wonnaminta, Brougham of Netalie, Dickens of Wilcannia (son of Charles Dickens), and a host of others,—hearty, courageous, and enduring.

No longer are rain and flood bringing gladness and destruction all at once. The demon Drought has laid his angry palm upon the land, and it has shrivelled up.

It is midnight. We have travelled a long day over an agonised plain. "We" are the driver, my friend Hanna the Superintendent of Roads, a woman with a patient baby at the breast, a policeman, and two prisoners. Through two hundred miles of desert, without sleep, this mother held the child with weary arms,—no, not all the time, for the Superintendent had a heart and gentle arms. But at midnight we are come to Burke's Cave, an historic spot —sadly historic. For here began the bitter fate which dragged the valiant Burke and the faithful Wills to lonely graves, and gathered down a fruitful expedition to a tragic end. Cold and hungry, we stand at the door of the humble hostel beside the cave. We are admitted, and all crowd into the giant chimney, where warmth comes again to us. The days have been hot, but the nights are chilly. Though September, it is spring-time in Australia. Yet no one catches cold in these nights— so dry, so clear is the air. Roast mutton and brownie are given us to eat, and with a billy of tea beside us we are comfortable enough, prisoners and all. Resuscitated, the Superintendent and I seek the cave with a slush-light. The stars are palpitating in the sky; near by is the pawing of newly-harnessed horses. Around us is the voiceless Australian plain and a dark heavy line of cheerless forest. Within the cave a dog lies

BURKE AND WILLS' MONUMENT.

asleep on some bags of chaff. The Superintendent holds up the slush-light, and runs it along the scores of names carved on the hard wall. But Burke's initials are obliterated, entirely vanished. "Here they were," he says. "Years ago I saw them here; but they are gone." And in this cave we remember the statue in Melbourne of the young and noble-minded Wills, the brave and enthusiastic Burke, and the deeds of the generous and devoted Grey.

And standing there in the cave, one might be pardoned for a misty eye, as the thought rises of the awful mockery that followed them as they crept on from post to post, to be a sacrifice to their own success at the last; to fall victims to the unforgiven act of some one who blundered. Sitting on the box-seat on the coach, I had read out to the Superintendent, Jim the driver, and the policeman, the tale of the lives of Burke and Wills, from the Rev. G. Grimm's excellent book of the Australian explorers. Jim was not likely to be moved easily in the emotions, but he gulped a little as the tragedy neared its end. The warrigals in the traces rattled on shoeless and untamed; the wheels rumbled over the aching ground; the voice of the reader rose through the dust. These men of the plains were silent and grave as the words fell that told of the burial of poor Grey, and the return of the leaders to the spot on the Barcoo, where they had ordered the rear-guard to stay. But Wright, the subordinate, in whom their hope lay, had never come. There were three of them left to face death —Burke, Wills, and their faithful follower King. But let Mr. Grimm tell of the end in his own straightforward way: "On the second day Burke succumbed, and felt his end to be near. He was a brave man, yet he shrank from dying alone, and he entreated King to stay with him till all was over. His dying request was religiously observed by his trusty friend, who held him in his arms until he breathed his last. Then King returned to Wills. It was all peace, for he too lay quietly asleep in the arms of death. Beside his body lay his journal, in which he had made his last entry with a trembling hand, noting the aspect of the weather, and adding, with a stroke of pleasantry even yet, that he was like Mr. Micawber, 'waiting for something to turn up.'" Behind me the policeman turned his head away, the Superintendent had his hand to his forehead as if he were scanning the plains, a whip went sharply across the flanks of the leaders, and Jim said in a husky voice: "It was all along of that damned Wright!"

What country can show a history of heroic exploration like to this? None; for in none was the problem of travel so ominous. And in this cave one thought too of Sturt, who had passed through these wilds on his way to Rocky Glen at Mount Poole, where he and all that were with him suffered as suffer the damned. Later, it was my lot to travel over his very course, and to see a country where only an inch of rain had fallen in eighteen months. From the door of this cave such a vista of vicissitudes, such a marvel of achievement stretches out as must amaze all who attempt to view it. "Up there," says the Superintendent, pointing to the ravine, " is the grave of one of Sturt's followers, but the name is gone from the stone." One bright star was shining over the place, as if in immortal guard over the forgotten pilgrim.

It is morning now. All night there is nothing to do but watch the stars wheel down the sky; to feel about you a space of desolation; to know that death and life were here in desperate conflict; to hear only the cry of the driver, "Get up, you rubbish!" to see only a dim world ahead of you, from which, now and again, glimmers a handful of flame, to tell you that you are nearing a change; to know that another set of chaff-fed warrigals is ready; then, without the merry horn of the northland, to shuffle away again into the waste. At last there is a gleam in the east; a line of grey, a touch of purple, a suffusion of saffron and fiery red, and the morn stares in upon the land. But on what a land! Is this Arabia? There nears us from the line of grey willows by a waterless river-bed, a train of camels from some great company's station, driven by Arabs, and making for the *entrepôt* far to the south. The warrigals scent the camels afar off and they are wild; but we are nearing our breakfast station, and even they are affected by that satisfying proximity. Yet how can one eat? See, as the coach passes into a paddock, these eyeless lambs. Fallen through starvation and weakness, the ravenous crows have picked out their eyes. They strew our path, and far to where the plain becomes one leaden grey are white spots innumerable—dead and dying sheep. It is numb despondency, over which the carrion-crow cries a hateful requiem. This is not the crow of the northern hemisphere. However it chances, this knave has caught from the sheep a cry like its own, only it is harsh and desolating. It is not the hearty *Caw! caw!* of the meadows under the Great Bear. Yesterday we saw scenes of misery, but we had grown into them gradually, and their horror did not touch us so. This morning it bursts upon us. We are in a great charnel-house. Upon this barren land a plague of rabbits has descended, has spread, has swarmed ahead of the sheep, taken the place of the kangaroo, and eaten the land clean of grass and salt-bush and edible scrub.

Dire are the straits of this people; dire the needs of its enemies. For, see: four, five, seven feet up the boles of the little trees the rabbits have climbed and eaten the bark. Here is thought for Darwin, if he chanced to know it—that rabbits should climb trees. How might not this faculty grow until the rabbit had all the capacities of the monkey!

But here the warrigals rattle feebly in, and Mrs. Flynn greets us at the door. What does it matter to Mrs. Flynn that the sun is angry; that the sky is unresponsive; that the nights are miserably cheerless; that the heavens never drop their fatness? Her bountiful face sees only a tired mother, whom the Superintendent helps out of the coach, whose child the Superintendent carries to Mrs. Flynn. Good Mrs. Flynn, across these twelve thousand miles of land and sea between us, I send your own cheery greeting that gave us a gleam of light in the implacable landscape: "Oh, isn't it the fun of the world to be alive?" Kind soul. In the heart of that stricken country you kept the fun of the world in your heart, and you served the mother and the prisoners first of your lean mutton and damper. You served the prisoners first. Was that because you were Irish, or because you were a woman?

Weeks after. High noon on the plains and a cloudy sky. Is it so, that rain is coming? The darkness gathers in the horizon, grows, spreads, thickens. And now great wheels of thunder crack down the sky. What, Quin of Tarella, no joy at this? Here is plenty overhanging for your empty wells. You will not need to send your sheep travelling into No Man's Land, that haply they may find food and water. But Quin of Tarella has no joy in his countenance. It is a bitter kind of irony that says, "Wait." Turbulent, ponderous grows the sky. Then a volcano of thunder bursts like a split in the universe, and the storm falls on the world—a storm of wind. Only wind. It catches the earth, worries it and shakes it; but that is all. Not a drop of rain! And for many and many a day the jackaroo will still chop down the limbs of the mulga tree, that of its tonic leaves the sheep may eat and live. And for many a day also the clouds will roll up and threaten, and then march in sardonic procession away, leaving not a track of moisture behind. And all the while the sheep have gone from grass to salt-bush (in appearance like the alkali bush of the Arizona plains), and from salt-bush to the puntie, the peppermint, the turpentine, the hop, the cotton, the gidja, and the dead-finish bushes, for their food. And these now are swaying in the wind, overswept by the withered grass, and bending to the sterile plain. And then, suddenly, the hot blast passes, the sky is clear again, and one looks through a palpable and palpitating area of heat, the fiery waves rolling backwards and forwards. And now, blessed relief, is a mountain afar, in a blue buoyancy—Mount Lyall. What sweet expanse may lie at its feet? But consider. That is the mountain which the valiant Sturt saw as he fought his way into the heart of the continent in search of great inland seas. And he hurried to it—to look down upon, not a river, not a sea, but a white quartz desolation. And from this mountain, at whose base we stand, we turn our eyes further westward, and we know that there is the Great Stony Desert, and that at Milparinka still lies a boat in which Sturt hoped to sail on his to-be-discovered seas. Amiable and indomitable soul. You sought refuge in a land of living death. For then it was that the tubes of the thermometer burst; that the soles were scorched from your shoes; that your finger nails broke like glass; that your hair ceased to grow, and the ink dried in the pen. Yet in that region where you wasted and despaired, men are living, working now, —brave, defiant, conquering, and at what cost! "See here," said Quin of Tarella to me, "we are gambling with God." Yes, even that. For, in the hope of one or two good years of flood in six or seven, these pioneers live there, and as far west as Mount Brown and Tibbooburra and Mount Poole, playing a desperate game with nature. Between rabbits and drought this Land of the Golden Fleece fights a hard fight.

It is a white and dreary plain. There is a line of straggling gums beside a feeble watercourse. Six wild horses—warrigals or brombies, as they are called—have been driven down, corralled, and caught. They have fed on the leaves of the myall and stray bits of salt-bush. After a time they are got within the traces. They are all young, and they look not so bad. We start. They can scarcely be held in for the first few miles. Then they begin to soak in perspiration. Another five miles, and they look drawn about the flanks, and what we thought was flesh is dripping from them. Another five, and the flesh has gone. The ribs show, the shoulders protrude. Look. A poler's heels are knocking against the whiffle-trees. It is twenty miles now. There is a gulp in your throat as you see a wreck stagger out of the traces and stumble over the plain, head near the ground and death upon its back. There is no water in that direction, worn-out creature. It comes upon you like a sudden blow. These horses are being driven to death. And why? Because it is cheaper to kill them on this stage of thirty miles than to feed them with chaff at £50 a ton.

And now another sways. Look at the throbbing sides, the quivering limbs. He falls.

"Driver, for Heaven's sake, can't you see?"

"I do, so help me God, I do. But we've got to get there. I'll let them out at another mile."

And you are an Anglo-Saxon, and this is a Christian land.

It is the evening hour. The Traveller draws near a station homestead. His feeble horse pulls itself together for another effort, and whinnies as he sees a solitary horse in a paddock just ahead. At the right hand is a water-tank (a great wide hole dug in the ground), filled eighteen months ago by rain. Hundreds of sheep lie dead and dying round it, and thousands stench the plains. The sheep have either died in reaching the tank, or, getting to it, have plunged in, and have then perished, too weak to climb the low sides again. Thousands of sated crows stand in line upon the bank,—a black and menacing barricade; and kites and magpies hover overhead.

The Traveller has passed empty wells, and has shuddered at the tales told him in some shepherd's hut where he has sought shelter. He nears the homestead; he dismounts and makes for the garden,—an oasis kept alive by a woman's hand till water ran low. Then she forsook it sadly, this one touch of her past now withered and dead. Is there no one here? Is it, too, a scene of tragedy, with human victims? No: and yet tragedy too. To a sharp "Coo-ĕ-ĕ" there comes an answering call, and the manager appears at the door, a bearded, gruff, but kindly soul; and over his shoulder peers the face of a woman, sad and drawn. The great exhaust-pipes of nature in that burning land soon take the bloom from the cheek and the light from the eye. A shake of the hand, a "My word!" of apostrophic welcome, and The Traveller says, "How goes the unlucky game?" With a swift sigh of relief and a sudden uplifting of the arms comes the reply: "The last lamb is dead. Thank God, that's off my mind!"

And then the Manager said: "Come out and see how things look." Outside he added: "We were just going to plant a sundowner when you coo-ĕ-ĕd. Didn't want to say anything about it before the missus." Then he told the oft-repeated tale of a wanderer creeping to the very threshold of safety, and there dying, his hand upon the gate of that little withered garden.

By the grave we stand, the Manager with a Bible in his hand, a book rarely used by him, perhaps, but reverenced after his fashion, and necessary now. He wishes The Traveller to "do it over the cold 'un," but The Traveller declines. With coarse fingers blundering through the leaves in an uncertain fashion, the Manager begins to read at last from Ecclesiastes. A half-dozen verses gruffly fall, and then the words come,—

"*For what hath man of all his labour and the vexation of his heart, wherein he hath laboured under the sun?*

"*For all his days are sorrow, and his travail grief.*

"*Yea, his heart taketh not rest in the night. This is also vanity.*"

Then he closed the book, and said: "Well, he was a goner afore he was a comer; and I don't know as there's need to pitch a long yarn. He hadn't much for his labour under the sun; and a hot sun it is up here at 110° in the shade. He come a long way over the country-rock. He hadn't a drop in his water-bottle, nor a bit of damper in his swag. He'd got his fingers on the slip-rails, and was within Coo-ĕ-ĕ of drink and tucker when he went out

Coo-E-E.

sudden to the Never-Never Land; and went it alone. He couldn't have had much vanity, not with them features, and, my word! the Lord knows all about that. I hope if he gets as near to the homestead-gate Up There as he did down here last night, that, even if he isn't very fit, one of the hands will see him, and open it, and let him in,—if it has to be on the sly. It was at night he got here, and in the morning we found him; it's at night we cover him, and, rest or no rest, he'll not have to work in the morning. There isn't a place that's hotter than here, and this one ain't sent to *that* quod for punishment. Let him down easy and slow. . . . Drop in his shirallee and water-bag by him. . . . That's right. 'Scatter some sandal leaves over his face. . . . Now scrape in the country-sand. . . . The dingoes can't touch him there. . . . What's that you've put on the board, Jim? '*A Sundowner. Gone.*' And God forgive him wherever he's gone. . . . In the midst of life we are in death. Amen."

And another of several such tragedies that The Traveller saw was thus hidden away—a nameless refugee of misfortune in a nameless grave.

And now it is midnight, and the two, with pipes aglow, sit and blow away dark anticipations. Before the wife retired she had said, in response to the Manager's doubts of their being able to hold out for a week longer; to his announcement that Shady Jack's well was done, and that the Frenchman's tank was empty: "Hope for the best." And the Manager, through a cloud of smoke, replied: "My oath! but the best things never come off." To this the wife rejoined: "Yes, Dick, but the *worst* things never come off." Night after night this man had walked the room alternating between prayers and curses, as each day's record was another thousand sheep gone, another empty well, until at last he came to this apathetic endurance, to this grim courage of despair.

"I shouldn't care so much," he said, "but then my wife, my girls in there!" He drew his sleeve roughly across his eyes, and bowed his head on the table. For ten minutes he sat there, so. Then The Traveller saw him raise his head, start, spring to his feet, and listen with strained attention.

What was that? Something *pinged* on the corrugated roof above us. "Rain! rain! rain!" he cried, as he rushed outside, and fell on his knees with his hands stretched out towards the gathered sky. "Thank God! Thank God! Wife! Girls! Mary! Rain!"

Even so. The flood-gates of the sky were opened, and before morning came The Traveller was helping to put up a dyke on one side of the house: and the march of destruction was stayed.

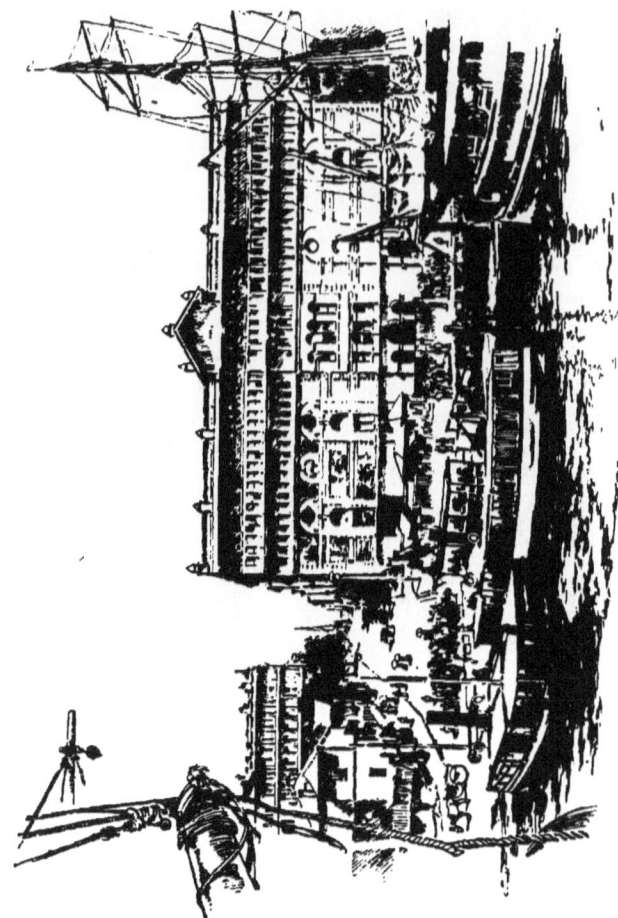

MORT'S WOOL HOUSE.

CHAPTER IV.

RURAL AUSTRALIA.

THE passage from the glimpses of Australia, given in previous chapters, to a proper perspective of the conditions and questions discussed in this and following chapters, should not be difficult. We are to consider a continent that was touched by Dutch navigators, a century after Columbus discovered America, but which only came to be considered as a place for colonisation when Captain Cook took possession of it for the English nearly a century and a quarter ago. The real history of the continent begins with the inauspicious function of landing a shipload of convicts at Botany Bay in 1788. For over seventy-five years some portion of the continent was given over to convict settlement. Western Australia was the last colony of refuge and imprisonment for outcast criminal England. It voluntarily sold itself into bondage long after the deportation of convicts to the other colonies had ceased; when the land was rising out of its shame, and when the proportion of the convict to the free population of the whole country was small. Legislation practically began in 1829, when New South Wales was given a Legislative Council of fifteen members, one-third of whom were appointed by the Governor for the time being.

Then the Crown began also the system of making

lavish gifts of land, and the process of wholesale alienation, which the background of resources of the country alone prevented from being disastrous. Freehold grants, with extensive grazing privileges, were followed by the system of sale by auction, and conditional purchase based on free selection before survey. Then came appraisement of rents by officers of the Crown. Later still the Government woke up to the fact that all the land could not be legislated for alike, and that it was very like building castles in the air to hope for agricultural settlement in a country where seven, and even ten, acres were required to keep a sheep. It therefore cut off conditional purchase outside certain limits. Meanwhile, the Minister for Lands was an autocrat, who himself settled the rents for thousands of leases. A local landboard a thousand miles away might decide one thing; he could, and did, decide another. But in New South Wales in 1889 this autocrat was deprived of so trying a function by a wise Government and a wise Minister for Lands, who succeeded in passing a Bill which provided for a central Land Court to adjudicate rentals; while in the one-sheep-to-ten-acres-country the leases were extended to twenty years. In all the colonies, with variations more or less important, this has been the process; and in all, likewise, the Minister for Lands has ever been the most important officer of the Cabinet. The area of freehold property, in comparison to leasehold, is very small, save in the compact colony of Victoria.

Government began with the idea of homesteading as in America; but that was a dream, which had not much fertility. The proportion of really good agricultural land in Australia is not large. In New South Wales, out of 198,848,000 acres there are only 1,000,000 acres under cultivation, or an acre per head of population; but there are about 145,000,000 acres under pastoral lease. In Victoria, out of 56,245,760 acres there are only 2,141,291 acres under cultivation; in South Australia, 2,762,273 out of 578,000,000 acres; in Queensland, 221,843 out of 428,800,000 acres; in Western Australia, 84,403 out of 625,000,000 acres; and in Tasmania, 1,527,388 out of 15,571,500 acres.

I desire my readers to think they are with me now on a sheep station in the far west of New South Wales. I might choose a station on the Darling or Fitzroy Downs in Queensland; on the Murchison River in Western Australia; on the Daly River in the Port Darwin district, or on the Murray River in Victoria; but the one to which we are to be immediately transported is complete and well-managed, and might be considered both a type and a standard. Its owner is successful. He is a man of force, activity, and general knowledge; he is also hospitable to a degree. It might be said in this connection that everybody is hospitable in the heart of Australia. It is only the nature of the kindness that differs. We might divide the hospitality as we divide the people. There is the station owner, or leaseholder, who lives on his run in good season and in bad, with his wife and children and children's children round him; the manager who represents a company, and has less real responsibility, and cuts a notch lower in the social scale; the bachelor, or set of bachelors, of good birth and breeding, who dispense their kindness without conventionality, and always with good liquor; and there is the owner, whose family lives in the metropolis, while he divides his time between the station and the city. According to their methods of living, the views of these occupants of the home-station—as the chief house on the sheep-run is called—develop. The first has all his household gods beside him, and all his brains, his labour, and his money are invested in the spot where are the household gods. It is therefore natural that he should make his *ménage* more and more complete, and that his views should filter through a moderately steady atmosphere. The manager comes next. He "sits down," as the aboriginal says, also with the thought of having a home ; but he will not spend much money on other people's property, and so he must depend upon the generosity and care of the company. The company, like a central government, cannot well administer in detail, and so the great company's station-homestead is generally less complete than that of the resident and well-to-do owner. The feeling of the last two is, as a rule, to get out of the country as soon as they have had a few good seasons, and can sell to advantage their interest, their stock, and their improvements. Had they the same ties and daily surroundings they might find, even in the isolation to which they are so much committed, a sense of permanency, and, therefore, a feeling of home. The stations near the coast and along the railway lines come chiefly under the category of the first and last divisions ; but the station to which I would transport the curious is four days' hard travel from a railway line. Hard travel in Australia means one hundred miles a day, often enough without a change of horses.

We are then at Wallaroona. One big central house of stone, bungalow-make, stands in the middle of a large paddock. Windows open to the floors, a water-bag and tin cup ever hang in the shade of the verandah, and on a table, in the same shade, lie the colonial weekly newspapers—a great institution—and perhaps one of the latest of the English or American magazines. The sun is setting behind a red-coloured mountain, where many a poor chap came a cropper at mining ; and, at our feet almost, there washes a lake of conserved water, the result of a great rainfall of a few days before. There is a boat on the lake, and clouds of wild ducks and pelicans hover near.

"If you've got your throat clear," said Cawdor, the owner, who had £50,000 invested in the improvements of the run—that is, buildings, wells, tanks, etc.—"we will go and have a look round before dinner. The ladies are in the school-house." On the way over to the school-house we had a run through the laundry and the kitchen, which, in all Australian country houses, are detached from the living house. The school-house was part class-room, part sewing-room. The class-room was used for service on Sundays, when Cawdor, under the persuasion of his wife, read the prayers, and supplemented them with a sermon from some austere divine. A permanent dressmaker was employed, who also, with an assistant, did the lighter tailoring. And here, with her daughters and her daughter-in-law (the wife of Cawdor's eldest) was Mrs. Cawdor engaged. Hard by were the son's house and the house of a married daughter. After introductions, Mrs. Cawdor asked me if I had had lunch.

"Yes, chops cooked in the open, and a bit of damper at Wild Bob's Well," I replied.

"Was Mr. Fitzgarrick there?" said Mrs. Cawdor.

"He was."

Mrs. Cawdor sighed. So did one of the daughters.

I continued: "A trooper and black-tracker were there also."

"Hunting for that villain Blake, who picked the eyes of Macallister's land for his selection, and, after cutting off poor Mac from the use of his tanks, stole his stock," said Cawdor.

"Oh, those homestead leases!" added Miss Cawdor.

"They ruined Mr. Fitzgarrick," remarked her mother.

"Let me state this question, to see if I understand it aright, Cawdor," I said. "The Government threw open this great west to selection; men came in with a small handful of cash, and settled runs where you and others had spent scores of thousands of pounds; picked out the best spots on your leasehold, and began to depasture five or ten thousand sheep, cutting you out of your improvements sometimes. They went under at the first flush of drought, and of course were ruined, after having seriously interfered with you, and done nothing to advance the settlement of the country. Is that it?"

"Yes, that is about it," replied Cawdor.

And since Cawdor and I talked together the New South Wales Government has concluded that beyond the River Darling there shall be no more homestead leasing. And so we see the far interior of Australia a peopleless, homeless country to all appearance; that is, one might travel for days and weeks and never behold a sign of habitation or human life. Great sheep runs are there, and large establishments, but they are oases in a desert which supports one sheep to eight or ten acres.

While we sat there a rouseabout came to the door. "Mountain Jim's back," he said. There was no "sir" in the remark of this lowest of station-hands to his master.

"Where is he?"

"Gone to have a coil."

"How is Mad Nancy?"

("That's the brombie that Mountain Jim rode," said Mrs. Cawdor in explanation.)

"Right as rain," was the reply.

Whatever a bushman may do to himself, he looks

after his horse, though indeed it needs little care, and has marvellous powers of survival.

The rouseabout continued: "He'll need a new outfit. Rags has it now."

"Let us go down to the store," said Cawdor.

The store was like an American country shop, where anything useful in soft goods or wearing apparel, groceries or ironmongery, could be had. Picking out the largest suit of clothes in the place for Mountain Jim, Cawdor handed them to the rouseabout.

"Let me see Mountain Jim," said I.

There he lay, on the floor of the barracks. From the walls, faces of innocent children and sweet-faced women—pictures clipped from English illustrated papers—looked down on a swarthy drunken giant.

"Been knocking down his cheque over at the One-Tree Tavern," said Cawdor. "What did it cover? Half a year's wages—forty pounds." And, looking up on the walls again, a sketch, done in brutal colours, caught the eye. It was an illustration of Adam Lindsay Gordon's poem, *The Sick Stockrider*, and beneath the picture of the dying bushman were the words,—

> "For good undone, and gifts misspent, and resolutions vain,
> 'Tis somewhat late to trouble—this I know,
> I should live the same life over if I had to live again,
> And the chances are I go where most men go."

Cawdor was unmoved. He had seen it so often. It was a feature in the life of the back-blocks.

"Let me see if I have got this matter clearly," I said; for I, too, had beheld scenes like this in many places in Australia. "The station-hand lives a life of comparative banishment and absence from those of his own rank, women especially, with whom he can associate. He works for six months or a year as shepherd, boundary-rider, or what not; then draws his cheque for his wages, gets leave, and goes to the nearest township to knock it down. His views of life, his philosophy, his religion, his *vade mecum*, are found in Adam Lindsay Gordon's poems of the bush—of riding, of reckless living, of romantic pessimism and stoic endurance. The pessimism has, in fact, touched all, more or less, who live in the heart of Australia. It began by a disbelief in Nature because it played such ghastly tricks; it followed with disbelief in Government because it refused to see that the country could not be legislated for after the manner of the coast-land; it grew to disbelief in the parson who was so seldom seen; and it came at last to a loss of faith in Providence."

"That is putting it bluntly, but it comes near the truth," said Cawdor, "if you mean a kind of disbelief that doesn't see always the *goodness* of Providence."

"Yes, that, together with a view of life which makes men victims of something or other; and this you surround with a kind of pathos borrowed from the melancholy landscape about you—and your *vade mecum*."

"You see too much for a new chum," said Cawdor. "If we're a bit pessimistic we fight all the same."

"You who have large interests do; but what about Mountain Jim's class?"

"Well, it's not a pleasant subject. Let us talk about irrigation, or water conservation, or local government," he replied.

"That is exactly what I wish; but before we do that, tell me Mountain Jim's history."

"It's an old story enough. Like many another, he took up a selection, married, and brought his wife and two children on it. Selections may be all right in the coast-country, where there's rainfall and less sun; but they are no good in the back-blocks. What can a man do with water and no grass, or grass and no water? It's too hot and hard to farm it, and there's no one to buy; and no market if he could be agricultural. He keeps a few cattle of his own—or some one else's—his children grow up round him without a bit of schooling, and with no ideas but horses and cattle. These they know all kinds. Sometimes the whole lot of them go wrong, with the pubs or worse. That was the source of bushrangers, as often as not, in the old days—the devilish hopelessness of the life. Mountain Jim went through all but the bush-ranging. His wife died from hardship and the heat, his only boy was lost in the Never-Come-Back Scrub, and here he is."

Two hours after, Gregson, a member of a squatting, and of a mining, company, Cawdor, Cawdor's Eldest, the bookkeeper, and myself were sitting in the bookkeeper's quarters after dinner.

"Gregson knows all about irrigation and water conservation," said Cawdor; "and if you'll add the evidence you've seen, and that which you heard when you travelled with the Water Conservation Commission three years ago, we shall be able to strike an average somewhere."

"The testimony offered throughout the whole of the back-blocks of Australia is that the land will grow anything, with plenty of water," said I; "but water cannot be had for the asking, and water conservation and irrigation costs money."

"It is a scheme," said Gregson, reaching over his glass to the Bookkeeper to be re-charged, "that looks lovely on paper. It looks cheerful, too, for promoters of companies who get founders' shares, and have little to lose;

but down in Sydney and Melbourne in the Parliament-houses they talk nonsense "—here the Bookkeeper interjected an unparliamentary expression as he repeated the word "nonsense "—" when they speak about making the wilderness to blossom like the rose, and all that poppycock. For irrigation there must be artesian wells, watercourses like the Darling or Murray, where water can be conserved by means of weirs and bywashes."

"But what about the great depressions on the plains, or lakes, as they are called, when they are filled?" said Cawdor's Eldest, meaningly.

"No good except to use like wells. They go dry too. There is scarcely a permanent lake or river in the back country. And if they were permanent and few, they are not of such tremendous value by any means. What is the good of water if you haven't grass within ten miles of it?"

"Irrigation doesn't come in there, of course," remarked Cawdor.

"You can't irrigate pastoral country; any bushman knows that," continued Gregson. "Now there's that lake of conserved water outside. You can let it off on the land, but it will soak the stuff up like lightning, and you'll get—what? A crop of lucerne if you please; but what good is that beyond enough to feed your horses in drought-time, if you haven't markets? It is all very well to try the scheme at Mildura and Renmark; but these places are beside a river, and not far from big populations. And more, they haven't been proved a success yet. The promoters succeeded in America; but that is a different thing. They had mountain ranges there and a different class of country; besides, there was the population to absorb what was grown. Irrigation for farming on a big scale doesn't pay, and it never could pay in this country. It may pay for fruit-growing, but you must have the demand, and you must produce as cheaply as the countries near by; as Fiji, Samoa, California, and Java, where fruit grows without the cost of irrigation. I've tried irrigation on the Darling, and I know what it costs. And men have tried it all over the country, and have succeeded with it. It's no trick. But it is only of use near large populations, and in Australia it costs more than anywhere else."

"Alfred Deakin and the Victorian Government seem to have faith in it," said Cawdor. "There's talk of the Government lending money at 4½ per cent. to Trusts for the development of the country. The Messrs. Chaffey have 500,000 acres at a penny a year for fourteen acres."

"Yes," said Gregson, "but that scheme is not finished yet; and they haven't built their rabbit-proof fencing (which they'll need some day), and they haven't yet produced, and they haven't sought markets. So far it has all been invitation to investment. Irrigation will pay under certain conditions, but it isn't a thing for which to give promissory notes on this continent. Experience puts it to me like this: a country should produce and develop on the lines in which Nature has favoured it. Competition is keen, and other countries, producing, on favoured natural lines, the things which we try to produce on artificial lines, will whip us, hands down. For instance, India can irrigate and produce wheat, and send it to us cheaper than we can produce it by irrigation, because of the cheaper labour both in production and in the arrangement of artificial conditions. And there you have my opinion straight, and for what it is worth."

CHAPTER V.

RURAL AUSTRALIA (Continued).

JUST as there are grave misconceptions of the Western Territories of Canada by politicians at Ottawa, so there is ignorance in the parliaments of Australia regarding the interior of the country. It is this ignorance which sanctions schemes that look well, and are patriotic in design, but with which the "old hand" has no patience or sympathy. He has seen, with a nervous disdain, the inconsequence of the "village settlements" scheme in Queensland, and the conditional purchase and homestead-leasing process in the far west; he has beheld serious mistakes made in Parliament regarding the conditions under which pastoral occupation occurs; and he foresaw the result of schemes which were based on inadequate knowledge. He knew that the only possible way for men to succeed in the interior was by carrying on operations on a large scale. Safety lay in wide acres, many wells, artesian or otherwise, and the depasturage of a large number of sheep. And all this meant capital.

Governments have been as slow to understand the difficulty of settling the country with small owners in the great interior, as they have been to provide a complete system of local government. Only about one-third of the population of Australia have the blessings of local government, and in none of the colonies may the system be said to be complete. There is not even in Victoria—and that colony is ahead in this question—the complete application of the principle as in Canada or in portions of the United States: that is, from school section to township council; from township council to county council; from county council to provincial legislation; from provincial to Dominion legislation. But a marvellous change has come over Australia in this respect during the past few years, and in Queensland and Victoria the systems are growing more thorough. The sparse population must, however, always stand in the way of the plenary form of local government which is possible in agricultural countries. New South Wales, with its million of people, has not yet attempted it. The results of the old system have been, naturally, unsatisfactory. A new fence, a set of furniture for a court house, a policeman's outfit, a pane of glass broken in a school-house window, a lamp for a dark street, must come direct from the Government offices in Sydney. A minister and his under-secretary did, and still do, all the duties of a township council. It is needless to state that this kind of government is the cause of much discontent. It has been the foundation of several attempts to divide New South Wales, and to make a separate colony of the Riverina, the south-western portion of the Colony; it is a force in the present attempt to divide Queensland.

To develop the opinions of Cawdor, Gregson, the Bookkeeper, and Cawdor's Eldest on the matter would necessitate a huge glossary attached to this book, and more space than can be given. But the Bookkeeper had a good deal to say, from a very practical standpoint, about arbitrary geographical lines. He produced books and accounts to prove his assertion that the trade of western

New South Wales did not go to Sydney, but to Melbourne in the rival colony; just as the trade of British Columbia does not go to Montreal, but to Tacoma, Portland, and San Francisco. Natural lines of division have been disregarded; and though New South Wales is doing its best to hold the west by the construction of railways, Melbourne and Adelaide continue to carry away the commerce of the Riverina.

"Let me put my finger on this question for a moment," said Cawdor's Eldest, "and I am only going to speak from experience. I've been in Queensland; I went to the Kimberley diggings in Western Australia, as you all know; I nearly lost my life station-hunting on the Daly River in the Northern Territory; and I tried the planter's life on a small scale in North Queensland. What got fixed in my mind was this: that the whole question of provincial or colonial division was wrong. Perth hasn't any real sympathy or industrial connection with Kimberley; Adelaide, in every sense, is as far away from Port Darwin as Boston was from Key West before the war; and Brisbane is simply out of all community of sentiment (commercial and otherwise) with Cooktown. The planter in the north wants cheap foreign labour—the Polynesian, the Chinaman—and protection on his sugar; the south, with the miner and squatter and dock labourer, is not disposed to give protection or foreign labour. Brisbane is too far away to radiate legislation properly. What is true of Queensland is true of the Northern Territory, and true of the northern part of Western Australia. And there you are."

Cawdor smiled approvingly, took a pencil, and ran it along the twenty-fifth parallel of latitude. "There is the great question of the future," he said. "America never had a greater. The interests of the south are not identical with those of the north, and the ultimate state of provincial divisions must be upon these natural conditions, or everlasting trouble will be on the track of all

From Harper's Weekly.   Copyright, 1891, by Harper & Brothers.
MOUNTED LAMP-LIGHTER.

governments. But with a central or dominion government, with provincial legislatures managing local affairs, and a moderate municipal system, and with the provinces divided according to the sun, 'honours are easy.'"

Gregson, who had been smoking placidly for some time, rose, took down a boomerang from the wall, and began to emphasise his remarks with it. "Well, you see, we've got to take this into consideration also, that the government is the great landowner and landlord, and there would be more difficulty in establishing local government here than in countries like Canada, where land is mostly freehold, settlements many, and ownerships small."

"That question of government as universal landlord is peculiar," said Cawdor. "It holds the country for the people after the most approved socialistic method, and yet, we are afflicted with dangers and evils as serious as those springing out of the feudal system in England. We get the benefit of easy settlements, but we are vexed by incomplete government, and are tied up here and there by restrictions which are tyrannous to a class, if not to the mass."

"Well, that's all right," said Cawdor's Eldest. "The class has to suffer. We want Australia for the Australians."

"Now see here," said Gregson, "what *has* that to do with the question? How you young beggars mix up things! And yet you only do what so many of the politicians do. What connection has socialism with 'Australia for the Australians'? If it is anything it is dead against exclusion of every kind.

"Democracy in Australia hasn't any political standard yet, any more than it has art or musical standards. It has had friction with Downing Street; it has had trouble with land laws; therefore, that party called Young Australia, of which you are, want to do away with Downing Street, and to have something new in the matter of landownership and occupation. I will put the thing squarely:

The young Australian is strong and successful ; he feels his oats, and desires prosperity more than anything else ; and he knows that he can get success under conditions as they are ; but he does not know how far the very conditions he grumbles at have contributed to his past success."

"Now let me sum up," I said, "merely to see if I have digested your ideas clearly. We are agreed that Australia is strongly democratic, while having also, in the older portions of the community, a personal loyalty to the Crown. The younger portion, not having known Joseph and being far off, have little direct sympathy with Buckingham Palace or Westminster. But the younger have patriotism, which is a less personal thing than loyalty. This patriotism may be trusted. Whatever spasmodic revolt against the present connection there may be, it is accidental not radical, and belongs to national full-bloodedness rather than national discontent. The political unrest that exists, the frequent change of governments, the ease with which Australians meet all political movements, whether executive or in lines of policy, are an indication of a discipline and ingrown sense of adaptation which are born with men in new countries. They go about as soon as they can walk, looking out for the main chance. They are industrial craftsmen, they are social and political craftsmen naturally. From squatter to planter, from the rabbiter's hut to the mining king's palace, from carpenter to premier, the passage is easy, or, if not easy, is accepted as easy. For instance, every one of these newspapers from the different colonies, lying on your table, tells of a change of ministry or of a moribund government. Do you worry yourselves about that? Not at all. You know that you will fare about as well with one government as another. Your free-traders are one-half protectionists in practice. You know that you will turn the incompetent government out in six months if it doesn't suit you. You are adepts at the political game; you are less perplexed by a change of ministry than by a slight fluctuation in the wool-market. As a people you are the employers, the masters of the politicians; you have yet to experience the extreme partisanship of England, Canada, or the United States. Your chief newspapers may be committed to a question, but not to a government or a man. The country has not yet been divided on great and divergent policies surrounded by tradition and grounded on political heredity. But that is fast coming. The growth of the country will eventually force it. For you are all students of politics, from city-cabman to boundary-rider. Political incompetency angers you, but you are not dismayed by political confusion."

"You are on the right track," said Gregson. "And about political incompetency,—was there ever a greater bungle than the Rabbit Act?"

"Well, we are slipping away from our original subject fast, but perhaps it is just as well. There are things that concern you more intimately and locally than the Australian Democracy; and the rabbit question is one of them."

"As if bad land laws and drought were not sufficient," said Cawdor, "we were sent the rabbits. We wanted to grapple with the difficulty ourselves, each man working away on his own lines, and getting some consideration by reduction of rents or longer tenure. But no. The government, being the landlord, appointed rabbit-inspectors and the elaborate machinery of a trapping system, all of which cost them at the rate of one thousand pounds a day; of which we must pay half and the government half.

I spent as much as four thousand pounds a month on my run. Some rabbiters earned fifty pounds a month, trapping. They could drink champagne, while I had to stick to my billy of tea. Plenty of squatters spent a thousand pounds a month for nothing. Trapping could not possibly destroy the rabbits; and eventually the government found that out, that is, after it had spent well up to a million. Now we have come to our original proposition to do what we can to stay this plague by rabbit-fencing, poisoning, and all that. Thank God, the whole of the colonies are not overrun, or there would be a poor outlook. Queensland, by dint of rabbit-fencing, has kept the invaders from New South Wales, and Victoria has not yet been slaughtered badly by them."

"And yet the country prospers," I said.

"Of course it prospers on the whole. . When we have crops they are enormous; when we have a good wool season there is a fortune in blossom, and we get free of the banks. If it occurs that we get two or three good seasons, we can send the girls to Europe and go ourselves to the Melbourne Cup."

Just then there came a tap at the door, and in response to Cawdor's hearty invitation to "kick it open, and never mind the paint," there entered a stalwart figure, in broad-brimmed hat and loose-belted clothes. After salutations, Cawdor said to me—" My brother-in-law Pride, a Queensland planter." After introductions and a liquid solvent of any strangeness that might exist, Pride said: "I dropped a sundowner at the Stranger's Hut. Poor devil! He has seen better luck one time. He wouldn't come up here, though I asked him; but I said I should send him down some tea and damper."

"There's some in the Hut," said Cawdor's Eldest; "he will be right enough."

"From where away?" said Cawdor.

"The wallaby track from the Palmer gold-fields,—hundreds of miles, of course,—and is making for Broken Hill. Good line, these Strangers' Huts. We don't have them on sugar plantations; planters live too close together for that, and they are not needed. But when you chaps run 600,000 acres of land, and live eighty or a hundred miles apart, it's a different matter."

And thus, in a bluff fashion, did these Australians tell of some of the most touching things in the character of the life in the interior of Australia. The Stranger's Hut is an institution. To it the wanderer goes, and finds a place to sleep and something to eat. The latch-string is hanging out always. But this is typical of the hospitality of Australia from end to end. Whether it be planter or squatter, line-fettler or selector, boundary-rider or homesteader, mounted policeman or shepherd, stock-rider or camel-driver, the same brusque heartiness and hospitality flows from them all.

"My wife," said Pride the planter, "insisted on my carrying this book to you—*Robbery under Arms*, by Rolf Boldrewood. She says, and so do I, that it is the best Australian novel yet produced. I said you'd be sure to have it, but she said I was to risk it, and if it was in your mob of books, to give this copy to somebody that would appreciate it."

Cawdor's Eldest replied: "Oh, we've got that all right; we saw it advertised in the *Athenæum* six months ago, and sent for it. . . . Perhaps you haven't seen our little library," he said to me. "Suppose we change the venue, and go in there." He opened the door, and we all went in, followed by the Bookkeeper carrying the commissariat. Pride ran his fingers along one row of the five hundred books, and said, "Do you chance to have

Carnegie's book on the United States? I want to look at something in it." Cawdor produced it, and the two were soon in an animated discussion upon the difference of growth between the United States and Australia; the unlikenesses regarding political needs; the antagonistic continental configurations and conditions; and the dissimilar character of the two democracies.

And here, in passing, it may be said that I draw no fanciful picture of the squatter and planter of Australia. This tendency to gather about them the best and newest in literature and to be keen on discussion is not uncommon. The squatter and planter make a landed aristocracy in Australia. They spend certain weeks or months each year in Sydney or Melbourne, or go to Tasmania for the hottest season,—that is, Christmas time,—especially if there are any young ladies in the family. Sydney and Melbourne have a goodly number of C.M.G.'s and K.C.M.G.'s. If the matter is studied, it will be seen that many of these have been conferred on men who have been successful squatters, and who have subsequently gone into political life. Not that the attraction to public life is what it was in the days of Wentworth, the father of responsible government in Australia; of Dr. Lang; of Deas-Thompson; of Martin; of Murray; of Foster; and in the earlier times of Parkes, Robertson, and Dalley.

So swift has been the rise and overflow of the advanced democratic spirit of the labouring classes, of the power of the miner and the Trades Unionist, that they send and have sent to parliament for years many paid representatives of their cause—working-men's members, Trades Union members, and miners' members; and at present they hold the balance of power in New South Wales. The squatters, therefore, do not, in these days, seek seats in parliament as they once did. They have simply struggled with their natural enemy;—for every one is the natural enemy of the squatter, from homestead lessee and selector who are at his very doors, settled down upon what once was his unencumbered lease, to the working-man of the cities, who beholds in him the representative of a wealthy, and, therefore, a privileged, if not a leisured, class. And whether the squatter hold the land by lease or has it in fee simple, the feeling towards him is the same. The working-man occasionally forgets that he, as a citizen, is the landlord, who gives the squatter the right to invest, with the help of the banks, great sums of money, and that from this investment comes the real wealth of the people. Every other industry sinks into insignificance before the pastoral industry in Australia. And thus in this country we see the peculiar circumstance of a progressive and active democracy, including, by reason of certain natural and climatic conditions, a class whose instincts and usages would be expected to tend towards the most conservative political and social practices. It must be said here too in justice to the squatter that, where homestead-leasing and conditional purchase for purposes of agriculture have been wisely and carefully introduced, he has offered no unworthy opposition. His bias is democratic, while large ownership and a kind of local (but unavoidable) monopoly urges him in another direction. The bias triumphs. He is freely with the state, which is socialistic in the management of its lands, in the possession and control of its railways, and in its paternal care of the people. This paternal care is exercised in the establishment of schools of art, libraries, and hospitals in the rural districts, and in the establishment of great parks, national art galleries, technical colleges, public libraries, and permanent endowed orchestras to minister to the artistic tastes of the people.

"Looking at the matter fairly in the face," said Pride, "it must be conceded that almost unconsciously Australia is, in practice, the most democratic country in the world. The Government does everything here except make the conditions very easy under which the squatter and planter can work. Until lately it has let the homestead lessee and selector prey upon the squatter."

"Might I just interpose here," said Gregson, "and say bluntly that the squatter did not bend his neck meekly to the yoke; that he did not hesitate to take advantage of the law, and let his children and all his family select on his own station to protect himself; that he paid men to 'dummy' for him, and that he made it pretty hot for the beggars who did pick out the eyes of his country? What is the use of posing as martyrs? We were getting it on the edge, and we gave it on the edge. We were not always fair when the Government and a bad land law were foul."

"Well, if you put it that way, all right," said Pride; "but that doesn't undo the initial handicap to the squatter, born of ignorance and prejudice."

CHAPTER VI.

RURAL AUSTRALIA (Continued).

IT is two years and a half since the little conference at Wallaroona was enacted, and the law has come into force which compels the abolition of Polynesian labour in Queensland ; and the danger of the planter's occupation becoming extinct in Australia is more than likely, save where the German, employing his wife and children in the fields, has begun it on a small scale in the south. But the German succeeds everywhere. He took the Rosewood scrub in Queensland and turned it into a garden ; he bought farming land and mallee wastes in South Australia, upon which Englishmen starved, and he grew well-to-do, as did the Swiss and Norwegians in the Warwick district of Queensland, or the Icelanders and Mennonites in Canada. The Englishman will not live like the German, and so Australia does not bid fair at present to become a successful place for small planters, though many planters, under the old system, have made money, and have done much to develop the country. Districts like Maryborough, Bundaberg, and Mackay, owe their success to the planter ; just as Mount Morgan, Gympie, and Ipswich in Queensland ; Bathurst, Broken Hill, and Newcastle in New South Wales ; Ballarat in Victoria, and Kapunda in South Australia, do to mining ; or as Perth and Gascoyne,

Melbourne, Gawler, Geelong, and Sandhurst, Sydney, and Goulburn, do to squatting. And there are portions of Queensland, of the Northern Territory, and of Western Australia which are adapted for nothing but cane-growing and other tropical productions, such as coffee, tobacco, rice, and spices.

For the year 1886 the rainfall on one of the most favoured sheep stations of the west was 1·44 inches. The rainfall for 1888, the planter's drought year, was twenty-six inches. Let us ask Pride, the planter, about that.

"Thirty inches isn't good enough," he says; "we want fifty inches and a turn. Sugar and rice and all tropical or semi-tropical products must have plenty of rain. Cawdor here doesn't get enough rain in a year to do me for a month."

Gregson had his note-book out. "On the station which my partner runs on the Fitzroy Downs in Queensland, we have better luck than either of you. Nature hasn't got all the squatters of Australia by the throat. It is you daring ones passing the safety-line that have to take the 'cat.' Listen. Here are the figures I noted last week with fingers almost frozen. McCracken thinks everybody is a burning fiery furnace like himself, and there I was, with the thermometer down to 10° F., scribbling this stuff for the benefit of the world. Take 1888. The rainfall for the year was 11 inches and 36 points; for 1889 it was 24 inches and 38 points."

"But what is that you said about frozen fingers?" said Cawdor's Eldest. "We never get that sort of thing down here, though we are further away from the sunline."

"Of course you don't. You are on a country with no bosom. The Fitzroy Downs are 1,800 feet above the sea, and a very good thing too; not too much rain for cattle and sheep, and yet enough to keep things moving well. But go a hundred miles still further west, beyond the Parroo, and out Thargomindah way, and you get the thing on the ragged edge as you do here. And about the frozen fingers. Why, on the Darling Downs, in July last, I found the glass of milk which I had left overnight frozen in the morning. And on August 16th I had to break the ice in my water-jug; yet the thermometer at noon was 87°. In December the thermometer rose to 112°. F. in the shade at noon. Now that is a country for Christians to live in, if they have got a few thousand pounds for a start."

"I wish I had gone there instead of sinking my money in sugar," said Pride.

"Instead of becoming a nigger-driver and black-birder, as Sam Griffith (Sir Samuel Griffith, the present Queensland Premier) says," replied Gregson.

"'Nigger-drivers!' He and the government know better than that. In the early days of sugar-planting there may have been black-birding, but it was confined to a very few, and it is done away with altogether now. And as for 'nigger-driving,' you have more sense than to place any faith in that charge. And since we are dealing with figures, let me mass a few. It cost, twelve years ago, £10 to introduce a Kanaka into Queensland. The Government, by compelling the payment of a sum to guarantee the return of the native to his home, and by other restrictions, has raised the cost to a sum varying from £23 to £30. Now it costs me £3 a ton to produce my sugar. If I had to employ white labour it would cost £5 and more, and that would be ruin to all of us. Besides, the white man will not work in the fields, as any can see who cares to read the evidence given before the Royal Commission of Inquiry of 1887. The whole opposition to the planter is unreal and unfounded, and the country will find it so. Now take my plantation. I paid the Kanakas, who worked in the fields in 1887—a good year—£2,300. I paid whites, that I employed in the mill and as artisans, etc., about the place, £5,700, to which should be added sums spent for medical attendance on the men, for food, rations, and buildings, all of which were supplied by white men, and amounted to £3,000. Let us add fencing, firewood, and contractors' work, represented by £1,000,—and what have you got? The payment of £2,300 to the blacks and the payment of £9,700 to the whites. We must add to the money received by whites of the district and on my plantation a portion of that £2,300 paid to the blacks. They naturally spend a good deal of it either during the course of their three years' engagement, or before they leave the country to return to their own homes. Any one can see that it is not at all a question of slavery, but of cheap labour. And now, Cawdor, I'll take another swizzle."

In the middle of the swizzle he paused to say: " I've made a cool £10,000 out of Broken Hill, and that helps one to bear the irritability of the chap who sits on the inside of the public manger."

And that being said we all rose to go and spend an hour with the ladies before we went to bed. How better shall we come to learn of the graces that surround life among the squatters, than by being told that the hour was spent in listening to the music of Mendelssohn, Chopin, and Schumann; the songs of Liszt, Pinsuti, Lassen, and Wagner? In this isolated home of the west these things seemed quite in place. These people lived their life within themselves;—the owner, with his bookkeeper, riding over his place to look at a well, a tank, a whim, a McComas lift, a mob of sheep or cattle, or perhaps to watch the breaking-in of a horse; the wife to superintend the management of the many departments of her household, assisted by her daughters, who, however, every day, might also be seen riding through the bush or over the plains, sitting their horses as none but an Australian girl can. The lass of the back-blocks has grown into horse-life. She has been in the saddle every day of the year; she has ridden a hundred miles to a dance, or to see a kangaroo battue, and no horse can throw her, no danger break her nerve. She has not the colour and warm beauty of the English girl; not the simplicity and piquancy of the Canadian girl; not the verve, artificial deftness of intelligence and wit of the American girl; but she has a litheness of body and mind, and a pretty, breezy directness quite her own. She loves Australia, but that does not prevent her longing for the sweets of Mayfair, and the crowded pleasures of Belgravia. She is never quite happy till she has been to England; yet she has been known to be happy without marrying an Englishman.

It might, however, be said that the custom is growing, for English gentlemen of marrying degree to look upon Australia as they have been accustomed to look upon America; and they have proved this by carrying to their English homes Australian brides who keep banking accounts of their own.

From Cawdor and Cawdor's Eldest, Gregson, the Bookkeeper, and Pride the planter, we can retort the real Australian. He who is most of the soil belongs to the interior. In the cities so much English influence is working, that we do not catch the most distinct outlines of the Australian. But where the influences of climate, soil, and natural movement are at work beyond the cities, there we get the sharp contour of a century of Australian growth. Whether the rural resident is an

Englishman or an Australian by birth, by the time he has lived ten years in the country he becomes Australian, as distinct from every other nationality. The Irishman gains direction and industrial confidence; the Scotsman adaptability and warmth; the Englishman leaves off his insularity and puts on elasticity: and the Australian is slowly evolved.

Australia is a success because its people are a success.

A splendid energy lies behind all Australian effort—a faith in the possibilities of the country; a persistency behind the pessimism that comes with drought, flood, and mining and land booms.

Coupled with this energy are self-confidence, freshness, aggressive assertion, and generous warmth. Because there have always been difficult questions to face; because unexpected circumstances have called for immediate action; because development has come by leaps and bounds; and because there have been struggles between class and class, there has been produced an upstanding race of men, irascible yet hospitable; strenuous and stalwart yet not robustious; explosive yet not troublesome; uncompromising yet generous; hardy, honest, and true. That is the true Australian. The rough persistency and selfishness of the Trades Unions are not Australian. They are English, with a sense of freedom borrowed from easier conditions of life, and a knowledge of power gained from the most perilous forms of American and English existence. It is engrafted Australia—Australia in the cities—which is ultra-democratic. Australia itself moves in ample assertion, but it is not without sentiment or patriotism. Its natural tendency is towards hero-worship; but the faculty has not scope for want of heroes. No great national crisis no violent danger, has drawn the different colonies together in bonds of common effort; and of late years but few of the best men have gone into public life.

A curious restlessness marks Australian character. This is due, perhaps, to vicissitudes of drought and flood, and to the speculative spirit pervading the country. From news-boy to Governor the fever of investment runs; if it be not in mining, then in land; if not in land, in racing; if not in racing, in ordinary athletic sports.

It is to this type of restlessness, energy, and daring that Australians, by birth and adoption, converge. Mountain Jim was acted on by the same forces which made for endurance and courage in others, but the conditions were not even with him; the hardest swelled against him, and he went down as thousands of his class have done. If drought is hard on the great owner, it is a deadly clutch at the life and hope of the small proprietor.

When misfortune comes there is not sufficient in the latent character and the indrawn influences to keep the man steady; he goes down in the struggle; and that is all too common a phase of life in Australia. Seven Dials and Westminster, Fifth Avenue and the streets of the Bowery, are not in greater contrast than these two sides of rural life in Australia. And yet in both, as in Cawdor and Mountain Jim, the same characteristics may be seen.

Although Australia has a north and a south (not as pronounced as the United States has, yet distinct), there is little radical difference in character. In Australia there are not great extremes of climate. Differences are incidental, not absolute. The northern man has a trifle more of freedom of speech and action than his comrade of the southern provinces. He has more fire and dash. The south being colder, tends to more sturdiness and reserve; yet it is but a variation in the type, not an unlikeness. The methods of living in the north and south differ slightly. In this there must be excluded the high tablelands in the centre of Queensland, where life is much the same as it is in New South Wales, Victoria, or Western

CAMEL USED FOR EXPLORATION.

Australia. The coast is tropical, and the people have learned to live as they do in India—with regard to the climate in dress and building. That is not the case, however, in Sydney and Melbourne, where, with the thermometer at 95° F., the business man, and nearly every other man, goes to his office in a black frock-coat and black silk-hat.

The most delightful thing in the life of northern Australia is its *sans souci* appearance. Existence is literally out-doors, and people live as if burglars were unknown. I have ridden past houses in the early morning, and have seen the verandahs littered with books, *bric-à-brac*, walking sticks, hats, lamps, and other articles, —and the doors wide open. Night after night things are left so, and they are not stolen. Stealing is punished in Queensland with the greatest rigour. A man might be guilty of manslaughter, and stand in better odour with the authorities than the thief.

I have ridden to a plantation late at night, turned my horse into the horse-paddock, entered the house, struck a match, found a sofa, lain down, and awaked in the morning to find life bustling about me, my breakfast ready on the table, and I an utter stranger!

Such is the freedom of the life. I was a traveller: I suppose I did not look like a vagabond; they appreciated the desire on my part not to disturb their rest, and they apologised for the hardness of the sofa.

Every planter has not merely one room in his house which is called the stranger's room, but several; and they are seldom empty. In the days when I visited Pride there were six guests beside myself there. Imagine a house through which the warm air will blow from side to side and from end to end; with a group of buildings as dormitories at the left, and another group as kitchens and stores at the right; and graced with all the comforts and with little of the conventional stiffness of metropolitan life; which has dignity without show, and elegance without heaviness; and you have the planter's home.

Conjure up roses and bamboos, oleanders and camellias, limes and oranges, laurestinus and jasmine, pine-apple and bourgainvillia, the glorious pawpaw and grenadilla, a tennis-court, and perhaps an observatory; and you have a planter's garden. Then put inside the house and garden a healthy generosity, a great self-reliance, a mind given to insisting bluntly on the wisdom of its conclusions, a hand ready to pour you out a glass of sherry, or indite a philippic against a politician who has opposed Polynesian labour; and that is Pride the planter.

There is a custom not yet dead in Queensland, for planters, when they meet together, to solemnly raise their glasses ere they swizzle, and say, "D———n to Sam Griffith!" An act, by the way, which was as unwise as it was unjust.

The planter does nothing by halves; he will not even be ruined by halves.

What you find of lightness and comfort in Pride's house you find in degree in all the north. Order and cleanliness reign. You may miss at times verdure and foliage, but never sweetness and light (literally). Villages and towns are swept and garnished, and the people love flowers. Go straight across the continent to Perth, Albany, York, or Geraldton, and the same thing may be found.

Added to squatting and planting life, or really anterior to it, is the life on cattle-stations. It, with mining, constituted the first broad development of Australia; but wool-growing is driving out cattle-raising. The pioneers held to cattle-raising as long as they could, but when improvement, fencing, etc., was required of them, cattle had to give place to sheep. And so it is that cattle-stations have been consigned to districts further and further north, till only a limited number exist in New South Wales. They are chiefly in Queensland, the Northern Territory, and in Western Australia. The life is much the same as it is in Colorado, with even more isolation. Boundary-riding, mustering, rounding-up, branding, shipping, and selling and hunting wild cattle, constitute the scheme of duties. In habit it differs little from the life of the sheep-squatter.

It would be impossible to get a true view of the life of the interior of Australia without a consideration of mining enterprise, its influence on the character of the people, and its part in commercial movement. Bendigo, Ophir, Turon, the Palmer, Charters Towers, Broken Hill, and Mount Morgan, are as familiar names to the world as Virginia City, Cariboo, the Fraser, and the Black Hills. Ballarat, like Virginia City, has been a name to conjure with. Mining excitement in Australia, as in America, attracted men of all nations, and not the least represented at Bendigo and Turon, at the Palmer and Charters Towers, were Americans. The rush subsided, and thousands who had been engaged in placer-mining vanished; but there remained a nucleus of each race to be absorbed in the Australian population, and to engage in mining as a legitimate and permanent industry; that is, in deep mining and in other normal occupations. In Australia can be seen traces of American influence on the people in the use of expressions peculiar to the United States. It is to be seen also in the business habits and the pleasures of Victorians. It is a cord in the cable of Australian energy. Australia is at base English in idiom, custom, and political practice; but the superstructure rising from this base has some configurations not English.

Like America, though in a lesser degree, it is absorbing many races—Germans, French, and Italians ; but the English element vastly predominates. In this it differs from Canada, which, having a French population, has not absorbed it, and is essentially Canadian, that is, distinctive in its type, owing to the fact that it has a population at its south, with a different political constitution and social organisation, constantly acting upon it. And between the English and the American influences Canada grows up a compromise. It is a fact worth recording that the manager and mining-manager of Broken Hill were Americans, and that Mount Morgan owes its success to the importation of an American who had had large experience in Mexico, and who introduced the chlorination process, through which alone the complete extraction of the gold was possible.

We have before noticed that the best land of Australia lies in the east ; that it is hottest in the north, and that the nearest side to Europe is the slowest to develop. Mining has only succeeded in the east. No mines have succeeded in Western Australia, though indications have been plenty, though rushes have occurred, and though for many years geologists have been benevolent with hints of hidden riches. The important mine farthest west is the copper mine at Burra Burra in South Australia. It is curious to note, that all the colonies which have pushed ahead fast have had an impetus from mining. South Australia has had but one real mining boom, if it can be so called. It occurred in a providential time when the Wakefield colony proved a failure.

A word regarding this unique colony ought to be interesting. The idea was to transport a colony *en masse* to Port Adelaide. Land was to be set at so high a price that the labourer could not acquire property, but must go on working for wages for a master who was to become "a lord of the manor" in Australia, and so enable "society to remain concentrated, engaged in agriculture, preserving the same relations that exist in Europe between the employer and employed, and avoiding the dispersion of pastoral pursuits."

The proposition actually came from the land of Hampden that, in a new country, the feudal system should stretch out octopus-fingers upon the land, and South Australia become a Quebec of the *ancien régime*.

"It was proposed," philanthropically remarks Mr. Wakefield, "to transplant not people only but society. ... In Canada, New South Wales, and other colonies servants, taken out by capitalists under engagements for a fixed period, invariably quit their masters, because in all these colonies every one can obtain land of his own for a mere trifle. South Australia will be the first colony combining plenty of labour with plenty of land."

The colony began, borrowed money, failed, and was on the verge of destitution and ruin, when land containing the Burra Burra copper mine was surveyed, and all classes of people invested in it. The investment, however, true to Wakefieldian principles, was conducted with regard to social distinctions. The quality bought half, and the common folk—tradesmen and such like—bought the other half. Was there a kind of poetic justice in the occurrence, that to the common folk fell the Burra mine, and that to the quality fell another mine which proved to be a failure?

That is the only real impetus from mining which South Australia has received, and her population, though she began in 1834, is only 342,000; while Victoria, which began in 1835, has over a million of inhabitants. During the last few years South Australia has received the benefit of the nearness of Broken Hill to Adelaide. In truth this famous silver field belongs geographically to South Australia. Broken Hill itself is a great jagged wall, showing the corroding wash of water, as if, where now a schist and mulga plain grows to a desolate horizon, a vanquished sea had rolled.

At Broken Hill the "rush" is long ended; and, as at the Queensland Fields—Charters Towers, Gympie, the Palmer, and others—the industry has settled down to a legitimate commercial enterprise. Charters Towers, or "Tors," as by right it should be called, has much the same appearance as Broken Hill—an oasis of success, in a land of questionable fertility. The peculiar characteristic of Charters Towers and Gympie is that they are virtually co-operative mining fields. They are worked from within. Foreign or outside capital does not rule them. The miners have shares, and are interested in the success of the mines. The chiefest of the Gympie mines are owned by practical miners. The result of this co-operative system is that mining in both these fields pays. In the best mine at Gympie the yield is but 1 oz. 3 dwt. per ton; but that makes the local company owning it rich. It is all deep mining—from 700 to 2,000 feet. At Charters Towers 1,700 miners labour; at Gympie, 1,400; at Broken Hill, 2,500; at Mount Morgan about 1,000. Gympie is an idyllic town. It is built, like Rome, on seven hills, and it has its "Apollonian Valley" sloping to the sea. Far from it is any sign of disturbing element, yet it is the centre of a strong and aggressive labour combination; just as Bulli the Beautiful, in New South Wales, though one of the loveliest spots in all Australia, has a record for violence that sits heavily on the hearts of the population of the colony; or as Nanaimo, an exquisite place on the Island of Vancouver, is occasionally the scene of bitter turmoil. But Mount Morgan is the phenomenon of Australia. Twelve hundred feet above the level of the sea lies the town of Mount Morgan; and the Mount itself, before it became the prey to the acquisitiveness of man, lifted its shoulders up 900 feet towards the blue sky. It is the mineral wonder of the nineteenth century. It has defied all the conclusions of geologists and the theories of scientists. Gold could not be found unalloyed with silver, it was said; yet it was found so at Mount Morgan. It must always lie in certain well-understood formations; and yet ever since they began to cut the hill down like a loaf of bread, the geologists have been quarrelling about the formation. One says it came through "thermal springs"; another, by "volcanic action"; "a precipitation that occurred with a chemical outburst," quoth a third; "belonging to the Silurian period," protests a fourth; "to the Palæozoic," insists a fifth; and so the enigma runs.

The hill is a mixture of all kinds of formations. Ironstone and silica, kaolin and French chalk, brown and red hematite, ochre and "country rock," are all thrown together in a happy confusion. At Gympie and Charters Towers one listened to the mighty stamps thundering the rock and gold into a pulpy mass. At Mount Morgan the greater portion of the stone needs little crushing; it is rotten, and ready almost at once for the chlorination process. So perfect is the system of gold extraction at Mount Morgan, that the company gets £1,000 a year out of the oil rags used about the engines and furnaces. The mine is valued at £15,000,000.

Three years ago Australia had a mining boom, and two years ago it had a land boom; and all the time there is kept up the fever of speculation. If it is not in land in Western Australia, it is in Rhaub, at the Malay Peninsula; if it is not in city property, it is in new regions where prospecting is being prosecuted. What strikes one most strongly is Australia's powers of resistance to constant shocks of one kind and another. There have only been one or two financial crises in the whole history of Australia. This is owing to three things—the great resources of the country, the constant inpouring of English capital, and the sales of public lands. At one time it was the custom in all colonies to let the proceeds from the sales of public lands cover current expenses of Government, and to be applied extravagantly on public works, at the solicitation of roads-and-bridges members. One has seen in a country district, where there was needed little more than a siding, a railway station which cost £3,000, a policeman's house costing £2,000, and a court-house costing £10,000. Those were prosperous days. Money was plenty, and there seemed to be little fear that the time would come when the people would say, Where is our heritage? The system was eventually stopped, and, what is strange, the people never have seriously taken to heart the evils that it brought in its train. Of far greater moment to them is the exclusion of the Chinese, the prevention of the deportation of French convicts to New Caledonia and the New Hebrides, and the success of the Eight Hours' Demonstration on Labour Day.

It is peculiar also to note with what imperturbability the Australian accepts sudden political acts of serious import. He knows no constitution that may not be set aside when necessary; he never permits a personal loyalty to St. James's to interfere with any local political purpose; he does not consider England's position with the other powers in the prosecution of his own designs. The New South Wales Government in 1888, quietly defying the courts, set aside existing laws without a moment's warning, in order to prevent the landing of Chinese immigrants who were coming to Australia under regulations established by the colony. There was no immediate danger to New South Wales or any of the other colonies. The agitation had arisen from a threatened inpouring of Chinese at Port Darwin, 2,000 miles away. The real reason of this attitude we have hinted at before. Men in new countries are not bound by tradition. They feel that they are making a constitution, not being governed by one; they are used to meeting difficulties with shoulders braced, and they have neither procedure, custom, nor habit of mind to suggest, to compel, parley. A topic seizes the country, and it at once becomes vital. Five years ago confederation was a nebulous thing; it sprang in a day into active life. This is said in spite of the fact that a Federal Council had already existed for some years. In it, however, the people never had an interest, and from it two of the colonies stood out altogether. To the people the Federal Council conveyed no other meaning than would a Parliamentary Committee of Advice—a kind of Advisory Board, which it really was—without power of taxation, or having any finality whatsoever.

But a central Parliament, composed of the people's representatives, seized upon the imagination of the public; and Wilcannia and Kapunda, Cairns and Bega, Echucha and Guildford, rural places at different points of the compass, were as alive to the force of the subject as were the six capitals, including Hobart. This could be readily understood by observing the rural newspapers of the country. In each of the capitals there is a newspaper which stands gravely and firmly by traditions of decorous treatment of all public questions. But these journals are opposed by others of the most unconventional and advanced types—a compromise between a popular Radical newspaper of London and a normal American daily. In a very few of the large towns there are those of the first-named type; but nearly every country journal does its work without gloves. It always has something to work for, something to fight. It is a miner's journal, a squatter's journal, a planter's journal, a homestead lessee's journal; or it is opposed to one class or the other, and it spares not neither chooses its words.

The heart of Australia is decisive in its characteristics; it is either with the inhabitant altogether, or against him altogether; and the inhabitant is either with a cause heart and soul, or defies it, attacks it, or despises it heart and soul. And this character works down to the cities by personal contact and through journalistic channels. It meets other forces not Australian, amalgamates with them, and there is evolved a working class having instincts both European and Australian (chiefly Australian); what is European being a persistent demand of fresh privileges and better advantages, without that fresh spirit of generosity, if not equity, which the real Australian possesses. One can only properly understand this who has spent some time on a sheep station, or in a township or village of the far interior. The towns close to the large cities are colourless, are uninteresting reproductions of metropolitan life; but Charlesville in Queensland, Bourke in New South Wales, Moama in Victoria, Gascoyne in Western Australia, or Jamestown in South Australia have a distinctive idiosyncrasy. They are the centres of a peculiar life—of the variations in the Australian type. The squatter drives in from his station to attend a meeting of the Local Land Board, or to post the editor of the local newspaper on a new phase of the land, or rabbit, question; the homestead lessee, with more modest turn-out, rattles in (all people in the back-blocks drive fast) for his month's stock of tea, sugar, and tobacco, —the great necessities of the far west; the selector comes swinging down the red-sand streets, where even the gum-tree finds no home, and the imported pepper-tree struggles for life, to seek some favour of the agents of a far-off Government; the shearer, on a brombie which he has bought for a couple of pounds, shuffles up to the public to knock down his cheque; the sundowner, with his swag on his back, posts through to the nearest station; the stock-rider, "sitting loosely in the saddle all the while," gallops in for a change as he travels his cattle to the south; a daughter of the plains rides swiftly to the post-office for the weekly mail; a mounted police- man in his blue coat and grey breeches, spurred and armed, becomes a welcome guest at the chief hotel; the local justices of the peace meet in conclave, full of desire for ready justice, and maybe innocent of law; the In- spector of Tanks meets his enemy, the Superintendent of Roads, and they "shout" for each other, while they breathe out violent criticism on their separate depart- ments; and the mayor, who seldom fails in accepting magnanimously the fealty of all parties, conspires with all as to what public man shall be the victim of the next banquet. For let it be remembered that the Australian (hospitable fellow) loves this function before all others, and looks upon the payment of a couple of guineas, to give a feed and provide an entertainment of speeches for a Royal Commission, a travelling minister, a curious

BLACK TRAPPER AND MOUNTED TROOPERS AFTER BUSHRANGERS.

member of Parliament, or a local magnate, as money spent wisely and well.

To be hospitable ; to be uncompromisingly zealous in converting those who do not think as he does ; to work all questions out by experience and not by faith or theory; and not to borrow trouble—is the Australian's idea of the whole duty of man. It is not twenty years since, in and near the largest cities, the citizen had to resort to the piercing conviction of rifle bullets to convert the bushranger of the Ben Hall, Dunn, and Kelly type ; it is not thirty years since the little affair of the Eureka Stockade at Ballarat showed the decisive temper of the people. It is still the custom in the north to make proselytes of the most ignorant of aboriginal races by the power of lead and saltpetre ; but a few months have gone since the Governments of New South Wales and Victoria signified their intention of curbing the lawlessness of strikers by the action of Nordenfelts ; and only seven years are numbered since, with a firm desire to be doing something active and missionary-like, the Soudan contingent left New South Wales to assist General Wolseley in constraining Egyptian rebels to remain satisfied with the *status quo*. From all this the reader may, perhaps, catch the outlines of rural Australian life, and may see also how it bears in upon and affects social and industrial developments in the great cities.

CHAPTER VII.

URBAN AUSTRALIA.

IN regarding urban Australia one instinctively puts the capitals in two groups—Sydney, Melbourne, Adelaide, and Brisbane in one; and Perth and Hobart in the other. Objection might be made to making Hobart a part of urban Australia, since it is the capital of an island distant 150 miles from the mainland; but it bears as close a commercial relation to Australia proper, as Vancouver Island does to British Columbia, or as the Isle of Wight does to England, socially. At the same time it preserves a character for complacency, morality, commercial and industrial lethargy, honesty and simplicity, quite its own. Perth, cut off as it is from the rest of the continent, is insular in its ideas, and different from the other capitals in its political practice and social economy. Hence, these two small capitals are set by themselves, to be considered apart, or rather to be counted, in a summing up, as a modification of all general estimate. In regard to beauty of situation Sydney and Adelaide may be placed together. Sydney, by many people, would be made to stand alone; but there is a dignity given to Adelaide by Mount Lofty, in whose shadow it is built, that warrants the association on which I have ventured. The first glory of Sydney is its Harbour. The entrance to it is only five miles from the heart of the city; and all the south shore has residences or public buildings to the very gates of the sea. Melbourne is forty miles from the entrance to Port Philip; Adelaide is six miles from Port Adelaide; Brisbane is twenty-five miles from the mouth of the Brisbane River; and Perth is nine miles from Fremantle, where the beautiful Swan River flows into the sea. As a picture Sydney is splendidly composed. On its right it has the sorrowfully renowned, but lovely Botany Bay, and on its left it has the rugged and delightful Broken Bay. Its outworks are stupendous cliffs, breaking here and there into glens that slope to sandy beaches; beaches which may not, however, become bathing resorts, such as Long Branch, or Brighton, or Cacouna. Sharks have their abodes too near for unrestricted dalliance on these shores. The city is built on the south side of the harbour, but it has its little Brooklyn across the six minutes' stretch of water that lies between Circular Quay and Lavender Bay. The main harbour opens out into a dozen other harbours, but it is in the main harbour that the picturesque elements of the life of this first city of the continent may be seen. If a great creative artist had sought to combine beauty and utility, he could not have done so better. The composition is close enough for the spectator to get a fine focus of interest, and yet there is a vast suggestion in it, owing to the vistas of water that stretch away between the hills of sombre green eucalypti. In Port Jackson the nations meet. One has seen an English, a German, and a Japanese squadron in these waters at one time, and at others an English, a Russian, and a French squadron. At Circular Quay the Orient and the Occident jostle each other: Cockney and Malay, Teuton and Lascar, Gaul and Mohammedan, Slav and Chinaman, American and Fijian,

Briton and the dusky *protégé* of Exeter Hall, Australian and the world. The same thing occurs at Melbourne, but the picture is more scattered there; Williamstown, the landing port, is far away from the city, and it is not a naval station. Sydney gives the impression of beauty, of soundness, and of home; Melbourne of progress, of courage, of success, and of expansion ; Adelaide of comfort, of well-to-do-ness, and something akin to godliness, —for it is gloriously clean,—and of home also. Brisbane is new, brawny, uneven, and half finished. One thinks of Topeka, Kansas, in considering it; and that is to suggest a greatness which is yet to come. It has its coat off, as it were. It stands up with muscles working vigorously, and conscious of great latent power. It scorns to seek the shade, but bares itself defiantly to the glaring semi-tropical sun. Sydney naturally has the most shade trees ; Melbourne has few ; Adelaide has only enough to clear her of the imputation of bareness. Perth and Hobart are humbler, but, in some respects, more favoured sisters. Although Perth is in slightly higher latitude than Sydney, it has none of Sydney's close heat; its atmosphere is dry and buoyant. Hobart is regarded as a kind of sanatorium for South Australia, Victoria, New South Wales, and Queensland. Both places have natural beauties, but Hobart far surpasses Perth. Mount Wellington at Hobart gives the place dignity, and the lovely valley of the Derwent, the Norfolk River country, the Huon Road with its big-tree splendours and fern-tree gullies, the hop fields and the little farms, lend a sweetness to Tasmania, not found elsewhere in Australasia.

Architecturally Sydney is impressive, Melbourne is imposing, and Adelaide is satisfying. One of the handsomest groups of buildings in Australia is that in George

Street, Sydney, which contains, in one block, the Cathedral, the Deanery, the Synod Hall, and the Town Hall. Next in importance ranks the General Post Office, which has a breadth and a simplicity in effect very striking. The Post Office colonnade, where the nations meet to get their letters, is an example of a refreshing and commendable style of architecture adapted particularly to Australasia. At Circular Quay one sees the inflow and the outflow of all peoples; at the colonnade of the General Post Office all peoples Australianised. None of the older colonies of Australia have followed generally a style of architecture, either business or domestic, really adapted to the climate. It is only in Queensland where anything approaching a southern style has been attempted. There the arcade, the colonnade, the wide verandah, the airy balcony, the building merging to a cool and spacious centre, are found. The same convention which keeps men in high hats and frock-coats in a hot climate, held Sydney devoted to its brown-stone piles for a long time. In later buildings the revolt against this condition may be seen, though in both Melbourne and Sydney the bare, solid integrity of Northern architecture is dominant. Unpleasant people have said that the splendid extent of public architecture in Melbourne gave the impression of a city "built by the yard." Expansive and broad-shouldered, certainly, this metropolis looks, but it is consistent in its general contour. It is new, powerful, eager, and conscious of a fine commercial strength. Its architecture suggests all that by its very contrasts—by the Parliament buildings, suited to a city of two millions, dwarfing to meanness neighbouring buildings of form consistent with an earlier and more pioneer-like growth. To put wealth and progress and success in ample visible expression,—that is youthful, it is natural, it is Australian. Melbourne must have the largest public buildings on the island continent; Sydney must have the largest organ in the world. Sydney has splendid yachting waters, and leads in that particular; Melbourne has a racing carnival that is fast becoming a rival of the Derby and of Sheepshead Bay,—that far surpasses both in all that it involves.

"Palaces and piles stupendous" rise from all quarters of these two great cities. Within the last five years coffee-palaces of twelve and thirteen stories have been erected, which, in Melbourne at any rate, strive for prominence with colossal post office and white and gorgeous halls of legislation. The prevailing tone of the architecture of Sydney and Hobart is brown; of Melbourne grey; of Adelaide and Brisbane white; of Perth brick red. Sydney coils in upon itself; Melbourne grows outward. Sydney's streets are narrow; those of Melbourne are wide. The one moves rather heavily, the other goes lightly; the former is proud of its cab and omnibus system, the latter of its tram and railway systems. Sydney boasts the best houses on the continent; Melbourne the best hotels; Adelaide the best sewage-system, and Brisbane the greatest common sense and liquidity. The last-named place has flotsam and jetsam in its front gardens, instead of brogmanshia, dog-roses, and cactus. Sydney is the most politically congested; Melbourne the most commercially daring; Adelaide the most thorough according to its resources; Brisbane the most proportionate in its growth, the most advanced politically; Perth the most conventional; and Hobart the most religious of the capitals. The vice-regal residence at Melbourne is a cheerless palace; at Sydney it is a kind of Irish castle to let; in Adelaide, Hobart, Brisbane, and Perth it is a home. Because

TOWN HALL, SYDNEY.

of the simple homeliness of Perth and its vice-regal residence, one could scarcely wonder at Sir William C. F. Robinson, the present Governor of Western Australia, choosing that colony for a third term, instead of one with much greater emoluments.

Government House, Melbourne, typifies the genius of the Victorian people in its immense area of architecture. It is conspicuously democratic, just as that of Sydney is serenely traditional. Each after its own order. The double-decked, lumbering, but convenient tramcars of Sydney, which are in reality part of a railway not a tramway system, would be a horror unendurable in Melbourne.

Melbourne relieves its street traffic by railway systems into the suburbs from different points, as well as by its tram-lines. Sydney's tram system runs over one line and one street to a certain point of division. But it has at last been decided that cable or electric tramways are to be laid in different streets, and the railway is to be brought in from Redfern Station, the centre of all the systems of the colony, to Circular Quay.

Socially these colonies are very English in custom and tradition. They differ from Canada in this. Canada, in the west particularly, has been acted upon by American as well as by English influences, and she has given away here and has taken on there. Australia is not a compromise of any kind. The spirit is essentially English; the tone only has been affected by pioneer life, by crude environment, and by the dominating occupation. The dominating occupation is wool-growing; it involves much freedom and outdoor life; therefore society has breadth and verve. It inclines to directness and heartiness; therefore extreme polish and fashionable *ennui* are as rare in the men as delicate, social deftness and emotional languor are in the women. The constant contact with an English influence, either by education or visits to England, or by the regular wave of English intercommunion, keeps society from forming customs as distinct to Australia as India or Canada possesses. What may be called the squatting class rule society, with the gracious help of Government House. This last factor is important. Government House in the colonies is all-powerful; more so than in Canada, infinitely more so than is the White House at Washington. American society does not catch its tone from White House, and indeed can get along very well without it if need be. As a place for functions it has its social uses; but to be on or off the White House list means nothing here or there. That which is best in American society stands where no passing favour or disfavour of White House can reach it.

It is different in Australia. As veers the favour of Government House, so veers the favour of the people. And, perhaps, in the absence of the "claims of long descent," rightly so. There should be a standard of some kind, some polite tribunal in social life, as there is a judgment-seat in professional, political, and commercial life. The verdict of the tribunal may not be followed by the masses, but it is followed and accepted by those who lead in the higher areas of thought and social practice. Below a certain stratum socially—what might be called the Government House stratum—vice-regal patronage to any public affair, unless it be an outdoor event, has no influence with the masses in Australia. The Governor and his wife may go to entertainments, theatres, concerts, and that sort of thing, and the mass of the people remain unmoved; they are independent of any suspicion of being in leading strings. But let a function in which the masses are interested occur, some democratic enjoyment or demonstration : then the appearance and presence of the Governor is a signal for the greatest enthusiasm. It is not given to Government House; it is given to the high personage who has become sufficiently one of the people to attempt to enjoy what they enjoy. It is not so much an obeisance to St. James's as it is a patriotic applause of their own actions. That kind of loyalty is not a thing to be traded on too much. It is noble, but it is selfish, and it will bear no strain. Hence it is that the Governors of the Australian colonies, being wise men in their day and generation, appear at gatherings and functions where Governors of other of Her Majesty's dominions, such as Canada and India, might not be found. Such Governors as have shut themselves up from popular recreations and demonstrations have had rather sad times of it. Not to participate in and enjoy the sports of the people is a crime in Australia never to be forgiven. Sports play an enormous part in Australian existence. People live, virtually, out of doors most of the year. It is not a land of firesides; there is little crowding about the hearthstone. There is, therefore, something more of independence than is seen in colder lands, perhaps less firmness to domestic bonds. From year's end to year's end the tide of recreation flows. If it is not a rowing race, it is a cycling tournament; if not a yachting regatta, it is a pedestrian match; if not a trotting event, it is a running meeting. In the last-named we have the dearly-loved sport of the Australian. What would be thought of the Governor-General of Canada if he attended a trotting race? In what favour would the President of the United States stand if he were to be seen every day for a week at Sheepshead Bay, alternating between the saddling-paddock and the Members' Stand, responding in due season to the call of " 4 to 1 on the field ! "

GOVERNMENT HOUSE, SYDNEY, 1787.

or " 6 to 1 bar 1 " ? And what would be thought if the ruler at White House carried the point still further, and entered a horse of his own for a sweepstake ? It is all a matter of custom. What, indeed, would be thought of the Governor of Victoria who did not appear at the Cup meeting in November, or the Governor of New South Wales who did not attend the Spring and Autumn meetings at the Randwick Racecourse in Sydney? He would be much reviled for leaving undone what

GOVERNMENT HOUSE, SYDNEY, 1887.

the President of the United States or the Governor-General of Canada would be execrated for in having done. But the rulers under both conditions do what is expected of them; and at the Melbourne Cup Meeting, where 150,000 people (more or less) assemble year after year, not only the Governor of the colony may be seen, but four or five of Her Majesty's representatives from different parts of the continent. Flemington is to the

Australian what Kandy is to the Buddhist. He may get excited over a Chinese Bill; he may become heated, and cripple trade at the time of a strike; he may appear nervous enough to stone his political prophets; he may venture a short sum of savings on a Beach and Hanlan rowing race; but his affections, his spirited emotions, his genius for risk and investment prostrate themselves in eager devotion before the Melbourne Cup. The average Australian may not know the estimated value of the public works of the colony, the amount per head of population in the savings banks, the names of past statesmen of note, or the date of the Responsible Government Act and its initiation; but he can tell you how much was paid for the Flying Pieman; what was the time to a second in which Phantom or Arsenal won the Cup; and of all governors he looks back to Sir Hercules Robinson, whose presence, in the grave words of a big newspaper of Australia, " gave the turf a great impetus, did much to foster breeding, and raised the tone of sport generally."

It is almost impossible to conjecture the ultimate effect of this love of exciting sports upon Australian national life. The elementary investment and risk in it is part of the general commercial existence. The great saving clause seems to lie in the fact, that these racing and other sporting events are not attended with viciousness, brawling, or lawlessness of any sort. A race-meeting is as orderly as a tennis tournament; and among 150,000 people the police have little or nothing to do in the preservation of order. The sense of reserve and personal pride is high in the character of the people. To them racing is a recreation, not a dissipation. One general result is plain, however; any sudden financial trial or crisis would cause confusion to the energies and commercial interests of the people. Australia is not a.

country where self-reliance is developed to its fullest extent; it is not frugal. The private wealth of each individual in the colonies is represented by £300, while the population increased in fifteen years (1873 to 1888) by seventy-five per cent. Australian governments have been lavish in the expenditure of public money, borrowed or locally realised. During the last ten years Australia has spent on permanent works—such as roads, bridges, and buildings—and remunerative works—such as railways —nearly £635,000,000. This, of course, has given a vast deal of employment; but the extent of public works will not be so great in the future as in the past, and there will be a consequent restriction to employment from this source. In New South Wales alone from 1876 to 1886, the sale of Crown lands varied from nearly £3,000,000 to £1,225,000 sterling per year, and part of these moneys was spent on public works. It is not likely either that mining will pay in the future as it paid in the past. There has been a steady decline in the general production during the past fifteen years. Mines have yielded in all Australia values to the extent of £355,168,826. This, of course, gave a great impetus to commerce. The wool clip for the last twenty years in New South Wales and Victoria has been about £274,000,000, or an average of £13,700,000 per year. The total clip in Australia for 1891 is valued at £20,000,000. There is invested in sheep-farming in the five colonies £300,000,000. It is, however, noticeable that, in all the colonies, the last ten years show a production which, taking two years as a unit, remains almost constant. That is, while there may be a decrease in value through two years of drought, alternating with an increase through two years of plenty, the plenty years do not greatly increase upon each other. In New South Wales for 1879 and 1880 the record of values was as 6 and 7; in 1881 and 1882 as 7 and 7; in 1883 and 1884 as 9 and 9; in 1885 and 1886 as 7 and 7; and in 1887 and 1888 as 9 and 9. In Victoria and Queensland the ratios were much the same. The deduction is that the limit of wool-production is being reached under present leasing conditions. Should this be, and the population goes on increasing while public works grow (of necessity) less, there must come greater effort on the part of the people and greater enterprise in manufactures and agriculture, which yet have not strongly seized upon the energies or the capital of the country. Will the people be prepared for the new conditions?

I think they will. They are not a race of weak-knees; they have breathed pure air; they have a sense of social and political freedom, and work stares them in the face. The poorer classes—labourers and artisans—will, when the time of trial comes, turn towards the interior for sustenance. At present it is a difficult thing to get workmen or servants in the heart of the country. The centripetal power of city life is so strong that Sydney always has a number of unemployed. The supply there is greater than the demand. Much might be made of the cry of the unemployed of Sydney and Melbourne, but in reality it has not serious significance. During four years' residence in Australia I saw many gatherings of the unemployed, whose cry was No work, and Destitution. But it represented no considerable amount of distress. As a proof of that the proceedings of the Labour Bureau established by Government may be considered. It offered to give work on railways and at the National Park, at four shillings a day, to those who would appear at a certain time. In the first place the unemployed refused to take four shillings a day,—(beggars, it must be remembered for whom a too kind Government was providing),—

they wanted five. And when this was refused, but fifty per cent. of them appeared at the appointed time to take the work provided. That was the experience on several occasions. Life is not severe in these cities. Men know that if they spend their last penny in grog they can, at least, sleep in the parks. At one time, when a cry was going up about the outcast and unemployed in Sydney, I secured a policeman, and, in company with a reporter, moved about in the haunts of these out-door sleepers at midnight and after. Some apparently deserving cases were met with, but the majority had come to an unprotected condition through vice, or similar causes. The cases could all have been met by the Charity Organisation Society, which does such good work there as in England. Any distress that is now felt among working men in Australia is the result of centralisation.

The population of Sydney, Melbourne, and Adelaide is considerably over one-third of the population of the three colonies of which they are the capitals. And the most striking feature of all is that the capitals are the only cities, strictly speaking, in the country. From the 360,000 of Sydney * there is a drop to the 15,000 of Newcastle, the next largest city; from the 360,000 of Melbourne † the step is to Ballarat with its 40,753. This may be traced to the fact that Australia is not essentially an agricultural or a manufacturing country. The squatters trade directly with the metropolis, and there is only left the selector and small settler, who, in nine cases out of ten, trade with the squatter. There is, therefore, little to contribute towards the building up of large or numerous cities outside the capitals.

In previous chapters I referred to the paternal Govern-

---

* According to a recent census, over 383,000.
† According to a recent census, over 383,000.

ments of Australia. I have emphasised it in referring to the unemployed. I will carry it further, and say that the newspapers teach, and politicians and people accept, the principle that it is the duty of the State to see that no man shall starve; in other words, that it must either feed him, if he is starving, or give him work to do. Australian Governments have done both. Democracy has worked with a robust frankness. There has been no "softly does it" in the political creed or practice. The parks, the Botanical Gardens, the Domain, and the National Gallery of pictures are (in some colonies) thrown open to the people on Sundays, and with a result the straitest member of a strait sect would not challenge. Wise as past Governments of Australia have been in providing places of rest and resort for the people, those of the present time are not less so. The Centennial Park embraces 1,000 acres, its main drive being 2¾ miles in length. The sumptuous way in which the people treat themselves may be further accentuated by the statement that there are works of art in the National Galleries, painted by the best of the modern men, valued at £130,000. Each year, in the three principal colonies, there is expended at least £15,000 in works of art or sculpture for the galleries, gardens, or parks. The railways carry the children to the State schools free, and education in Victoria and Queensland is free, and in New South Wales, Tasmania, and South Australia virtually free, the rates being very small—in New South Wales but threepence a week for each child.

One of the most striking elements in the democratic habits of the country is that of assembling for out-door speaking. On Sunday afternoons, in Sydney and Melbourne, the people gather in the parks, or on the quays and beaches at the watering-places, and are harangued by the lower orders of preachers, politicians, and philanthropists. It is the love of excitement, and of doing something with an air of public importance, which causes so many to join the ranks of the agitators. As a final proof of the fatherliness of the Australian states, it may be mentioned that a permanently endowed orchestra has been established in Melbourne, jointly by Government and people, and an accomplished conductor has been brought over from England to take command of the musicians. The Victorian Government paid Frederic Cowen, the composer and conductor, £5,000 for six months' work at the International Exhibition in 1888. Sydney is following in the wake of Melbourne in this particular.

One of the dangers arising from the fortunate conditions under which living and comfort may be attained in Australia is already seen in the area of university education. Not three per cent. of the students at the State universities—charters are granted to none other—go through their course supported by their own hard-earned funds. It is a common thing in Canada, in Scotland, and in the United States, to see numbers of students graduating from the universities who have earned enough by teaching school, or some other occupation during a part of the year, to send them to college during the other part. As instance Queen's University,—of deservedly high standing in Ontario,—where four-fifths of the students are of this hardy, ambitious, and noble calibre. The reply to this would be that the Australian is not obliged to work under such hard conditions, and that the other is a virtue by necessity. That is partially true; but there is not in Australia the hungering after education and professional position that exists, say, on the American continent or in Scotland. The young Australian worships commercial success more than any other. He is political and mercantile; he is ambitious, but he is not self-denying. Perhaps this is seen more plainly in the working of the system of common schools than anything else. Teachers are trained for their profession. That is good. They are civil servants, and are paid by the State; they enter the profession to stay. What is the result? Teaching in public schools is at best dreary work; the temptation is towards the mechanical; and this is, in most cases, the deadening thing that sinks on teacher and school. The teacher has no higher place to strive for; his surroundings are ungenial; he is without much ambition, and the plastic minds before him catch no fire or fervour.

One does not dare to conjecture how far this Australian system, which does not make for aspiration in certain channels, may ultimately affect the general weal; nor does one wish to advance the doctrine that men cannot become ambitious, self-reliant citizens, unless they have had to struggle against odds. I merely point out a characteristic and a fact, and say that there is at present not the same strenuousness of achievement in Australia as in the other countries I have mentioned. Men do not work so long or so hard there as they do elsewhere. The mechanic can earn from £2 to £4 a week, and earn it the year round, since there is no winter to stop the work of the bricklayer, the carpenter, the builder, the farmer, the dairyman, the ditchmaker, and the labourers and artisans employed on public works. The artisan can live for a sum varying from 15s. to 18s. a week, if he is a single man, and can rent a house at from 10s. to £1 a week, if he is a married man. Fuel costs him little, meat is cheap, and amusement plentiful. Professional men consider the amounts earned in Canada or Cape Colony ridiculously small; and civil

Tramcar, George Street, Sydney.

servants are paid at a much higher rate than the civil servants of the Canadian Confederation.

As some evidence of this higher pay and greater freedom of money, one has but to look at the immense number of waggonettes and hansom cabs plying the streets of the capitals, the multiplication of clubs and theatres, and the crowds that on Saturdays and Sundays seek the resorts outside the city. Sydney has eight clubs, which may be said to be "in society"; and Melbourne has a like number. All the small towns also have clubs of varying excellence and wealth. Sydney and Melbourne have, each, three extensive and admirably appointed theatres, running every night, and attracting the best of London talent, as they attract large audiences. It is a common thing for a play to run fifty nights, and sometimes plays run ninety and a hundred nights; this, too, in theatres that will hold from 1,000 to 2,700 people. The managers do not depend on the fashionable folk for their patronage, but on the middle and poorer classes. We saw in a previous chapter how, in order to get recreation in a lump, as he was obliged to do, the shearer, boundary-rider, shepherd, or station hand, in the interior, as typified by Mountain Jim, knocked down his cheque; how the squatter and well-to-do rural resident goes full-pocketed to the Melbourne Cup; how people recreate themselves in the city by daily and weekly draughts of pleasure;—and now what conclusion remains? But one: that frugality is neither a constant necessity nor a habit in Australia. We have also seen enough of the Australian to catch something of his political idiosyncrasy. We should be prepared at this juncture to follow him into constitutional and political fields, and, observing some of his habits, his acts, and his bias, venture on a forecast of his future.

CHAPTER VIII.

URBAN AUSTRALIA (Continued).

UNTIL lately the Australian colonies have been provincial to a peculiar degree; as much so as Upper and Lower Canada were in the Fifties and Sixties, and without any of the reasons for being provincial which the Canadians possessed. Rivalry in Australia became jealousy, and jealousy bitterness. It is no part of my task to say which of the two great colonies, so closely vieing with each other in wealth, progress, and population, was the most to blame in the family feuds which waxed fervid on slight provocation. If New South Wales initiated anything that affected the general welfare, Victoria promptly offered it a wet blanket; if Victoria put on a stock tax, New South Wales refused combination on the Water Conservation question, or caused uneasiness in the matter of riparian rights; if New South Wales criticised an actor, an artist, or a singer, Victoria promptly took him up. St. Paul and Minneapolis, Toronto and Montreal, are not qualified to be on the plane of envy where jarred politically and loved socially these two cities.

But a better day is dawning. It has been erroneously stated that New South Wales refused to join the Federal Council through reasons of jealousy, and because Victoria appeared to be coalescing with the other colonies, having in view her own dominance. There were grounds more relative than this. New South Wales, through its public journals, and in the speeches and writings of its politicians, took a position of strength. It constantly and emphatically insisted that the Federal Council was neither "fish, fowl, nor good red herring"; that as a piece of political machinery it was incomplete and imperfect; that it had no powers beyond that of an advisory board; that it was not representative or popular in a political sense; that everything it decided had to be adjudicated upon by the separate parliaments; that it could not deal with finances; and in any emergency where it ought to be of use it would be empty of result and helpless. It aimed at much and signified little.

This view was borne out by experience. The Federal Council never achieved anything further than to bring an influence to bear upon the settlement of the New Hebrides Islands question, consisting of strong but justifiable protest against the deportation of French convicts to these islands and to New Caledonia. England's position in this case was difficult, as it was in dealing with the Chinese question; but in both she had to give way to her blunt, outspoken offspring. Australia did not care whether England was involved in difficulties regarding treaties or not. Self-preservation was her only thought. And she won in both matters, as she won in the New Guinea question, when Sir Thomas McIlwraith, the type of a laconic, strenuous, and wide-thoughted statesman, after repeatedly urging England to take what should be hers, and not let the Dutch and the Germans swallow it all, sent down a commissioner, and annexed the country to Queensland. It is this same statesman, so jealous for the integrity and dominance of the Anglo-Saxon in the South Pacific, who has also threatened separation at times,—and meant it.

Devotion to provincial interests has been shown in nothing more than in the tariffs fixed between the different colonies, as ignoble and as shortsighted in policy as if Missouri put a tax upon Kansas productions, or England upon those of Scotland. Reciprocity has been held to in principle by New South Wales only, though she has been forced at times to protect herself against "cheese, butter, ham, and eggs" from Victoria and New Zealand. Whatever may have been the faults of New South Wales, she has always been alive to the wisdom of free trade between the colonies, as she has nominally preserved the principle in her dealings with the outside world. It was, however, this colony, so long accused of stubbornness in its attitude to the Federal Council, from which came the present movement towards confederation. It said, moreover, through its great newspaper, the *Sydney Morning Herald*, a free trade organ, and through the pronouncements of its Chief Minister, Let the question of tariff be sunk in this discussion: we are willing to trust to the judgment of confederated Australia, as to whether the dominion shall have Protection or Free Trade. This comes from the colony that has always fought for the principle of Free Trade, and has almost continually had a majority in parliament to support it. Such a view of the question was not magnanimity; it was broad, high-minded advocacy, and consideration of the interests of the whole continent. The time had come. A scheme of military and naval defence was necessary; it could only be dealt with properly by the colonies combined. The feeling for confederation was latent; Sir Henry Parkes, the Sir John A. McDonald of Australia, saw the hour; the country knew its man; and his proposals carried the question to a remarkable convention which had for its object the drafting of a constitution for the Commonwealth of Australia, and the bill of this convention to the Parliaments of the colonies.

This is an evidence of the capacities for expansion in Australian thought and character; it also shows that provincialism was more the work of politicians than the will of the people. Politicians of a certain type have fed the selfishness of the population for their own ends. It was not any idea of the homogeneity of race that raised the hue and cry against the Chinese in Australia; that has legislated against Polynesian labour for northern Queensland; but industrial selfishness—quite justifiable, perhaps, but selfishness. The Chinese crusade was a mad one. It involved Sir Henry Parkes and his government in a needless strife with the Supreme Court of the colony; it did injustice to Chinamen who had come to the colony under existing laws; and it ended by the passing of a new law, in which, not prohibition, but restriction, was compelled. Robustious politicians agreed at last that they had made sufficient capital out of the affair for party purposes, and finally permitted the entrance of one Chinaman to every 300 tons of a vessel. There were 44,000 Chinamen in all Australia ten years ago; there were at the time of the agitation 50,000. For ten years the departures have equalled 65 per cent. of the arrivals. To the credit of the chief newspapers be it said that they did not share in the vulgar campaign against the Celestials. They pointed out the law of the question; they counselled a policy which did not utterly disregard the question of trade between China and Australia; which had a little international fairness and consideration. Nowhere in the world are there newspapers of more dignified, unpurchasable temper, than the long-established, conservative journals of these five colonies. They, with their weeklies, fill the place of magazines to the people, so varied and extensive is their matter. The Saturday's issue of the *Sydney Morning Herald* often contains twenty-four pages; and the Melbourne *Argus* is nearly as large, and quite as able and upright. In a crisis such journals can be trusted; they go far to steady the waves of popular feeling which occasionally take possession of this very decided, confident, and adaptable people.

Though provincialism in Australia has done some harm, it has also done good, and perhaps, in the long run, it will make for the general benefit. There are old politicians of the type of Sir John Robertson (lately dead), for many years Premier of New South Wales, who declare that confederation will result in political dead-locks, arising from the struggle on the part of each colony to secure the greatest amount of benefit and patronage out of the Dominion Government. These antagonists also hold to the belief that independent rivalry is calculated to develop the greatest amount of energy and wealth, and that confederation will sacrifice the better and larger colonies, such as New South Wales, to the smaller. Provincial autonomy they hold to be a gospel of commercial and political security. Wise men, on the other side of the case, point out, however, that there are matters affecting the whole of the provinces, which can only be dealt with by the whole; and that therefore a combination of some sort must be made: It is, then, a question whether there shall be the elaborate inconsequence of the Federal Council, or a body, representative and comprehensive, and having finality in its legislation. They admit the force of the argument based upon the strength of provincial competition,

SOUTH HEAD, SYDNEY.

٧

of individual and separate effort under conditions peculiar to each; but they also show the commercial value of political solidarity; the superior national credit and cheaper rates of interest that would ensue with union; the greater economy in legislation; and the important fact that the colonies are not now merely fighting for success with each other, but with the world.

There is an element of national depreciation in the segregated character of all political action in Australia. Until very lately a man from Australia spoke of himself, not as an Australian, but as a Victorian, a Queenslander, a South Australian, and so on. Nothing could indicate more the pardonable pride of separate effort and the lack of a national spirit. The same tendency existed in Canada until confederation. In the east it soon was absorbed in the broadening horizon of larger political conceptions; but in the province of British Columbia it is still the habit to speak of a man from the east as a Canadian; thereby drawing a line between the British Columbian and his right of nationality, bargained for so Shylock-like twenty years ago. British Columbia bears the same relation to the eastern provinces of Canada that Western Australia does to South Australia and the other provinces; with the difference, that a desert makes the dividing line in Australia, while in Canada it is the Rocky Mountains. There is this difference also, that the West Australian is not averse to confederation, knowing that by such contact he has everything to gain and nothing to lose; in that unlike the British Columbian, who replies to the fervour of American invitation by amiable commercial dealings. The east of Canada was willing to sacrifice much for British Columbia. These sacrifices were made, more for patriotic sentiment and solidarity than for immediate commercial advantages. It was legislation for the future; it was a far-reaching political policy. In the course of the ever-expanding discussion going on in Australia now, it may be taught, and wisely taught, that under certain conditions there is an ultimate advantage in momentary sacrifice; and that, should the older and more prosperous colonies make concessions to the others, the success of those others in the confederation represents a contribution to the general success. The sacrifices that any colony in Australia might be called upon to sustain could never compare with those which characterised the making of Canada.

Western Australia would be willing to give immense grants of land—such as it is—as her contribution to a transcontinental railway. In Australia nothing is needed more than this. There are now railway lines connecting Brisbane and Sydney in the east, with Melbourne and Adelaide in the south. Between Adelaide and Albany there is a gap of 1,500 miles; but there are no engineering difficulties to be overcome, because there are no mountain chains. Every movement that brings Australia one day nearer to England is a commercial advantage of importance: a railway from Adelaide to Albany would do so. In Australia there is no radical race question to be reckoned with in confederation; the sheet is clean for the drawings. The question of Polynesian, Chinese, or Coolie labour for the North is a thing to be decided by future political organisations.

As an indication of how mutable the executive of the Australian colonies is, it may be mentioned that since a constitution was given to Victoria in 1855 there have been twenty-four ministries, their average life being about one year and four months. Such an unsettled state of things would naturally suggest political brusqueness, to say the least. It has been worse than that. It has been, on occasions, more burly than parliamentary, more physically exciting than edifying. The lobby, the very chambers of legislation, have been made arenas for personal assaults, and for language that was worse than personal assault. Public offences have been condoned. It has seemed at times' impossible to convict any one, however culpable, of political malfeasance. This, however, has not been general in the parliaments of Australia; in some it has been rare. It has been most frequent in the two oldest colonies,—in New South Wales and Victoria. A confederation will, undoubtedly, cure much of that. It will give the people higher standards of political conduct, and better men will be elected. There being more at stake, and less likelihood of overturning an unsatisfactory government at short notice, a greater sense of responsibility and a wiser practice of selection will prevail. The prevalence of a tendency to palliate irregularity—political, commercial, and social—has been regarded by passing spectators as the result of the early history of these colonies. It has not been unusual for men who were sent compulsorily to Australia to attain high positions in the State. But, as a refutation of any unusual emphasis of the "convict taint," it may be noted that the most moral, religious, law-abiding, and arcadian of the Australian colonies, is Tasmania. Into Tasmania altogether 25,000 exiles had been sent, when transportation ceased in 1854. In Western Australia 10,000 had been absorbed between 1850 and 1868, when transportation to Australia finally ceased. Nowhere in the world does there exist a more simple, homely, and less vicious population than the Tasmanians, though people are still living there whose mark was once the broad arrow. We must trace the stream of tendency to other sources as well. In an active and growing community, any natural or hereditary evil receives impulses which are not excited in less strenuous civilisations. The hot pulse-beat of a semi-tropical climate—more sensuous in New South Wales or Queensland than in Tasmania—is not conducive of tenacity to an austere morality, whether it be political or social. But life in Australia, unaustere though it may incidentally be, is not vicious, however much at times the strings of dignity may be strained.

The rapid influx of people in, and after, the golden Forties helped to make a population inclined to democratic vigour rather than to democratic righteousness. The element of legislative selection, sitting lightly on the shoulders of responsibility, fitted itself in place beside laxities of other kinds. The whole movement of Australian life makes towards strength, while it, at the same time, makes towards latitude rather than severity in social and political conceptions. There is no innate evil in Australian life; it is too earnest, too active, too ambitious for that; but it perspires freely, and it has a long rope. Out-door politics, so common there, are conducive to interest, ease of understanding and change, but not to stability. In the same way the religious habit suffers from the summer life which the people lead. They throng the seashores on Sunday; they fill the harbours; they recreate themselves with no more sense of wrong in the matter than they would discover in the corruption of a politician or a government. Yet it is not a lack of appreciation of high standards that one notices in Australia; rather a sense of palliation, if these standards are not reached. In a country where employers pay men a hundred per cent. more wages on twenty per cent. less time than in Europe, the dangers referred to are likely to have greater scope for a period. Such evils as possess Australia are those that spring from prosperity, ease, and pleasure. It requires a strong nature indeed to stand, without excitement, an abundant exercise of freedom, and the joys of sudden opulence. And that is what the British emigrant to Australia has experienced; in it the young Australian has been educated. But there comes a time in such communities when the sense of prudence, reserve, and carefulness reasserts itself, and a greater general and organic safety is evolved. This is coming to Australia, just as it has come elsewhere, as it is coming in California and British Columbia, where like conditions existed, and still do exist.

And just as we leave this part of the subject, an illustration of how a wide liberality, coupled with great good feeling, characterises the Australians, may be gathered from the way in which the 4th of July passes in Australia. The American has always been a favourite in Australia; he is of a country that more nearly appeals to the imagination of the Australian than Canada,—for instance,—because it is much larger in population, and more *en évidence*. This is no disloyalty to the British connection; it is an admiration of activity, skill, big development and success; which the Australian dearly loves. When, therefore, the American Consul has arranged for a huge picnic or celebration on "The Glorious Fourth," there have been present the Premier, Ministers of the Crown, a Chief Justice, and perhaps a Lieutenant-Governor. When an unofficial party of Americans arrange a less demonstrative, but characteristic gathering also on that day, editors of papers, Ministers of the Crown, and politicians are present, the affair has public notice, and something more than cousinly congratulations occur. A Melbourne man glows with pleasure if he is told that Melbourne is like an American city. And so it is, commercially and in configuration, while its social habits are still English, made pliable by the broad-shouldered squatters, who here and there elbow the customs of Belgrave Square and South Kensington out of the way.

Australia is only beginning to think about its destiny, though it has always had a few rare and prescient spirits who have foreseen its position in the south; men who have prophesied, and even worked for, federation. As far back as 1857 a conference was held to consider the desirability of union. It reported in favour of it. But the people of Victoria were then in the first experience of separation; Queensland was working for the same end, and the two conceptions were conflicting. Strange to say, at the present time, Queensland is enduring the pains of separation, or of preparation for it. The situation is not, however, a confusing one. Northern Queensland, desiring division from the South, knows that it would be easier to secure it before the general confederation takes place. The South seems at last disposed to grant the demand. The colony will, if the bill introduced into the Queensland Parliament be carried through, become three provinces in a Queensland confederation, while this confederation will again be absorbed in the dominion or commonwealth. It is a noticeable fact that Queensland, the most northern of the four chief colonies, is the most advanced in its ideas. In all public movements it has been in the van. It threatened all kinds of things if England did not alter her policy in the South Seas; it refused to take a governor that it did not like; it demanded imperatively that Western Australia should have Responsible Government, and, at the same time, it led in what was called the National movement, which, interpreted, is Australian consolidation and supremacy in the South Seas. And this much must be said for Queensland, that she has a group of the ablest politicians on the continent; men of decision, vigour, political grasp and ample conception. She has sometimes breathed out slaughter upon the most cherished traditions of the Crown, but she has always come serenely into allegiance again, having carried her point. She holds to the creed, that the time must come when New Caledonia, the New Hebrides, Samoa, Fiji, and Tonga, shall become part of an Australasian confederacy. Her predictions may or may not come true,—the chances are they will not,—but it does not alter the value of the conceptions of the stalwart politicians of Queensland. They at least see something of what should have been, of what would have been in the matter of supremacy, if England had not, during the past twenty years, pursued a *laissez-faire* policy, and resigned herself to the mild, but sometimes fatuous guidance of Exeter Hall. England might have had all of New Guinea; she might have bought or bargained for the New Hebrides; and New Caledonia, Samoa, Tonga, and Fiji might have belonged to one confederacy under Anglo-Saxon dominance, both commercial and political, if she had acted in the interests of Australia. It is for Australia's good that these important islands should be dominated by the English race. Tonga has been ruled by English missionaries and German traders; Samoa by German traders and French priests; New Caledonia and the New Hebrides by the French Government; and half of New Guinea by German and Dutch pioneers. England has not, of late years, desired, or sought for fresh responsibility of government in the South Seas. She refused it in the case of Samoa. Germany has desired political influence and commercial supremacy, and has made a strong bid for it. France has contented herself with using her islands as England used Australia fifty or a hundred years ago. One cannot wonder at that impatience so succinctly expressed in Australian cablegrams to Downing Street, when such matters as the annexation of New Guinea, the Chinese Question, and a disallowed Divorce Bill come up. These cablegrams are always quite explicit, and consider nothing of any interests save those of Australia. The meaning of all demands is not to be misunderstood; it is in brief: "We belong to the empire, and you are responsible for our well-being. It is your duty to care for us and protect us; our commerce is valuable to you, you cannot afford to throw us over. Upon that base we build our demands. You have treaties with other nations; you have European anxieties; you have other interests besides those of Australia, which you must safeguard; but we have nothing to do with that, we must be safeguarded first. We are selfish, supremely so, but that is as natural to us as it is to you."

Nothing is more remarkable than this difference of attitude between Australia and Canada. In Canada, Downing Street is a name only used in political quarters; it would be "caviare to the general"—save, perhaps, in Newfoundland. There is seldom any friction between Ottawa and Downing Street, and Canadians do not find the yoke to gall their necks. Australia is so far away; it feels itself so out of intimate connection; it has been so jarred by intercolonial jealousies and excitements, that, when it approaches Westminster by cable or letter, it does so with peculiar local vigour and strenuousness.

Yet it all suggests a lively hope and energy. The temper of Australia is active; it moves, it insists on

From Harper's Weekly.—Copyright, 1891, by Harper & Brothers
THE PARLIAMENT BUILDINGS, MELBOURNE.

advance ; it has no difficulty in ranging itself in line with a movement or policy ; it is not easily shocked. And when Ministers of the Crown and politicians, having the confidence of the people, predict independence for Australia with an elected governor, there is no quiver to the public sensitiveness. If this were proposed at the present it would not be considered with favour ; but, as a possibility of the future, it has a glamour not out of accord with the blithe and confident imagination of the young and ardent Australian. It is, however, probable, that with confederation will come a steadying and elevating element in Australian life, which will be shown in a continuance of vital esteem for the British connection, and in a grave regard for the benefits accruing from that connection. The signs do not point so much to severance, as to the widest possible freedom within the boundaries of the Imperial connection. It is possible for Australia to have the soundness of the Canadian federation without its race difficulty, and the breadth of the American Union without its eruptive forces.

Australia's political dangers lie in the direction of over-estimation of the commercial possibilities of the country ; in the development of the northern half of the continent ; in, perhaps, too accentuated an estimate of its power and position; in wholesale legislation, as, for instance, that against the Chinese ; and in a general tendency to disregard the conditions on which a foreign policy may be successfully prosecuted—for a foreign policy Australia must have in due course : her position in the south necessitates it. Her social dangers lie in too much ease of living ; in the disregard of economy and prudence among the working classes ; in an excessive centralisation ; in the radical growth of the doctrine that the State owes the citizen a living; in a too extensive dependence on State aid; in the speculative spirit; in a somewhat heated sense of political and commercial power; and in the too amiable influence of climate.

As a sign of the confidence and belief that sometimes passes current as statistical soundness of argument, a reference to *Hayter's Year Book* is necessary. It is there stated, as it has been solemnly repeated in journals outside of Australia, that upon the basis of an increase of population, at an average of 42 per cent. during every decade, the following computation is justified. In 1901 the population should be 5,678,029; in 1951 it should be 32,782,290; and in 2001 it should be 189,269,663. This is a comfortable doctrine and a simple calculation. There is, however, left out of consideration all thought of the possibility of sustaining such populations; of the adaptability of the country for industries warranting such an increase; there is exhibited a disregard of the severe limits to which pastoral settlements—the largest source of Australian wealth—have already pushed their way; and an optimistic confidence in the power of the Australian to develop his country, irrespective of the forces, good or evil, which mark its climatic and continental environment. It is the same confidence, in the mouths of certain politicians, which asserts before the bristling teeth of the navies of the world, that even as the United States in the time of the Revolution fought, and won victory over one of the chief powers of Europe; so could Australia, having the same population as the United States had then, repel invasion, and possess her homes in peace and quietness. It is a similar cheerfulness which sets aside thoughts of give and take, on any lines, with China, the great menace to Australia's future; and not merely restricts, but practically prohibits Chinese immigration. It is a tendency to see but one side of a question, and that not always the broadest side. This is not the fault of the newspapers, but of the politicians of the burly, happy-go-lucky, vainglorious kind, not uncommon in Australia. It must be said, however, that there is also a class of politicians, composed of such men as Sir Henry Parkes, the Hon. James Service, the Hon. Alfred Deakin, Sir Thomas McIlwraith, Sir Samuel Griffith, the Hon. Duncan Gillies, the Hon. Dr. Garran, Mr. Bernhard Wise, Mr. William MacMillan, Sir Graham Berry, Mr. Bruce Smith, Professor Charles Pearson, Mr. Edward Clarke, Dr. Cockburn, Sir John Forrest, Sir John Downer, Mr. Edmund Barton, and Mr. George Reid, who temper their hopes with facts, and their aspirations with judgment. Yet all are acted upon by the general feeling of the masses, and by the process of fertility in promise, which has been a suave prerogative of many Australian politicians; not of them exclusively, but of them in a sense of suffusing fulness and attractiveness. It must be said, too, that, out of comparatively plentiful resources, Governments have, in the past, been able to satisfy the demands of their supporters. With plenty of money through sales of Crown lands, it was not hard to glut the roads-and-bridges members; with a Civil Service of infinite expansion, the sons of patriots could be provided for; with an ever-varying tariff the sections of commercial and agricultural support could be hypnotised. But the process is grown more difficult. Australia is fast coming to be governed by committees. The cobra-like elasticity of the Civil Service of New South Wales has received some check through the Act of 1884, which takes appointment to the Service out of the hands of the Colonial

Secretary, and regulates it by examination and probation. The railways in most of the colonies have also been put into the hands of commissioners independent of Government and responsible to Parliament ; and, in New South Wales, a permanent Public Works Committee, composed of responsible men, is established, to pronounce upon the suitableness of all public works proposed to be undertaken, of value over £60,000. Thus is the system of patronage being wisely curtailed in Australia. What it has been may be illustrated by the story of the farmer who brought his boy to the Chief Secretary of New South Wales, and said: "See, you have educated my boy at your public school, your high school, and your university till he's no good to me ; now you take care of him." . . . He was given a berth in the Service.

It is possible that the Australian confederation will be confined to the island continent and Tasmania. There are difficulties more considerable in the inclusion of New Zealand, 1,200 miles away, than in the federation of Newfoundland with the Dominion of Canada. It is much easier to preserve a connection between states with only arbitrary boundaries, than between those divided by the sea. Dependent islands seem to form in themselves distinct bases of government, and to have an abridgment of political sympathy at their shores. This is the stand taken up by the New Zealand people in the question of Australian federation. If such close relations as Vancouver Island and the mainland of British Columbia find difficulty in fusing their political elements, it may be safely considered that New Zealand and Australia would find still greater trouble in doing so. It is a question, indeed, whether Tasmania and Australia will work together harmoniously ; though since Tasmania has everything to gain commercially by the connection, it may not affect her as it would New Zealand, which is large enough to be considered a rival to any or all of the Australian provinces. Islands build up races with a genius, predisposition, and character of their own. The New Zealander is of a different type from the Australian, and the Tasmanian varies from both, just as the Irishman is different from the Englishman or Scotsman, or the Corsican from the Frenchman. It would appear that the safest federation to be formed, and the one beset by the fewest political difficulties, would be bounded by the shores of Australia proper. There is force in the plea of New Zealand, that one of the most important reasons for confederation is flawed so far as New Zealand is concerned. The Defence question called up the federation spirit; it has been used as a final argument to convert the sceptical; it has solidified sentiment in the colonies. But New Zealand cannot see how there can be any real union with Australia on the Defence question; she conceives, and not without cause, a system of defence of her own, not bound or trammelled by the weight of discussion or command of a parliament, a four days' water-journey away. So far as the land forces are concerned, the objection is certainly strong.

Australia is enthusiastic in military matters, as the Soudan Contingent may bear testimony. Although the regular land forces of the whole continent only number 976, and the naval forces 362, there are 21,170 militia volunteers and reserves for land defence, and 1,297 volunteers and reserves casually employed. New Zealand is left out of this calculation. It is remarkable, however, that with her population of 620,000 she has over two-fifths of the land forces, while her naval forces number within 400 of the naval forces of the other colonies combined. Military exercise is part of an

Australian's recreation, and great pride is taken in the efficiency and regularity of drill. The most popular branch of the service in the country is the Mounted Infantry. This body has an appearance of smartness, enhanced by the close dress of brown, and a rakish felt hat adorned with a feather, lately seen in London. Cadet Corps have also been started in the public schools; they are fast becoming popular, and are as useful as popular. If these are not sufficient to repel an invasion by Russia, or a phalanx drawn from 300,000,000 Chinese, they represent a possibility of coming strength which may easily be under-estimated. The earnestness of the Australian Governments in the matter of defence may be gathered from the fact that the colonies have combined to maintain a naval squadron, purely Australian, but under the command of the English admiral in command of the Australian station. The fleet consists of five cruisers of the *Archer* and *Rattlesnake* classes. The cost of maintenance of this fleet, amounting to £91,000, is to be paid by the colonies, and they are also to contribute the interest on the first cost of the fleet up to £35,000. Besides this Australian squadron there is also the regular British fleet of a dozen or more cruisers, corvettes, gunboats, and sloops, moving in Australian waters.

Against all dangers that beset Australian life there may, therefore, be seen the element of a great activity—the latent strength and the conquering faculty of the Anglo-Saxon race. The climate, if it encourages a certain buxomness, does not feed sloth or dissipate virility. If it helps to contribute towards that large drink bill of £5 5*s.* in Victoria and £4 8*s.* in New South Wales for each inhabitant per annum, it presents an out-door life of marvellous variety and sturdiness, which counteracts the influence of high living. The amount spent per inhabitant in Victoria for wines and liquors is three times that of France, and three and a half times that of the United States. The sum spent by New South Wales represents 8·5 of the average income; in the United Kingdom it represents 8·2; in France it represents 7·7; and in the United States it represents 4·2. It must be said, in passing, that the Australians have the patriotism to drink their own wines and beer. Under this head the ratio of consumption of native products to foreign importations is as 4 to 1. Lest the potency of this patriotism may not be sufficiently appreciated, reference might be made to the fact that the wines contain from 24 to 37 per cent. of spirits, while the beers have an average of nearly 14 per cent. These figures are not quoted to make out a case against Australia, but to show the comparative luxury in which the people live.

When all dangers to the national life are regarded, when the causes for good and evil are both considered, one comes back to that point of view where, with all irregularities subordinated, the general configurations and the whole action of development are spread out: and there is seen a young, valorous, buoyant country, a robust and progressive civilisation, which is reviving in these latter days the glory and the puissance of a decayed South.

PART II.

VICTORIA, SOUTH AUSTRALIA, NEW SOUTH WALES, QUEENSLAND, WESTERN AUSTRALIA, AND AUSTRALIA ALL.

CHAPTER IX.

MELBOURNE AND ADELAIDE IN 1888, AND THE CENTENNIAL EXHIBITION.

THERE are two impressions which most people receive when they first arrive at Melbourne : the first is the spacious appearance of the place, and the other is the wonderful activity of the people. Taking a cab at the Spencer Street Station and proceeding up Flinders Street to Swanston Street, thence to Collins Street and Bourke Street, the traffic seems tremendous, and the people are tremendous too in their enterprising pedestrianism. It would be impossible for the casual observer of this city's life to come to any other conclusion than that the capital of Victoria is the busiest place in Australia. The city has the appearance of a business centre. When mingling among the people socially, one gets the impression of a population who are given to entertainment more than simple hospitality, and whose life is one of money-making. You cannot escape the feeling, go where you will, that the chief end of life in Melbourne is to make money. Education is good enough in its way. Art, music, are pleasant ; domesticity is, perhaps, valuable in one's old days, when the capacity for the enjoyment of excitement is gone ; but the making of money is a perennial pleasure. Of course, just at this season it would be expected that Victoria should put her best foot forward, that she should present to her visitors a smiling face. That she has done so there can be no doubt. She has consistently lost no chance of letting the world at this time see her at her best. Victoria is written all over this Exhibition, and the world is made to believe that she is really the "hub" of Australia. All that is what a live young country would be expected to do; it is the very soul of enterprise. Therefore, from Premier down to peasant, every man and every woman preaches Victoria. It is a text chosen on all occasions, most often, perhaps, laughingly, banteringly, but it has a basis of intention and fact. Talk with a member of the Ministry, and he will tell you of Victoria's desire to be fraternal; but one can see also that the fraternal spirit is an elder-brotherly thing. It says: "I must be first, and then I will be gracious. I must lead the van, and then, behold, we are the very best of friends." And most of the other colonies have given in to her superiority. The Queensland Premier, the other day, enlarged upon the vast friendliness of Victoria and the northern colony, which declared the kindred nature of their policy. New South Wales, because she believes in her real superiority, has held her peace, or else has maintained a severe dignity. No one could visit the New South Wales court at the Exhibition without, perforce, saying: "This is the best of Australia." Men from all parts of the world, indeed, have said: "This exhibit of coal, and minerals, and wood, and wool, tells more of the great resources of this continent than anything else in the Exhibition."

But having thus formed a basis for after remarks, I should like to put into form some notes which I have taken, regarding the commercial appearance of Melbourne. Reference has often been made by strangers to the great traffic there is in Spencer, Flinders, Swanston, Collins, and Bourke Streets. This is apt to be taken as the general condition of Melbourne. If one does not study the conformation of the city, and keep one's eyes open, one is apt to believe that the place is a mass of traffic. It is, however, afflicted with congestion of traffic. If one takes a tram at the head of Collins Street, near the Treasury, few passengers, as a rule, will be found upon it; but as it nears Swanston Street it fills, sometimes uncomfortably, and so it continues till the tram gets to Elizabeth Street, and then the passengers drop off until Queen Street is reached. From Queen Street to Spencer Street, except at train time, there will be few or no passengers. And this, it must not be forgotten, is Exhibition time. I have come several times in a tram from the Federal Coffee Palace, which is at the corner of King and Collins Streets, and have been the sole occupant until Queen or Elizabeth Street was reached. This would occur at almost any time of day. The same thing would take place in Bourke Street, with this difference, that in Bourke Street is the traffic to the Exhibition Building, and from Queen Street there would always be crowded trams. The weight of the traffic is, on this account, now in Bourke Street. The real and great business life is, therefore, within a square, bounded on all sides by at most three-quarters of a mile. This means a congestion of traffic; it means that the body of outside commerce is thrown into a small space, and the result is an appearance of enormous activity. All the wood, coal, timber, and produce traffic, which, in Sydney, is not thrown into the main streets, but is seen about Sussex Street and elsewhere, is crowded here into the principal thoroughfares.

If one consider the vast harbour frontage of Sydney and the division of the traffic among such places as Circular Quay, Miller's Point, Darling Harbour, Pyrmont, and Balmain, it can be clearly seen that much of that traffic not noticed in Sydney, one cannot help but observe in Melbourne. One would not care to say anything for Sydney at the expense of Melbourne, but the two cities stand under view at this time especially, and the appearance of things excites interest and analysis. If, therefore, a stranger landed first in Melbourne, and went on to Sydney, he might be under the impression that Sydney was not so active as this capital of Victoria. There is no doubt that people move more quickly here, that they decide on all things with more rapidity, and that they have large elements of push and enterprise. But as to the comparative solidity,—that is another question. A Sydney man does a deal of thinking before he enters into a bargain; a Melbourne man sees a chance and takes a risk. The Melbourne man is especially speculative, and given to throwing the dice, as it were. Commercially the Sydney man is often so deliberate that he misses his chance. The Sydney man has not made the most of his opportunities; the Melbourne man uses them all, and is not averse to discounting the future. New South Wales has been, and is, prosperous because she has mighty resources, and has withstood bad management and lack of commercial enterprise and energy. Victoria has played every card in her hand, and has lived fully up to all her advantages and opportunities. She has drawn upon all her resources. She has sent out her pickets in every direction; and with what result? We shall look at that a little later on. She has not been content with doing business within her own borders, but she has established

COLLINS STREET, MELBOURNE.

her branch houses in the other capitals, and particularly in New South Wales, because it is free trade. She has taken every advantage that tariff and a selfish policy could give her; and yet many are disposed to question her superior prosperity.

Now let us see. In 1887 the total value of trade in New South Wales was over 20 per cent. more than that of Victoria, while the value per head of the population was over 26 per cent. more. As for exports, such figures as these are somewhat startling, while they are true. The total value of exports from New South Wales in 1887 was over £7,000,000 more than from Victoria. But this is for one year. In eleven years the average export of home produce from Victoria per head of population was £12 13s. 9d., while in New South Wales it was £16 10s. 6d. These are perhaps some of those figures that can be made to prove anything, but they are authentic nevertheless. But take last year again. The total tonnage of vessels inwards and outwards for Victoria was 3,858,243; that for New South Wales was 4,322,758, giving a balance in favour of the latter of 464,515. These are stubborn figures, and they help one to understand better the relative merits of the two great cities commercially. But while dealing in figures, if we turn to *Hayter's Year Book* we shall find some interesting reading. On page 515 it may be seen that the average amount for each depositor in the Victorian Savings Bank is £17 12s. 7d., while that in the New South Wales Savings Banks is £31 6s. 2d. Now, there is no test so accurate, so satisfactory, of the wealth of a country as the savings of the people. Mr. Giffen, the well-known English economist, in an address before the British Association, said that the vast increase in deposits in the savings banks during the past ten years in England was a proof of the more even distribution of wealth and the general prosperity of the people; this, in spite of the depression of trade, which, he contended, had not affected the people in general, but the capitalist. If, then, we consider these facts in connection with our impressions of commercial life in Sydney and Melbourne, will it not appear that those who bemoan the backwardness of the mother-colony have been pessimistic without a cause?

While speaking on the Exhibition generally, it might not be out of place to supplement what was said about the New South Wales court and the splendid exhibit of natural products, by some figures which will go to show that the mother-colony has a sound basis on which to build. She has her coal and she has her wool. Both are sources of great wealth for her. She has all that Victoria has, and more. She would be able to stand a season of depression better than Victoria. The wool exports of Victoria for 1886 were 4,999,662 bales, and the wool exports of New South Wales for the same time were 7,201,976 bales. What does this mean? The most careless thinker can see that, exclusive of the question of exports, there is the producing power of the soil, which is so much capital and so much guarantee of national prosperity. Victoria must, in the future, largely depend on her manufactures and on her agriculture, and, to some extent, on her minerals. New South Wales can never have the same success in agriculture, because of the difference in the rainfall, and the greater general adaptability of the Victorian colony to farming purposes. But New South Wales will always have as much success, proportionately, in agriculture, as Victoria has in pastoral pursuits. As for the industries, *Hayter's Year Book* gives some figures which are indicative, at least, of a soundness in the manufacturing interests, which speaks much for their continued and ultimate prosperity. *Hayter* puts the matter very simply in a few figures. During the ten years ending 1886 there was an increase of 13,085 in the number of hands employed in Victorian manufacturies; while the increase for New South Wales was 20,851, and the number employed altogether in New South Wales in that year was slightly over that of Victoria. But taking the later period of three years instead of ten years, from 1883 Victoria shows a decrease of 1,084 hands employed, while New South Wales shows an increase of 10,541. Now, protection or no protection, it would appear that "the tall chimneys" in New South Wales are puffing away their smoke to a good deal of advantage. Does it not seem that she is getting along very well without bonuses and bounties, without coddling and coaxing? The younger colony has been working hard for her bread and butter, and in doing so has bidden the continent look at the sweat of her brow and the labour of her hands; but easy-going New South Wales has been pushing along in her quiet way, putting up a tall chimney here and a small workshop there, until, in the race for sustenance and production, she has reproduced the fable of the hare and the tortoise. Given to ruminating as she is, disposed to pounding away on old lines, adhering steadily, as she has been accused of doing, to worn-out theories, she has somehow been building her wealth upon a rock, which even bad government and extravagant expenditure could not destroy. Could she have been destroyed, ere this she must have succumbed to the desperate pressure of evil report and internal discord; her wise men must have driven her over the steeps into the sea. But, while keeping her way, impeded only by the foolishness of some of her counsellors and the turgidity of her genius, she has achieved a position which one dares to compare with that of Victoria. All this would, perhaps, not have been recorded, were it not that a Melbourne paper has been announcing the superior prosperity of Victoria, while responsible men whom one meets here are declaring that she is, like George Washington, first in everything. Victoria has been "crammed with distressful bread"— the bread of a genial and splendid progress; and looking round her, like Chanticleer on his harem, she crows and challenges the world and her brethren, quite as modest, but not less worthy, to come and gaze upon her. One can feel her saying, always: "Now, look about you. I am mighty and valiant. I have built here a city in less than a man's lifetime, the like of which the world has not seen produced under the same conditions. Give honour unto me, for I am full of puissance, and wear my armour bravely." Well, she *is* valiant, bountiful, and rich.

Here in this capital of South Australia, where I continue these impressions, are quiet and repose, and here is a city of homes, where the sky comes down between the working-man's dwelling and that of his neighbour, and the pulse-beat of the people's life is normal, or, perhaps, a little too slow. But it is safe. As Richelieu says, "Safe and formal." Perhaps so, but still safe and healthy. The life of Melbourne is irritating in its restlessness and anxiety—an anxiety which springs from a fluctuating, experimental, and speculative commercial system. Strong, buoyant, full of nerve, prompt in action, impatient of control or resistance, Victoria is. It is a splendid colony, the garden, if it please you, of Australia, in point of natural gifts and agricultural endowment; and what it lacks of solidity, and what it exceeds in sordidness, will, her best friends must hope, be overcome by experience and the conservatism that comes with age. The country that could produce a Black Wednesday must have some strange trials before it finds its real place of vantage and stability.

Leaving Melbourne was rather a relief, after all the excitement, and official and social dissipation of Exhibition time. Already officialdom had departed mostly, and only the stragglers remained in the big city. In the Adelaide train, which I took one sunshiny afternoon, there were Chief Justice Way, Principal Grant, a very notable Canadian, a member of the New South Wales Upper House, a couple of members of the South Australian Parliament, and some ordinary folk like myself. The South Australian sleeping carriages are adapted to increase a man's self-respect, if not his vanity. South Australia is generally looked upon as slow, but I can count several things in which she is ahead of her neighbours. She has better sleeping carriages ; she has better refreshment rooms ; she has a better system of sewerage ; she has a better method of conserving her natural resources, as evidenced in the conservation of forests and some serious attempts at the conservation of water ; she is providing more or less completely and effectively for the education of agricultural students ; she has a professor in music at her University ; she has better roads ; she has better organisation and discipline in her school system ; she has had larger ambition, and has undergone greater sacrifices than any of the other colonies in providing cable and railway communication. This is, I know, a heavy list. It is a long impeachment against the other colonies, and it requires substantiation. I may not be able to prove everything, but as I am only giving impressions here, they can be taken for what they are worth. As for the railway carriages, thousands of people can testify what this sleepy little colony has done. Travelling in them is a comfort—a decided comfort. Beautifully upholstered compartments for four give ample sleeping accommodation and easy sleeping. The cars run so lightly that one can write and read with great ease, and the whole movement of the train is rapid and regular.

As for refreshment-rooms, South Australia heads the list. There is a good refreshment-room at Goulburn on the New South Wales line, and at the Albury refreshment-room a palatable cup of tea and a fairly excellent meal can be got. There is a descent though, in quality, at Junee and Seymour, and the up-grade of value begins again when one leaves Melbourne for Adelaide. Excepting the rooms where one can get a cup of tea and a sandwich, and selecting the regular meal-rooms, one would pick out Ballarat in Victoria, and Murray Bridge in South Australia, as examples of the best.

After we left Murray Bridge, there was the Murray River winding off among the hills; there were the cottages of German farmers who have lived here for a generation, and who took up land under the old 80-acre system, and gradually accumulated the comforts of a home about them; frugal fellows like the Scotch, good pioneers, good citizens. The only thing the German has done that does not recommend him is his having brought the stink-wort, a wicked weed, into the colony, for the purpose of curing bacon. It has not cured much bacon, but it has spread over a great deal of country, and, like the wild mustard and dandelion, is fit for nothing but to destroy crops. I was about to add thistles to the list (Scotch thistles), but they are benefactors instead of destroyers. So, after all, we have nothing to condemn the Scotsman for as a pioneer, except, perhaps, for beating us all at a hard bargain. Principal Grant, who lately travelled in New Zealand, and a prominent stock farmer in the South Island, from near Dunedin, told me that the Scotch thistle is doing a double office there. The cattle eat it readily, and it also plays a most profitable part in loosening the soil and adding to the facility and power of cultivation. The stink-wort does no such office, and therefore the German is debited with it. And here it might be mentioned that there is a very large population of the Germans in South Australia. A generation ago hundreds of them came out under the scourge of religious intolerance, and settled in the hills of the Mount Lofty Range, where they have lived ever since as farmers, market-gardeners, and wool-growers, adding to the national prosperity. In some of the suburbs of Adelaide one would think that one had stepped into a German village, so German is the life.

In the journey from Melbourne to Adelaide we get glimpses of thriving towns and a comparatively fertile country. The first of the important towns was Geelong, the inhabitants of which are called Geelongeese. This name, however fit in euphony, was applied to them for their advocacy of a railway, which ultimately carried away their prosperity, and left them lamenting. But the Geelongeese have always had pride enough to think that their burgh should have been the capital of Victoria. Perhaps they still look forward to possessing the capital of federated Australia. In Victoria we saw, in passing, stretches of wattle planted along the railway line. These had been started as an experiment, and it has proved successful. The bark is used for tanning, and is valued at £7 per ton. It is better than the oak bark, and is fast coming into universal use, while large quantities of it are shipped to England and elsewhere. In South Australia there are a great many wattle plantations, and it bids fair to become a prosperous industry here. We passed a good deal of mallee-scrub land on the journey, as well as fine farm land.

While speaking about the Germans I omitted to mention the care which they take of their farming implements and stock. The first thing a young Englishman does, when he comes out here and takes up land, is to make himself comfortable first, to build himself a good house, and surround himself with conveniences: his stock and appliances of his trade are the last thing thought of; but the German is different. He is content with wattle-and-dab, with a mud hut—with a hole in the ground, indeed, so that his stock is well cared for and his implements properly housed. It was suggestive, both in Victoria and South Australia, to see along the railway line farming implements—strippers, rollers, harrows, and ploughs—lying out in the bad weather, uncared for. That is slovenly farming. No matter that the fields were green and the wheat bade fair to be a good harvest; that the houses stand in gardens, where the brogmanshia, the heliotrope, the flame-tree, the tea-roses, and the sweet-smelling carnation bloom; if the tools of the workmen were left the sport of the elements and the sign of the sluggard. The mallee scrub, it is not unlikely, will become more valuable than if has been in the past. It is a fine wood to burn, and if a coal famine should happen, the colonies will have to depend upon it. There is fortunately no lack of it, and it can be laid down in Adelaide for 6s. to 8s. per ton. Its value too as a heat-giving power is about one-half that of coal, so that if the supply were constant there would be no great loss to the community generally. The steamers and the gas companies would feel the calamity most. In Adelaide there is no excitement regarding the present strike at Newcastle, and people are prepared to face the thing squarely, though sympathy, it can be safely said, is not at all with the workmen. In fact, Adelaide is not a place where the people would become very excited about anything. One guessed that as, upon Mount Lofty, one looked out towards it, 1,500 feet above the level of the sea: and when we came winding down past the pretty residences, and the quiet places where the market gardener had comfortably ensconced himself, we felt we were coming to a steady and slow, but healthy city, socially, politically, and commercially.

One of the first things to strike the stranger in Adelaide is the cheapness of cab-hire. It is carefully regulated by the Government, and, what is more, the regulations are obeyed. One can get a hansom cab for three hours for 10s., and for 2s. 6d. per hour after. Everything is as green about the city as a bright sun and plenty of rain can make it. It is a pity the same cannot be said of the great interior, for business men and station-holders tell me that up country there is no rain; that in the Darling country there is no feed; that from Menindie to Bourke no patch of grass is seen to refresh the weary waste of sand, while the river is nearly dry. How different from two years ago, when the Darling was a deep brawling stream which rose above the banks, and flooded the country for miles on either side; when the river plains were carpeted with a miracle of native flowers; and far and near on the wild country, between Wilcannia and Menindie, Sturt's pea, with its flaming top, was seen; and the sandalwood tree, the myall and the jarrah were washed of their dust, and the pall of grey was lifted from the land! Somehow I dread to face the desert, because the memories of that far west were kind ones, and I had seen the squatter at his best. But I shall be in the midst of it in a day or two. I shall see Broken Hill and the mines where more than shafts have been sunk; shall see the crushers that crush more than ore; shall find the places where men have made fortunes, and where others have saddled themselves with heavy debts, besides having lost their all. But unless one gets into the heart of the business circle here, one does not know of the working of the forces that help to give prosperity to this colony, or cast a cloud upon its hopes. Broken Hill was expected to do much for Adelaide, and it has done something, but not nearly as much as was anticipated. Sydney supplies far more goods to Broken Hill than does the capital of South Australia; and Melbourne more than both. Adelaide ought to have profited more. There are smelting works not far from Adelaide where the ore is melted down, and so the city gets a good deal of benefit from the mine that turns out its 92,000 ozs. of silver weekly. Hope is high here regarding the return of these mines, and the heart of the population has been made happier by the announcement of the Treasurer in the Assembly that there is a surplus of £173,000. There have been hard times here for several years, and the people have been forced to learn the lesson of economy. They have been stopped in luxurious courses, and have been made to understand that fortune is not with them always. Public and private enterprise has been crippled, and retrenchment has been the order of the day all round. Mr. Playford, the

VICTORIA SQUARE AND KING WILLIAM STREET, ADELAIDE.

Premier, has pleased the community by giving it a surplus of revenue. As the result of the protective tariff, it may not be so enduring as the country could hope, but it gives hope, and that is all-important. The public debt is large, but not unusually so, considering the magnitude of the public works entered upon, such as the transcontinental telegraph and railway lines. A public debt of £19,397,700 looks startling for a small colony of 340,000 of population; but it is not indebtedness, strictly speaking. There are assets: the railways and the telegraph lines stand there to represent money, and though as yet they do not pay, some day perhaps they will. There is something concerning the Assembly here, which other parliaments might take into consideration. It meets at 2 o'clock in the afternoon, and rises at 6.30 as a rule. Blessed observance.

Commercially Adelaide is not very sound, and the most patriotic of its citizens say that the unsoundness is not cured by the fact that so many stand at the street corners, and cry, *Ichabod*. One would not find a Victorian doing that. He has too much pride, too much ambition, too much self-confidence. Unhappy is that country or that city where the people, like the Israelites of old, hang their harps on the willows and refuse to sing. The world believes in you very much as you estimate yourself, provided you have resources and are willing to fight for the portion you demand; and so I do not wonder that sensible and loyal men feel that injustice is being done to this city by the children of its own household. But looking upon Adelaide with the eye of the uninitiated, one would say that it was most prosperous, contented, and home-like. It preserves the last of these qualities to an extraordinary degree; and there is no swagger of any sort, from the Governor down. There are some fine men here, too,—able, thoughtful, representative men,—who remind one, in their sterling merit, of Sir John Hay,* the President of the New South Wales Legislative Council; such as Sir Samuel Davenport, Sir Henry Ayers, Chief Justice Way, the Hon. William Angas, Sir John Morphett, the Hon. Mr. Tompkinson, Mr. Barr-Smith, Sir John Downer, the Hon. J. C. Bray,† and others; men of courtly presence and steadiness of thought, and who are the backbone of the moral and social life of the community.

It would be impossible to visit Adelaide without becoming interested in vine, olive, and fruit culture generally. A little thought given to the matter impresses one with the belief that South Australian prosperity will date from the time that "their corn, and wine, and oil increased." The vast district to the north, the continuation of these plains whereon Adelaide is built, will never be a source of great wealth to the country. The fringe of land at Port Darwin may be used for sugar-culture and mining, but such wealth as may spring from that will not affect the interests of the south to any great extent. It may be safely concluded that, when the north becomes strong enough, it will ask to be cut off from the south, and the desert will be divided between the two colonies.

It does not appear that the colony will ever be a very wealthy one,—not so wealthy possibly as Victoria or New South Wales,—but there is no reason why it should not be safely and comfortably prosperous. There are some evils, however, common to all the colonies, which work to particular disadvantage here. In the first place, this

---

* Sir John Hay has died while this book is going through the press.

† Mr. Bray has since been knighted, and accepted the position of Agent-General for South Australia in London.

generation of farmers are not careful, frugal folk; in the second place, they will not be taught what they can best grow to work their land to advantage; and, worse than all, the labourer will not fulfil the conditions whereby people of this world, of different occupations, live and let live. A short time ago, a sturdy, sensible fellow considered that he could start a fruit farm at the foot of the Flinders range, 100 miles away; and, taking advantage of plenty of water and a fine mountain climate, grow as proportionately wealthy as the German market-gardener nearer the city in the Mount Lofty range. But with his first crop his hopes ended, for he found that he could get no women to pick his strawberries and olives—only men at 8*s.* a day. What industry could thrive under such conditions? He was ruined. Others have fallen by the way in the same fashion. And the farmers prefer to work on, striving to make five bushels of wheat grow to the acre, rather than go into the fields with their families, and cultivate the grape, the olive, and the strawberry, and find their living in 10 acres, where they cannot get it now out of 300 acres. Prominent men have told me that the farmers as a class are poor here. They live on borrowed money. They buy machinery on credit, and give their creditors a bill of sale on it. With such farming is it any wonder that South Australia's back should grow heavy with public debt? One of the oldest members of the Upper House told me, in the presence of Sir Henry Ayers, that he had had no rent for two years from his tenants, and that he had even furnished them seed, but he was determined to give that system up, for the farmers would not help themselves. Sir Samuel Davenport, whose place I visited, did not speak hopefully of the farmer and his interest in fruit-growing. He seemed to think that the farmer is slow to learn; that he is better pleased to grow hopelessly poor on his five and six bushels of wheat to the acre, than to educate himself to the surer and more pleasant occupation of small vigneron and olive planter. The farmer of this generation insists on living well,—both he and his family. He will not bend his back to the yoke, as did the Scottish and German pioneers before him. And the future of agriculture here is not bright.

One day, in company with Principal Grant, I went, at Chief Justice Way's invitation, to visit his stock farm "Kadlunga." I began then to gather information which has given the cue to much that is recorded here. It was shortly after seven o'clock when we started from the railway station, and the whole day or two days were before us. It was not long before the smelting works came in view which represent the source of that 92,000 ozs. of silver which Broken Hill furnishes Adelaide every week. Trucks were loaded with ore, and scores of men were at work. But, as I shall have an opportunity to discuss the mining question from Broken Hill itself, we will let it pass here. Perhaps the two most interesting things on the route were the Government Sewage Farm and the Agricultural College. The sewage farm confines about 160 acres. All the sewage from the city is carried in mains to this farm a few miles away. It is then pumped up and deodorised, and distributed over the farm by troughs. The principle seems to be a right one; and it is avowed that the process of deodorisation is so complete, that some learned and healthy councillors of the city, to show their faith in the completion of the work, drank some of the deodorised water. The agitation for this sewage system is very strong in Melbourne, and it is likely to be introduced there. Adelaide is remarkably well drained, and

Melbourne and Sydney are anything but that. The initial cost of the work is borne by the Government, and the municipality pays the interest and manages the works. The farm returns fairly in its crops, as fairly as any Government farming would, for no one has ever much faith in the money-making capacity of a Government. If a Government can make five per cent. out of anything, an ordinary individual, given the same capital and opportunities, ought to make ten per cent.

The Agricultural College has had its ups and downs, and is not yet in a position where it can be said to be entirely successful. The first principal laboured hard for its welfare; but he came into aggressive contact with a farmers' association and with the Government, and he resigned. The present principal works along bravely, like a man with one hand tied behind his back. He is the only professor, and on his shoulders rests the burden of all the teaching. He has not sufficient apparatus, and he is expected to lecture to students on scientific farming without scientific appliances; and, worse than all, the land which he is working is far from being the best. It is said that the Government deliberated on the matter thus: "If a poor farm can be made to pay, what an advertisement it will be to the Agricultural College! What a proof it will be that scientific farming is a good thing!" So, handicapping the principal on every side, and giving him five times the work they ought to have done, they now shake their heads sagely, and are by no means sure that scientific farming is as good as it has been proclaimed. Those who would be expected, however, to be good judges, say that the college has done as well as is possible in the circumstances; and that the farmers have been much benefited by it, inasmuch as it has at least stirred them up to consider theories, and give their opinions on practical farming. But what college could prove a success that had not the facilities wherewith to prosecute its labours and perform its functions? Past experience has shown that agricultural schools and model farms can do much to direct the labours of farmers, and if an institution of the kind is needed anywhere it is in South Australia. Against the first farmers, the old pioneers, no one can be found to make complaint. It is the late immigration—those who have to some extent taken the place of the old settlers—which comes under disapproval.

Not far from the Agricultural College, on the other side of the line, is the Labour Prison of the colony; and further on is the ambitious town of Gawler, with its 2,500 inhabitants and its many workshops wherein the Government locomotives are being made. It is pleasant, when one has been saying what might be considered disagreeable things, to express opinions of a more complimentary type. On the way to Kadlunga I came across a practical man, who is largely interested in land. He pointed out land to the extent of 12,000 acres which he said had been thrown over by farmers as unworkable, through lack of water. The land was bought at a song, and one of the owners, being a scientific farmer, proceeded to search for water, and having at last found it in the sandhills, proceeded to irrigate; and now the barren soil yields its five and six bushels to the acre; and this, he tells me, pays the small farmers when they have enough under crop. What would the English, the New Zealand, the Canadian farmer, think of five bushels to the acre?

There was a place in the hills pointed out where, it is expected, water will be conserved to irrigate the great plains which stretch down to the sea. The cost is estimated at half a million, and the results will be, it is confidently believed, commensurate with the expenditure. The great reservoir will be fed from the streams in the hills, and the power of gravitation will do what is so difficult to do on the River Darling, where water has to be pumped at a cost in proportion to the height of the river and the amount to be distributed upon the land. Already conservation has been tested in the Flinders range, where water is supplied to several mining towns and to the small farmers of the district. Time was when the people up country bought all their vegetables in Adelaide from the German and English market gardeners; but, of late, vegetables have been grown in these watered districts, and the process of production and consumption goes on. The possibility of water conservation is always reasonable in the vicinity of mountain ranges, and that has been one of the secrets of the success of the Chaffey Brothers in southern California. They got their water largely by the force of gravitation, and were able to distribute it over the land with greater facility, and at reasonable cost. At Mildura, in Victoria, they do not find such advantages, and one is not certain as to the absolute success of their project. Of course, it is too early to venture an opinion; but unprejudiced men have not been slow to say that there is no great wave of public interest in the matter, and that selections cannot be disposed of as freely as when these Canadians first opened up the irrigation farms. For the sake of the country it is to be hoped that the venture may prove prosperous. The Chaffey Brothers have certainly gone into it with their eyes open. They have not undertaken the task as tyros, and their efforts, if successful, will stimulate water conservation and irrigation in other parts of the colonies. Remembrances of a past experience with the squatters and farmers on the Darling are not, however, calculated to arouse much hope for the far west of New South Wales. "The land," said they, "will grow anything, if it has moisture; but it absorbs water at a terrific rate, and the supply is the thing. Where is it to come from?"

The farmers of South Australia cultivate wheat mostly, and their hay consists of wheat or oats cut green. Along the line one noticed fields which had been stripped; a system believed to be in other countries pernicious; but here it is a custom, and machines are used for the purpose. There were some fields, too, of last year's hay, faded and discoloured, and the un-initiated might regard it as a wasted growth; but it is just as valuable a food as if it had been cut last year in season. The sheep along the line in many places did not look well. They had eaten the fields bare. The owner will, in a short time, turn them out in the roads with a shepherd, to let them pick the grass there for a few weeks, and give his fields a chance to rest and a new crop of grass to grow. Then he will bring them back again, and so work them through a bad season.

Getting out at Saddleworth, we took coach to Clare. We passed through a beautiful piece of country,—the best that I have seen in South Australia, and as good as what was seen in Victoria or in the Hunter River district of New South Wales. One did not see, however, the general evidences of careful farming which strike one in parts of Victoria; but the country had had plenty of rain, and it was fresh and green. Here and there were olive groves and vineyards and orangeries. Old-fashioned, one-storied stone houses dotted the pleasant valleys, and one thought of the vast and desolated Australia of the north, the place of heat and sand and scorching winds. We passed, at the rate of eight miles, and even nine, an hour, the little towns of Auburn, Wakefield, Seven Hills (where the Jesuit College is, with its vineyard and wine-making students), and Dombrook; then, in a sudden rain, we came to Clare. On the way we had seen the splendid Treloar vineyard, and had heard repeated the labour difficulty, and the statement that large farms could not be successfully worked, because of the difficulty of getting labourers at decent wages, or, indeed, at all. We had discussed the wisdom of the policy of South Australia in charging a pound an acre for land, when, in other new countries, land that would grow 40 bushels of wheat to the acre could be got for nothing, and with plenty of time to pay it in. We found occasion to consider why it was that the labourer and the small farmer actually opposed immigration, while at the same time they folded their hands when they might be labouring for their own prosperity, and, through it, for the prosperity of the country. But these subjects brought little that was pleasant in their train, for the mind followed it up to the present agitation and threatened strike in Sydney, and this was not a charming thing for meditation. Among the sagest and ablest of public men here, the opinion exists, that the only cure for the evil—the only way to get the equilibrium again—is by union of the employers, and by boards of arbitration to adjudicate between the employés and the employers. Since the evil exists, this is the one reasonable and least irritating way out of present embarrassments.

The stay at Clare was a pleasant one. It was natural that at lunch one should choose South Australian wine for a beverage, and so two brands were set before us. One was called "Constantia," and the other was a "fine old red wine." Both were rather indefinite, considering that the name of the wine-maker was not on the bottles; but we tasted them nevertheless. They were very sugary and heavy, and would be slow poison to one of a bilious temperament. The people here do not drink dry wines. They prefer the heavier and sweeter wines. This and other things shall be spoken of more definitely elsewhere. South Australian sweet wines cannot be sold in the London market. This was told me by a dealer who is out here now from London, buying up wines and establishing connections. We visited the school, having been waited on by the Board of Advice of the district; and I was glad we did so, because it was the first opportunity I had had of seeing the working of the South Australian system of education. This school at Clare contrasted favourably with the schools in the interior of New South Wales and Victoria. There was an air of brightness and activity in the faces of the children, and the methods were intelligent. What had struck me elsewhere at times was the mechanical method of imparting instruction, the simultaneous process improperly used—the beginning of dulness and inattention. One could not help but notice, at this well-taught school at Clare, the necessity for young men of active brains, ambition, and education, as teachers. South Australia is particularly fortunate in its Inspector-General. He is a man of wide grasp, of great educational experience, a born disciplinarian, an acute observer, and a good organiser. The system of teaching shows the effects of his labours. One thing may be said fairly,—that he has secured in the schools the most admirable discipline. I saw at Clare what I had seen in so many schools in the Darling district—ophthalmia. It was not so marked in the children of Clare, but yet the pupils' eyes told tales of suffering.

Leaving Clare, we wound among the hills behind a pair of three-year-olds, which carried us along, at the rate of eight miles per hour, over some of the best roads in Australia. There can be no doubt that there are better roads in this colony than in any other colony in Australasia, if we except Tasmania. In places they are like billiard tables, and in and around Adelaide they are simply unsurpassable. On inquiry, we found that these horses were fed on nothing but hay, and sometimes not that. They were turned loose in the fields, and left to grow rugged and hardy on grass; and they do so. The Australian horse is the hardiest in the world. It seems to be with him a case of the survival of the fittest. Those that endure the experience of growing hardy outdoors become splendid animals, and the South Australian horse is quite equal to that of New South Wales, and much superior to that of Victoria.

Passing on, we came to the fine estate of 60,000 acres, the stud-farm of Mr. John Angas, where there were some splendid short-horned Durhams destined for the Agricultural Show in Melbourne. Mr. Angas had done good service to South Australia in importing some of the best blood that England has produced; and the effect of it is seen in the stock on many of the farms. Crossing an immense paddock, a herd of blood cattle passed us, and one could not help but wish that these stud-farms were more plentiful than they are. Two thousand guineas is a great deal to pay for one yearling, but it represents improvement of stock. Close to Mr. Angas's place is that of Chief Justice Way, who goes in, more particularly, for cultivating blood sheep. He has succeeded well, and his estate of 5,000 acres has upon it some excellent flocks. There, too, are young olive and orange groves, and, as at Mr. Angas's place, fruit and flowers make the place very fair. This, of course, is valuable land ; and, while speaking of value, it might be in place to mention here, as an example of what the land is worth in King William Street, Adelaide, that a 70-feet frontage was sold lately at £500 a foot. In Collins Street, Melbourne, land has been lately sold at £1,500 a foot. This, of course, is the result of the land boom, and is an inflated price.

And now a little matter in parenthesis. The postal rates in Victoria and South Australia are very high. It is not encouraging to think that one must pay twopence to send a letter across the way, in either of these cities. The ancient and worn-out theory still prevails that, in order to get revenue sufficient, the postal rates must be kept up. Has not that been contrary to all experience? As Principal Grant, the most acute of observers, said to me, Has Rowland Hill lived in vain? He further made this calculation: New Zealand mutton is sent to England now at a penny a pound; letters cost sixpence a half-ounce ; at that rate a letter costs 192 times as much as the same weight of frozen mutton, or a dead sheep goes 192 times cheaper than human sentiment * and the interchange of the commercial communication which provides for the sale of the mutton. And, as another gentleman added, Is not a man more than a sheep?

It was easy enough to get people to talk about the prospects of South Australia and the sources of its wealth. It was not so easy to arrive at entirely satisfactory conclusions ; but many notes, retorted, amount to this : that the climate of South Australia is eminently adapted for fruit-growing, and that the vine and the fruit tree ought to be sources of enduring prosperity; but the thing

---
* The rates have been altered to 2½d. a pound since 1889.

standing in the way at present is the backwardness of the farmer to learn the cultivation of fruits,—also, the insufficiency of labour. Now, this is not the opinion of the large proprietors only, but of people of sound sense, who have quietly observed the working of the fruitgrowers' operations. The growers investing the most capital have had much enthusiasm taken out of them by the difficulties with labour, and the struggle naturally has also been great to secure an outside market for South Australian wines. They all seem now to be working steadily on, because they have committed themselves to it, and are bound to see it through, while, of course, having gone into it chiefly because they preferred it to any other occupation, they have a fondness for it. The market for the wines has increased in London during the last few years, but, even now, there is little sent to England compared with the vast amount of wines consumed. The largest grower about Adelaide is Mr. Thomas Hardy, and he, of course, has established a good connection in London; yet it is only a handful of trade after all. It is hardly yet recognised as a thing of importance by the London dealer. At the most, Australian wines can only be said to have been fairly introduced, and to have appealed to a certain small constituency of buyers and likers. The Indian and Colonial Exhibition did much to advertise them; but this introduction, auspicious as it was, could not guarantee either an even standard of excellence in the wines, or a steady increase in patronage.

There seems to be a good deal of trouble in keeping up the merit which, perhaps, a particular brand has shown in one vintage. The art of blending is one of the great secrets. This art is not thoroughly understood in Australia. The best producers acknowledge that they are but experimenting, while there can be no guarantee that one year's vintage will give the same degree of merit in a particular brand as the last. Customers have been delighted with some particular wine, and have renewed their orders, only to get a wine which, bearing the same name, was different in quality. Even in France, Italy, and Spain, the same difficulty occurs; but in these countries the art has been mastered, and the wines do not vary greatly. The climate, the particular season, the pruning, the treatment, must all be studied, and a science be based upon experiment. This is being done in Australia, but the work is yet in its novitiate. The industry must progress slowly. Its progress is slower than it ought to be, because it is not yet looked upon as a national industry. In California they have already arrived at the conclusion that the Land of the Golden Gate is to furnish the world its wine. The result is that viticulture is being taken up all over the state, and Californian fruits have gone to supply the markets of the East. The cultivation of the soil in Australia is evidently too much on the lines of a land different from it in climate and power of production. A farmer might grow rich on 200 acres of land in England; he sometimes starves on 50 times that here.

What is wanted first is a belief in the industries, —such as vine-growing—that are natural to the country; and secondly, a conviction that success in cultivation can be mastered. But what can be expected for an industry and for a country where the labouring classes will not work as they should, nor the small farmer exercise faith and invest muscle and money? There does not seem any good reason why the women of the labouring classes and small farmers should not undertake the light labour of the vineyard, the olive grove and fruit garden, at a moderate and profitable wage—profitable at once to both employer and employed. But the women, with few exceptions, will not work in the fields. Nor will their husbands let them. They prefer to let mortgages accumulate and debts grow; to see things going behind every year, and to watch the increase of dangerous agitation, than to help turn the wheel. It is a strange democracy that cries, among other things, that woman is the equal of man, and is, therefore, entitled to share his responsibilities and vote, and, at the same time, says that she must not labour as a man or after his semblance. Surely Australia is peculiar in this. Go to any other country in the world, the most republican and democratic, if you will, and you shall find that women and children work in the orchard, the hopfield, and the garden; and do labour which is more adapted to them than to men. To engage men at 9s. a day, as has been done, to pick olives and strawberries, means, of course, loss and ruin. Women and children could well afford to do the work at 2s. 6d. to 4s. a day, and would be getting a good wage then. These are the wages that such men as Mr. Thomas Hardy and Sir Samuel Davenport are willing to pay, and are paying, when they can get women and children to do the work for them; and, as they are nearer the city than some others, they can succeed better.

As to the adaptability of the climate and soil for vine, olive, and fruit growing, there can be no doubt. There lies a difficulty, in fact, in the peculiar affection of the soil for the vine. The grape grows too fat and sugary, and the result is that the wines are more or less heavy. They have too much alcohol, and to reject this alcohol and to lighten the wine is what puzzles the growers. There are one or two Frenchmen who have been brought out here purposely to treat and blend the native wines, but as yet the success has not been complete. One occasionally tastes a good wine with little alcohol in it, but not often. I sampled some at Bankside, a vineyard belonging to Mr. Thomas Hardy, and it was a very good wine; but, pure and sixteen years old as it was, it had too much alcohol. The labours of those who are experimenting will, one believes, be finally crowned with success; but most of the young wines are badly alcoholised. I was much amused on going through Bankside to find an autograph note written by Mr. George Augustus Sala, in a visitors' book,—amused because, like another distinguished man, "G. A. S." could not tell a lie. He loved good wine too well, and so he contented himself with writing this: "George Augustus Sala, London, England: Astonished and deeply interested in the vineyards, the oranges, lemons, and olive groves, and especially the various vintages which Mr. Thomas Hardy has kindly permitted him to inspect. August 4th, 1885." Now, I do not think that G. A. S. committed himself there. He was "astonished and deeply interested." He did not say he was "delighted," but "deeply interested," in the vintages, etc. How deep? Pottle deep? I fancy not. G. A. S. is too much of a *connoisseur* and a judge of wine generally to play the jolly fat friar in the cool cellars at Bankside. While referring to this note, I wish to quote another as an example of what an Oriental thinks of these wines of Bankside. It is from the pen of General Wong Yung Ho, and is in a fine Roman hand. Men who doubt Chinese scholarship and grasp of English might study this,—

"We have this day visited the Bankside vineyard, the property of Mr. Thomas Hardy, and we feel deeply interested in everything that are grown here. The wines made therein are of a very excellent quality, especially Oomoo, which gives every one a judicious flavour. And we wish to see that some of these wines will find a handsome market in China as well as in Europe. It is gratifying to us to see that Mr. Hardy has done his best to improve the quality and increase his products every year.

"(Signed) GENERAL WONG YUNG HO."

Is there not a hurried nervous movement about these sentences of General Wong Yung Ho? The perfect freedom, and even license, of the English used, is full of suggestiveness. And what struck me as peculiar was the amount of bad penmanship generally in the book ; and not only that, but the gay and joyous manner in which the signatories told their experiences. There were no adverse criticisms, there were no half-hearted compliments. George Augustus Sala began the book, and his was the only reserved flattery. There were the names and opinions of English and Japanese naval officers, of an earl or two, and of hosts of town councillors and travellers. It seemed as if every town council in the colony had made a pilgrimage there, and had engaged the vestry clerk of the village church to compose the panegyric. I never saw more real *abandon* in writing. There was an exhilaration in the sentiments expressed which one would hardly expect in a cool cellar, and with only musty, dirty old bottles about. Says a well-known actor : " You have only to use French labels, and any one would believe that they are drinking the best French wines." I asked young Mr. Hardy why he spoke of them in the plural. " Well," said he, " he tasted them in the plural." Added to this was a diagonal line from a pretty colonial actress, saying in inky modulations, " And don't you forget it !" The young man said to me, "And you know we don't forget it—or her." I know the signatures of several gentlemen who have recorded their opinions in that book, and somehow I could not recognise them. I do not see why a man should try to disguise his signature because he has been in à wine-cellar. I could quote a hundred delicious things that the ladies said,—ladies whom many of us know,—but that I am forbid to tell the secrets of the prison house. Our highest sentiments, at times, might seem to the cold, unfeeling world as if worn upon our sleeves; and so no further shall I go in telling of those deep, those underground annotations.

These side remarks and quotations, I think, tend, if read aright, to bear out some of my previous notes about the fat and sugary nature of the grape, with its accompanying exciting qualities, when pressed and bottled. In connection, however, with the development of the wine industry here, it might be well to show how much wine there is actually made in South Australia. In the 1887 vintage there were 500,000 gallons, and in the 1888 vintage 799,000 gallons; while the stock in the colony on May 1st, 1888, was 2,000,000 gallons. Last year was one of the best years that the vine-growers ever had; hence the increase of nearly 3,000,000 gallons. The grapes ripened easily and evenly, and were not scorched by the sun. The exportation, however, has not increased visibly in the year. There was a rush after the Exhibition, and then there came an ebb in the demand; and it will need all the push and energy of the agents in London and the houses here to get a steady patronage in England. Such as it is now, it is confined to the dry wines. The sweet wines are not popular. One does not wonder at it. They are far heavier than the heaviest of the Mediterranean wines, and are too robust. Yet South Australians seem to prefer them. An opinion by Mr. Hardy is worth noting in reference to the means for getting an English patronage. He said to me, in substance, this: "It would be a good thing for a wealthy company to purchase all suitable wines when about six months old, and mature them before shipping to London. This would ensure an even sample being maintained from year to year. To procure this even sample is a great difficulty when growers themselves have to mature and ship. The company could have its own house in London; but this would not be necessary perhaps, because, if it could always supply a standard wine of even quality, customers could be found in London to dispose of it, as is done with other goods of which the quality does not vary to any great extent. The company could have an expert in the colonies to advise regarding the treatment of the young wines while yet in the grower's cellars, so as to get as uniform a sample as possible." He further said that in his opinion "the free interchange of Australian wines through the colonies would do a great deal to develop the trade in wines both here and in England. Such increasing trade as there is with London is in a full-bodied dry red wine of Burgundy character."

Now one or two things may be gathered from these notes. In the first place, the growers feel that they have a heavy contract—to cultivate the vine, treat the wines properly, and provide for sale and market. Each grower could hardly afford to employ an expert, nor could the growers as a body be expected to employ one on a mutual co-operative plan.

The difficulty regarding labour prevents the production of wine on a vast scale by any one man, and the efforts of most, if not all, are necessarily cramped, and not satisfactory even to themselves. They recognise the faults of their wines, and they wish to better them by every possible means; but, as Mr. Hardy says, "We cannot do it all at once—we must experiment and work out the problem carefully and scientifically." It does seem, however, that much could be done by securing a Frenchman, trained in wine-making in France, to treat the wines in every vineyard if Mr. Hardy's idea cannot be carried out; and even with a company the skilled foreign workman in the vineyard would still be of great value. Sir Samuel Davenport has a French vigneron, and he has had a good deal of luck with his wines. He is a careful and moderate grower. His year's vintage would come under 40,000 gallons, perhaps; but the quality of the wines is very good. He was one of the first growers in Australia, and for the past thirty years he has sought to improve and cultivate.

All admit that, as yet, it is impossible to produce an Australian champagne. They are willing to leave that to France and Spain for a while still. Such Australian champagne as I have tasted has been of a peculiarly unpleasant quality. It is dangerously heady, and particularly stubborn in leaving one in the morning. My remembrance is of one glass at a dinner in Melbourne; but I am quite satisfied. Both Sir Samuel Davenport and Mr. Hardy devote themselves to olive planting as well as vine growing, and they have been very successful thereat; but again comes in the question of labour. South Australian olive oil is now in much demand in these colonies, and a trade with England is slowly opening up. The oil that I saw in the large tanks at Sir Samuel Davenport's place was pure and sweet, and beautifully fruity. It was appetising to stand beside one of the big vats and inhale the perfume of the amber fluid. Mr. Hardy in 1887 produced 800 gallons of olive oil at Bankside, and in 1888 he produced 4,500 gallons. This is a large increase, but the increase has been steady all over the colony. Mr. John Angas has a vast number of olive trees, and now nearly every large farmer goes in for cultivating the olive, as well as the almond and the orange, to some extent. Bankside, when I saw it, was a pretty sight. The almonds were in blossom, and the oranges were ripe and loading the trees to the ground. On the floor of one of the rooms in the establishment was a great pile of raisins, and there were rows of muscatels in boxes up to the ceiling. There is not, however, a large trade in them as yet, because foreign raisins have been coming in here at such low rates. Since protection, however, has come to bless the vignerons, there are hopes that the Bankside raisins may supply the market. There are also large fruit-canning establishments on American lines here, and the South Australian fruits are fast becoming popular. That is, I was going to say, a marvel, because Australians have not, generally, much faith in home productions.

On looking over my notes, I find that Mr. Hardy said to me, when pointing out the different wines, that he sent every fortnight to London from 20 to 40 hogsheads of No. 1 claret, sold at 18s. a dozen. No one has so large a trade in South Australia as he, so that this may be considered the largest export made. As to the olive, general figures could not be obtained; but Sir Samuel Davenport said that, in his small way, he produced about 1,600 gallons every year. Of course, none of the vignerons are satisfied with what they are doing. They would like to extend their operations, but they cannot. One thing is certain, however, all are earnest in the work, and if they do not produce great things, it is because the Fates deal hardly with them. When Australia fully wakes up, as California did, to what she can do, and believes in herself, and also, as California did, secures the best French treatment she can get for her wines, the industry will grow properly. It is only struggling bravely now. It is idle to insist that Australian wines are pure. People want purity, but they want something else. They want less alcohol, and no less palatableness. When this is got there will be joy in the household of Australia.

CHAPTER X.

SOUTH AUSTRALIA IN 1888: FOREST CONSERVATION.

AT Adelaide I saw Mr. J. Ednie Brown,* the Conservator of Forests, and had a talk with him about the important and unique work of his department, so necessary in a country like Australia ; but talking was, no matter how interesting, unsatisfactory. Seeing was the only thing that could make one understand what this forest conservation means to South Australia. Mr. Brown offered to accompany me to the Bundaleer Reserve if I would go. By no means willing to leave the subject where it was, I gladly availed myself of his offer, and one morning early we started for Jamestown, near which place is the reserve. We went over some of the same ground that I had covered, a day or two before, on my way to the estate of Chief Justice Way. After leaving Saddleworth, however, new country opened up, and the rest of the journey was interesting enough, if similar to all that had gone before. This district through which we passed is, perhaps, the best farming district in South Australia. There were not evidences of great prosperity, but there were no indications of poverty. Branching off at Petersburg, we took another train for Jamestown. Miles off, on the treeless plains, we could see the village nestling in groves of

---
* Mr. J. E. Brown has since been made the Conservator of Forests for New South Wales. Mr. Brown is a Canadian.

trees; and this was the first token that I had of South Australian forest conservation.

Here was a little place, which had been a dust-heap a few years before, transformed into a garden. Here were the Tasmanian blue-gum, the New South Wales iron-bark, the South Australian sugar-gum, and the West Australian red-gum. Here were the pepper tree, the bunya bunya, and the Cape acacia, all healthy, and some of them 40 feet high. This was not done with Government money, but by corporation funds. The people borrowed £1,000 after the first experiments had proved successful, and spent it in beautifying this, hitherto, desolate place. The streets were lined on either side with trees, there were reserves of fine varieties, and there was a recreation park where a good landscape gardener had been at work; and the gum, the pine, and the cypress were growing beautifully.

One could picture to oneself what this place was eight years ago, when Mr. Brown went out one day and said, "I am going to plant some trees here." The people laughed at him. They said they understood the place better than he did, and that the trees would die. These "old identities" knew it. They knew that Jamestown was destined to remain desolate till the end of time. But the Conservator planted the trees nevertheless, and the next morning there came a rain, the first rain in weeks, and these trees "grew and multiplied, and replenished the earth." One uses the words "multiplied" and "replenished" advisedly, for this is something which bears upon the conservation of forests. The process of natural regeneration is now recognised in the working of the Forestry Department, and it is found that, in the case of the sugar-gum particularly, the seeds generate, and a new growth of trees springs up where the old ones were. The confidence begotten by these first successes, "aided and abetted by Providence," as the Conservator says, has never been shaken. This is as fortunate for the country as for him, and now South Australia has waked to the fact that she has another developing industry. An enthusiastic politician said that he looked to the Forestry Department to pay off the deficit of the country, and to bring affairs back again to a prosperous condition. This is perhaps a little sunset-like, but it has its good effect. Not only has Providence been favourable; there has been a systematic and capable management to drive the thing to a prosperous accomplishment.

After brushing the accumulation of dust from our clothes we sallied out to see what had been done round the village, and here and there a farmer stopped Mr. Brown as we passed through the streets, and told him how he was getting on with his trees,—for the Government gives away to all that ask trees to plant; and, more than this, it gives also a bonus of £2 an acre for not less than five acres of cultivated trees, with a minimum of 170 trees to the acre, after five years' growth. As we walked along, one man met us, who had already applied for, and got, £160 in this fashion. He had planted already 15,000 trees. Another had planted 20,000 trees. In the colony altogether over 2,000,000 trees have been given away, and 80 per cent. of them have been successful. In the northern district the cultivation of trees is being carried on extensively, not only by the Forestry Department, but by the farmers generally, and the great plains are now being relieved, here and there, of their depressing barrenness. With it, too, the farmer has taken heart, and the very land itself seems to have benefited by it, and to have caught the contagion of prosperity. Land that thirteen years ago could have been bought, and was bought, for £1 an acre, cannot be bought now for £9, and plenty of it is worth £7 an acre. Not directly to tree-planting, perhaps, is this due, but the reserve has improved the value of property in the district, and there is more ambition to achieve good results, so great is the effect of a thrifty influence in a country.

The people of Jamestown have pride, and they have shown it. The record of 60,000 trees for one village is remarkable, and yet there does not seem one too many. In this country, too, there is not long to wait for the result of labour to be seen. Corporations have not to invest money in the hopes of a return in twenty-five and thirty years, as is the case in America where trees take long to grow. Here they grow 8 feet in a year, and I was shown trees which were six years old, and yet which are splendid shade trees between 40 and 50 feet high; this, with only an average yearly rainfall of about 18 inches. As to the trees that are given away, one cannot do better than to give a list of them, to show, too, how broad the intention of the department is, how thoroughly the work has been entered into, and on how many lands contributions for the reserves have been levied. From east and west, north and south, seeds have come to play their part in this forest growth of South Australia. I take my information from an order list of young trees for which a farmer may make application. This particular order was for 1,000 sugar-gums. The list was made up as follows. (I have not given the botanical names, for that does not signify to the practical man.) Among the gums there are the Tasmanian, the sugar, the West Australian red, the karri, and tooart, and the South Australian blue, red, and manna, gums. I did not see the New South Wales iron-bark on the

list, though it is cultivated on the reserves. Then
there is the white mulberry, the olive, and the privet.
Among the pines there is the Aleppo, the spruce fir,
the cypress, and the white cedar. There is the English
oak, the cork, and the English elm; the English and
American ash, the catalpa, the sycamore, and the white
acacia; the weeping and the osier willows; the upright,
and the grey, poplar; the Canadian maple, the tamarisk,
the walnut, and the pepper. Of them all the sugar-
gum is the most common, as it is the prettiest and
cleanest of the gums. Everywhere it may be seen with
its slender drooping leaves, cool-looking, and, with its
smooth bark, something like the beech in appearance.
The Tasmanian blue-gum does not flourish so well as
the sugar-gum, but the red-gums succeed. Last year it
cost the Government for trees given away £300—that is,
this amount was put upon the estimates for the purpose;
and 213,061 plants were taken away from the several
nurseries, the names of which are Bundaleer, Wirrabura,
Mount Brown, Kapunda, and Mount Gambier.

It was a fine day that found us on our way from
Jamestown, across the green plains, to Bundaleer. We
travelled in a buck-board behind a spanking pair of
horses, at the rate of twelve miles an hour. Close outside the town we could see the river at the base of the
hills, running away off to the north. To our right was
the scene of this year's planting operations—3,000 acres
of land under the plough. Here and there on the plains
was a comfortable farmhouse, and the condition of the
occupants could be gathered from the remark of the
Conservator that "that man could write a cheque for
twenty thousand pounds, and this one for forty." Their
cattle were grazing on the Bundaleer reserve. This is

permitted on the conditions that they fence in the wooded district, while the Government reserve the right to resume at any time. Running through the plain was a creek, rejoicing in the soft-sounding name of Belalie. It was not long before we were driving along the edge of the big wood plantation. This was the cleanest, healthiest forest I had seen in Australia. Straight, bold, and strong grew these sugar-gums, Tasmanian blue-gums, and red-gums. With all the beauty of the natural forest, these trees of six to eleven years' growth had a freshness which the natural forest does not possess.

Down a well-kept road we passed till we came to the entrance of the plantation, and were met by the chief forester, a plain, practical man of few words, a rustic labourer—as seemed, indeed, all of Mr. Brown's subordinates. He knew I should notice this, and he said to me: "I keep men about me who are practical foresters. If there are to be any theories they must proceed from me. It is work I want, not fanciful suggestions." Men of few words were his subordinates, ready to listen, anxious to do, and keeping their plantations in the very pink of order. No evidence of unthrifty labour, no sign of Governmental portentousness here. Everything was of the simplest fashion. One did not get an idea of manufacturing—it was natural farming that rose before one's face. There were thousands of sugar-gums and red-gums peeping up from the beds, and clumps of mulberry and sugar-maple. The wind caught the thin needles of the pines, and sent a plaintive shiver through the air, while in the trees the birds sang as if they would split their throats, and the laughing-jackasses cackled loudly. "There were but few birds here, sir, when we first came," said the forester to me, "but now they be everywhere about, and they keep coming still."

Climbing the side of the hill we came to the great tank which caught the water from a shallow course scooped in the hill, and sent it down to the nurseries below by the force of gravitation. We had a splendid view from the hill, and we could see far off to the end of the reserve where the long line of trees ended, and the unwooded plain began again. "It is a big thing," I said to Mr. Brown. "Oh no," replied he, "a little thing yet; but a promise of what should be done. If they would but give me £100,000 to put into conservation now, we could do something worthy of the great necessity, but this is slow work; it is after all on a meagre scale. You see, this is a large colony, and these reserves are very small, and, well, you know —I don't mind saying it to you—I am an enthusiast, and I am anxious to do a work commensurate with the importance of the cause."

After a little time we drove over to another plantation, and it was far more beautiful in appearance than the first. "Here," said the Conservator, "here I should like to come and stay a couple of months with my family. I can conceive of no more pleasant spot for a holiday." After spending a while in the green places, examining the young trees, we started for the depths of the forest to see some of the oldest and biggest trees. We found some splendid specimens eleven years old and over 70 feet high, with boles that would make fine timber now. "Here are some trees," said Mr. Brown, "worth £5."

It was a cold night, and we heaped up the mallee upon the fire, and, with a couple of good cigars, set ourselves to the pleasant task of talking over the object that had brought me to this spot. My comrade was on a congenial subject, and he did not stint his information. There was no beating about the bush, only straightforward matters-of-fact made most interesting by the practical enthusiasm of the man.

"Eleven years ago," he said, "I began this work in South Australia. I knew the contract was a big one; I knew that to succeed would require devotion and enthusiasm, but I went at it, and the results have, at least, been encouraging. We have now 32 reserves altogether, and varying in size from 2,000 to 50,000 acres, with over 8,000,000 trees on them. If the trees which we planted eleven years ago were sold to-day, they would bring £30,000; that is, an average of £1 a tree. Bundaleer was our first reserve, and you are in a position to judge of what has been done there. I employ about 50 permanent foresters, and in the planting season about 150 men altogether. We put in now about 1,000,000 trees a year, but before 1885 we never rose above 300,000. The first few years were devoted to experiment; but now we know our ground, and I only wish we could plant 5,000,000 trees a year instead of 1,000,000. After twenty-five or thirty years' growth, these trees now planted will be worth £300 an acre. Of course we have not a large market now, but that will come with the increase of population."

"Markets come slowly," I said, "for all new industries; how has it been with you?" The Conservator replied, laughingly, "We have been no exception. At first the Public Works Department did not believe in us, and they would not buy our railway sleepers; but when we proved to them that we could furnish as good a timber as Victoria at 1s. cheaper for each sleeper, they began to patronise us; and in four years we have furnished 500,000 sleepers to the railways, and supply the Public

Works Department with all its hardwoods; and thus we have retained the circulation of £88,000 for the wood within the colony, the profit has been a South Australian profit, and we have given employment to our workmen. Then," said he, "we give the Public Works a better timber, because the old system of calling for tenders resulted in green, ill-seasoned wood being supplied. Now we are able to cut in time, and season properly, and at least five years is added to the durability of the timber. We have 40,000 sleepers on hand now, for the extension of the railway lines."

We discussed then the probability of the other colonies taking the matter up, and Mr. Brown was of the opinion that Victoria would, after her go-ahead fashion, begin forest conservation at once on a large scale ; and that she, profiting by the experience of South Australia, would put in a much larger amount of trees every year—"the six or seven millions that we ought to put in," said the Conservator. "Victoria imports £1,000,000 worth of timber every year, and South Australia imports to the extent of £300,000. Well, Victoria, with all her advantages of soil and climate, could, in twenty years, reduce her wood imports one-half by growing her own timber."

"Can you give me some idea of how you stand at present financially, and in the matter of cultivation?" I said. "It is easy enough to do that," he replied. "Of last year's trees we have 900,000 now growing. We expended £6,000. Our revenue for the same period was £11,500, which leaves us £5,500 to the good." "In other words," I added, "your department is not only costing the country nothing, but you are contributing to the general revenue." "Exactly," he replied. "During the eleven years we have been at work we have received from the Government £60,000, and we have returned them

£70,000, or a profit of £10,000. This small profit for the eleven years is due to the fact that during the first few years there was naturally no gain, rather loss. But this £10,000 does not represent our assets, for we have 8,000,000 trees, which, averaged up at a fair value, would make a large sum of money; and, as is quite evident, the values and the profits must increase year by year, for drought will not affect us a great deal henceforth. We know just about what rainfall will suffice us, and we plant our trees accordingly. We have a great pull over the northern countries, you see, because we can grow matured timber fit for cutting in ten or twelve years, while the colder countries, take thirty years and more. The time is coming when these northern countries will keep all their timber within their own borders, and then, every country, Australia among the rest, will have to shift for itself. It is for that evil day that preparation should be made, and it is not so very far off."

"And about the natural regeneration," I said, as the Conservator lit another cigar, and I piled some more mallee on the fire. "It's a good term, isn't it?" he replied. "Well, as an example, we took up a block of land, and removed 10,000 natural trees. During the third year we cleared from the block the wood-splitter and the grazier, and now there are 500,000 young natural trees coming up. So our system is to cut up a section of natural ground in twelve blocks, and reserve a block per year. By the time the last block in the twelfth year is resumed, the first block, on which the regenerative process has gone on, is ready for cutting again; so that you see we renew our strength like the eagle, and we have the same satisfaction as the farmer has, who knows that Nature is working away for him, while he is only giving her a chance to do her work. We have much to expect from this method of reproduction. You see, we are not only utilising our old forests, but putting new ones in their places." So the talk ran on. I hope enough has been said to give some idea of what South Australian forest conservation is. I left the Conservator at the railway station one cold evening, and he said, as we parted, " Don't forget to come to Bundaleer when you want a holiday." When I broke bread again I was in Broken Hill, swallowing its clouds of dust, and searching for a good hotel. I could soon look back with nonchalance upon the cold and weary journey from Jamestown to the great mining district of Australia—to the Barrier Ranges in New South Wales.

CHAPTER XI.

BROKEN HILL IN 1888.

I AM sure that many people, even in Australia, have but hazy notions of Broken Hill, of the country surrounding it, and of where it is. A doctor there told me that a letter came from a bank manager in Melbourne addressed to Broken Hill, South Australia. Another gentleman informed me that friends of his in Sydney grieved, in his presence, that Broken Hill was not in New South Wales. I have been shown a letter from a Melbourne gentleman, addressed to " Broken Hill, Queensland." This ignorance may not be general, but even a small percentage of it would be too much. Broken Hill has been, as a keen, non-investing man said to me, a Cave of Adullam. How many have sunk their all in wildcat schemes, in paper mines, in syndicates formed upon assays of ore that never came from the places claimed for them, we shall not know ; but here and there in one's circle of acquaintance one comes across the victims of speculation. The retired worker who had laid up sufficient to live in comfort for the rest of his life has been obliged to take up the burden again, and so he will hold it till the fitful fever is over,—his shoulder to the wheel that he hoped never to turn again. The mechanic who mortgaged his furniture, the draper who sold his shop, the clerk who left his counter, and the farmer who sold his farm, and came here buoyant and hopeful, have gone back ruined, hopeless men ; while the few spoilers have gathered in the harvest. Standing—Sunday it was—on the highest peak on Broken Hill, and looking down to the dusty, mushroom place beneath, one could not help but ask one's self many questions, which to answer is not to make one wholly cheerful.

It was a bright morning when I arrived, and there were many cabs waiting at the station. One could see little else, save dust, corrugated iron, smoke, and barren, scrubby hills and plains. Moving down through walls of dust, I was glad when the Australian Club Hotel was reached. It is a comfortable, spacious building, with balconies round it. I was fortunately told the name of this and two or three other hotels before I came, or I should have been in a quandary. I said to a cabby at the railway station, "Which is the best hotel here?" "Well, sir," he said, " it would be pretty hard to tell, for there are forty-seven altogether; but there's the York, sir, and the Grand, and the Australian Club, and Durant's, and the Royal, and the Masonic, and the Bonanza, and the Crystal, and——" "There, that will do," I interjected. " Put me down at the Australian Club Hotel." He did so. He charged me 2s. for the five minutes' drive, and as there were two others in the trap, he earned 6s. for his five minutes' work. I should hardly have said " earned " it. He demanded 6s., and he got it. This is on a par with prices generally at this mining field. One pays three guineas a week here for board and lodging, or 10s. a day at hotels that are—well, hardly equal to the Métropoles at Sydney or London. But these are prices that were established in the palmy days of Broken Hill, when the place was full of people and fun. The golden days are gone ; the honest level of value has now come ; and a large number of the people are also gone, and most of the fever too.

The sun is setting as I sit here writing on the balcony of the hotel, and between me and the rosy radiance there are vast clouds of dust rising, and heavy waggons go in slow procession, drawn by horses that once, perhaps, were fat and well-liking, but now are worn, fagged creatures that scarcely ever get a good day's feed—"a feed as is a feed." Here, too, go the long lines of ox teams; and one can hear the sharp crack of the bullock-driver's whip, as he urges his thin weary cattle on the last stage in their journey. Curtains of dust blow about them, and one's mind reaches beyond them, out to the measureless plains, where camels take the place of horses, and where the land is beginning to bear the pall that covered it in that terrible season of 1883 and 1884: when one fed on bread that was chiefly weevil, and salt pork and damper; no milk, no eggs, no decent living; when brave women succumbed to the dreary life, and fell sad-eyed into the Silence before the rain came to refresh the parched land; when men cursed their hard fate, and asked (with what anxiety none can tell) if the lane would never have a turn. But rain came at last, and the land arose from its death-in-life, and gave bread again to man and beast. Those days, however, can never quite come again, for there is this railway opened up to Broken Hill, and Wilcannia is now 150 miles nearer the markets than she was before; and that means much in a land where the most well-to-do squatters are reduced to one or two horses, as was the case in the dark days of which I speak. From the Barrier Ranges, lonely and inhospitable, the western folk will be able to get succour now; and yet, when one looks round, this does not seem like a feeding-place for the hungry many.

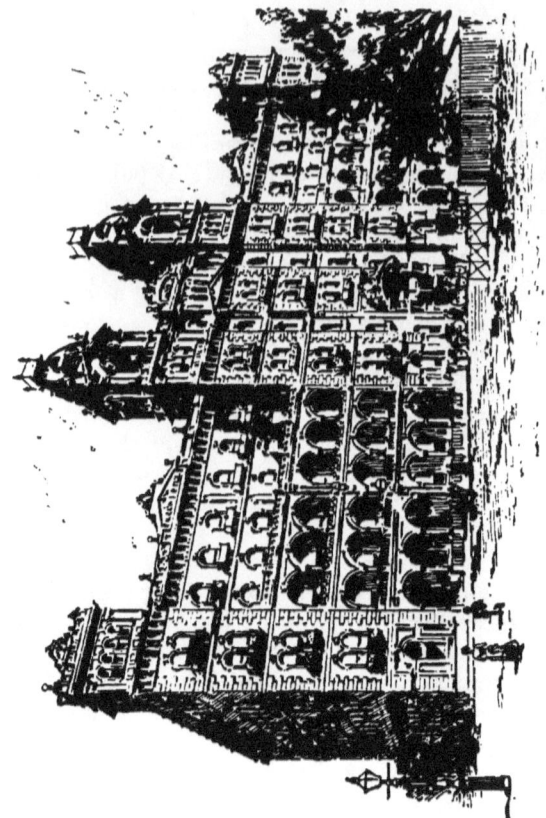

From Harper's Weekly. GRAND HOTEL COFFEE PALACE, MELBOURNE. Copyright, 1891, by Harper & Brothers.

Here are houses of canvas and corrugated iron, low places mostly, in which one would kennel a dog or a cow in more settled districts. Tents, lean-tos, and miserable shells dot the scrub land far and wide, while now and then a pretentious villa stands out conspicuously in the meannesses that surround it. A small dwelling makes a villa here, and the hotels are palaces by comparison. The hotels are certainly most creditable. The three principal ones are well kept and very orderly, and the cooking is fair. One or two of them are quite metropolitan in their arrangements, and the *menu* cards are written in aggressive French. There are boys in livery; there are silver plate, and side-tables, and French wines, and many courses. At the York Hotel, where I lunched, five *entrées* stared me in the face, and other things in proportion; and one felt that one would have to discard any notion of being free-and-easy because one happened to be in a mining town. Free-and-easy! The people who imagine Broken Hill to be a place where one lives like an aboriginal, had done well to have been with me at the opening of the Theatre Royal in Argent Street. I wish they could have seen mingling with the noisy miners the swells in evening dress who paid their 5*s.* for reserved seats, and came proudly in, undaunted by the ironical cheers of the underground toiler in his slouch hat and dirty jacket. There was a major in undress uniform; there was a volunteer captain in full dress; there was a fire-brigade captain in official attire; and maids and matrons in lace, silk, and muslin, as if they had stepped out of a boudoir at Darling Point, Toorak, or the South Terrace. But just here, perhaps, I might record something of that performance; for it marks an era at Broken Hill, or Willyama, as the natives call it.

On arriving at Broken Hill I was surprised to find

at the breakfast-table some actors and actresses whom I had seen play in Sydney and Melbourne, and I picked up the newspaper to find what it all meant. There I saw announced that on Saturday evening the first theatre of Broken Hill would be opened, and Grattan Riggs's company would appear in *The Irish Detective*. The building was to be called the Theatre Royal, and Mr. W. J. Cummins was announced as the sole proprietor. This was worth seeing, so I turned to the only man I then knew in Broken Hill, and asked him about it. He said, "You must come and see for yourself." So I did. This companion was one with whom I had travelled two years before across the plains between Wilcannia and Menindie; with whom I had tried to shoot emus and kangaroos; with whom I had cooked wild duck and boiled a billy of tea, and who is as hale and kindly a man as one could wish for a fellow-traveller. I count myself fortunate that, when I entered the breakfast-room the morning of my arrival, he should be the only man in the room, and his the first face that I should recognise. I felt myself safe at once,—safe as regards information and direction—and I have not been mistaken. So, together we went to the Theatre Royal. It is a pretentious place, and will hold over 1,000 people. It was all confusion in the morning at ten o'clock. They were fastening down the chairs, and the stage was covered with half-finished scenery.

An hour after I met Grattan Riggs. He was nervous about the evening, and I did not wonder. This helter-skelter population—who could foresee what kind of an audience it would make? I depended on the scene that would occur at this opening to get some of my best impressions of Broken Hill. I was not disappointed. I had seen a well-known actress nervously pace up and down the balcony of the hotel, with heavy eyes, studying a manuscript attentively, and then throw herself exhausted in an arm-chair, in apparent hopelessness. I discovered the cause afterwards. She was trying valorously to commit to memory a prologue which had been written for this opening, and though she had always been considered "a quick study," she could not learn these fifty-two lines. When I heard it that evening recited before the footlights I did not wonder at her desperation. I must quote a few of the lines here; but before I do, a short description of the scene might not be uninteresting.

Outside there was a wind which raised clouds of dust. Down Argent Street the people were pouring, and many of them had "more aboard" than they could well carry. In front of St. Leon's Circus, to which admission could be gained "at million prices," a band was playing with perfect independence of any concerted harmony; and the overflow of the theatre was marching in to see "Dick Turpin's Ride to York." Around the doors of the theatre there were hundreds gathered, but only those who had secured seats beforehand could gain admittance. When I got in, all except the dress-circle, or reserved seats rather, were crowded. The fashionables, as is their custom, came in just a little late, much to the delight of the dusty sinners at the back, who yelled with delight at the white neckties and claw-hammers. I remember distinctly that there was a band; no, two bands—one String and the other Brass; the String just to the right of the footlights, and the Brass at the other end of the hall, standing in a door-way. There was a shout when the outside curtain of chintz went up and revealed a "drop" which, according to a local journal, "is striking and artistic, full of the light and colour which scenic artists are prone to put into their pictures of Southern Europe, and reflects the highest credit on the painter." I cannot add anything to that; I do not wish to add anything to it. With the rising of the chintz on came the proprietor, and up rose the voices of the gods. He came forward swiftly, in a business-like fashion, and said that Miss E—— F—— would recite the prologue. He gave another sudden salutation and retired.

Miss E—— F—— came in dressed, so far as a man could judge, in a manner that was "rippin'." And here are a few of the lines of the prologue :—

> "Hail, Willyama! Patrons of the play,
> Congratulate us on this festal day!
> . . . .
>
> "To-night we come from histrionic glades,
> Where oft we played beneath Olympic shades.
> Methinks dramatic flight will never cease,
> Since first it reached the Colonies from Greece.
> . . . .
>
> "Here Scott and Moore will strike the minstrel lyre,
> Whilst Riggs and Kean will act with Attic fire.
> . . . .
>
> "To-night we hope to win the just applause
> Of a full house, obeying Nature's laws.
> I must away. I am no star of song.
> 'Tis naught-a-gal a pro-logue to pro-long.
> . . . .
>
> "We thank you for your presence here to-night.
> Ah, me! 'Tis a glad financial sight.
> But pray remember, when you leave your toil,
> Forget not to 'Cummin' to the Theatre Royal."

I am not much of a judge of poetry, I confess, but this strikes me as being bold and unconventional. It seems we have been ignorant heretofore that Grattan Riggs and company have been playing in Olympic shades. We know it now. We are also to be favoured with a visit from Scott and Moore, and Riggs and Charles Kean are to appear together—as Hamlet, no doubt, and the ghost of Hamlet's father. This is cheering. I do not know whether the house obeyed " nature's laws " or not, though I was there all the time,—I am not a scientist. There is, I believe, a brilliant bit of humour in that line about the " naught-a-gal." The author, it is said, understands it perfectly. I shall not soon forget the pathos which Miss F—— put in these words—

"Ah, me! 'Tis a glad financial sight."

She has said since, that she never felt so pathetically moved in her life. The joke about "Cummin" is generally understood ; it has no Scriptural significance ; it refers to the name of the proprietor of the theatre ; it is considered to be very clever ; it is poetry. When the fair actress (I believe that is the way it is generally put) had retired, in came the proprietor, who announced that " Mr. Captain Piper would declare the theatre open under the Royal Coat-of-Arms." Then the Brass Band, evidently impatient of delay, and thinking there was something particularly significant in the " Royal Coat-of-Arms," struck up " God Save the Queen," while the proprietor, with outstretched arms, firmly insisted that it should stop. It was a long time, however, before the bass and the big drum would desist, and meanwhile the audience stood in respectful, if noisy, acknowledgment. Captain Piper came on duly, and, I believe, read a speech, in which he reviewed the growth of Broken Hill, and said, among other eloquent things, that the population of the place had risen from 2,000 to 15,000. I have been told since that these figures are tokens of the capital imagination which life breeds in Broken Hill. I did not hear him deliver the speech ; but, as I saw his lips moving, and from the fact that, at the far end of the room, cheers were repeatedly called for him, I conclude that he did so. The String Band, which included a piano and a violin, and excluded all other instruments, ought, it is understood, to have played "Rule, Britannia" at the conclusion of the speech; but they did not do so, and so the generous orator urged them to their task. They found difficulty in discovering his meaning, and only arrived at last at it by passing through a medley of tunes till they sounded the chorus of "Rule, Britannia." Here the Brass Band, evidently incensed at being neglected, struck up "God Save the Queen." But the general feeling seemed to be against this, and the speaker, to encourage the String Band, began to sing "Rule, Britannia,'" in which he, with pathetic gestures, begged the audience to join. This was not achieved, but the Brass Band could not withstand the continued antagonism, and so one by one the players disappeared from the doorway, till the only one left was the first cornet, which insisted on playing as long as did the String Band. Finally, that part of the function was concluded by a vigorous and triumphant upper C note from the first cornet. Then the orator disappeared also, and the proprietor again came forward. I conceive that he delivered an address of congratulation to the man that had had the pluck to build such a fine theatre, and, before it was through, one understood that himself was the fortunate and heroic individual. The audience had a nasty habit of interrupting him, and so he had to pause and tell them that "if he stayed there ten hours he would say his say, but if they heard him out he would not keep them long." I have not the least doubt that he meant it, because he repeated this nine times at intervals. At every interruption he simply retreated a few steps, bowed, pulled at another finger-joint, adjusted his garments—I was going to say his "harness"—and began again. He triumphed. When, at half-past eight, he vanished, up rose the curtain and the play began.

There are a number of people here who feel something more than a temporary interest in Broken Hill, and they are struggling valiantly against metropolitan indifference to local wants of a sanitary and municipal character. The private interest in Broken Hill is large; but it is only a speculative and selfish one. Nowhere are the evil results of centralisation more apparent than in the Barrier Ranges. Broken Hill ought to be a corporation, but it is not; it ought to have sanitary safeguards, but it has not; and it never will have until local power is given. The summer is beginning, and the fever-plague of last summer will be repeated, because in all probability the effect of the drought will be more disastrous. The sixteen people who are in the hospital now will be five or ten times sixteen, and the vile odours of the place will breed contagion everywhere. "Do not drink water or milk at Broken Hill," said two Adelaide doctors with whom I chatted about this place before I left South Australia. To follow out that advice a systematic appeal to Guinness or Three-star would be necessary. I drink the water and the milk despite the doctors, but I take the water boiled. I know the practice is not a perfectly safe one up here, but I shall risk it during my short stay. The condition of this place is infamous. The odours sometimes are almost unendurable, and as the weather gets hotter,—well, let every man thank Heaven that has not to live in Broken Hill in the summer time. Dr. Thompson said to me, when talking with him upon this subject,—"Sanitary conditions! There are no sanitary conditions here. They are insanitary. When I first came I prepared a careful article on the subject, and it was forwarded by the Progress Committee to the Government; but it was never heard of again, nor have other representations received any attention; and the Progress Committee can do nothing."

Local control would do away with this evil state, but there is just this much against it, that there are many people who are here but for a day, and have no real interest in the place. They are not anxious for the responsibilities of local government, and so they say, Let us wait awhile. This prevents unanimous representation on the part of the inhabitants. To the reasonable man, however, it is evident that the affairs of this place can never be properly administered from Sydney, and that local government should, if necessary, be compelled, not merely granted. Broken Hill will not wither away like Jonah's gourd. It is destined to be a mining town of permanent importance. The fever of speculation is over, but there still remain mines of undoubted wealth, of resources which only require to be developed carefully and legitimately, to make an industry of value to the country. There has been gross mismanagement in many of the small mines. In the hurry and excitement incompetent men were appointed managers, and inefficient machinery has been purchased. There are mines here where the machinery has been changed three and four times, and frequent calls upon the sharcholders have shown them that mining means something else besides dividends.

Standing on a ragged edge of the lead of Broken Hill, and looking about, one could count scores of mines which may or may not be wealthy, but are quite hopeless as they are. Somehow, one could, from the height of 200 feet, see more clearly mentally the condition of affairs here. We had climbed slowly over the mullock and schist and ore to our place of vantage. It was a beautiful day, and when at last the vast and lonely plains on the other side broke upon the view, the effect was impressive. In front of us stretched endlessly the red sand and the mulga; far off to the hills, and between us and them, there were small homes of isolated miners. To the right was the village of South Broken Hill, with its population of 1,000 people. Four months ago it consisted of one or two tents and a shanty, and now it possesses at least one church and four public-houses. Away beyond this place stretched the treeless plains, till they melted into the amber sky. My companion, following my scrutiny, said: "Think of swinging your swag on your back, and starting out through these desolate places to find shelter or a place of human habitation." Turning round, and, with his arm sweeping the circle, he continued: "This was—and not so many years ago, either—the No Man's Land. Here was the refuge of the outlaw and the outcast. Here came the bushranger and the cattle-stealer from the clutches of punishment, and no law followed them. It seemed to consider that to be encompassed by this region of desolation was punishment enough."

Truly. For, looking beyond Broken Hill and South Broken Hill from the height where we are, we see what the land was half a generation ago. It offered little comfort to the wanderer, as it gave little to those noble men who risked their lives and lost them for the cause of exploration and discovery. Sweeping a half-circle again, and looking out beyond The Pinnacles,—three hills which rise pyramid-like in spaces as arid as the Egyptian desert—the realm of loneliness also meets us. It is a circle of depression, save in its centre where we are. Here at our feet is Broken Hill ; here to our right, straight along the line of the outcrop and the lode upon which we are perched, are the great mines—those terrible magnets which draw the fortunate and the unfortunate to them. There are North Broken Hill, the Junction, the British Blocks, Block 14, the Proprietary, the Central, and the South. These all are working on certain ground. Whether the lode ends with the outcrop or falls below is the question, and the hopes of thousands are resting on the answer to the enquiry. It is all a process of experiment now, and it is impossible to tell what may occur. As we sat there we could hear the engine in the Brisbane Blocks below us, driving the diamond drill, which is ceaselessly asking the earth if, a thousand feet below, it will find the inclined continuation of the lode, which has made the mines before-mentioned so valuable. Who can tell?

CHAPTER XII.

QUEENSLAND IN 1889.

At the Capital.

EARLY one August morning we drew into the station-yard at Brisbane, and ended our thirty-six-hours' journey from Redfern at Sydney. On our left was a hill, upon which stood, in the pleasant sunlight, a pile of buildings, having in architecture an educational flourish. A college they proved to be. Not the cajolings of the cab-drivers could quite drive away the first pleasant impression of Brisbane—not even the practical ejaculations of fellow-travellers. But the crisp yet tender air suggests something else; the mellow sun-warmth creates a wonderment. What is the association? It is Los Angelos, in Southern California.

Brisbane is like Los Angelos in the matter of atmosphere only. It has not the appearance of the pretty town of the south, which is not yet emerged from its languid, half-Spanish, half-Mexican thraldom; from that state which drew out some of Bret Harte's best work in poetry and story. No, Brisbane is not the least poetical. One does not drive through streets of limes and cacti, where the dog-roses stretch red hands over the fences, where johnny-jump-ups fill the door-yards, and where there are manifold hedges of the iris lily. Brisbane is in appearance scraggy, low-built, and premature. It is far from picturesque as a whole, and first impressions are not changed by closer inspection. There is a sense of disappointment, which grows deeper as the sojourn in the capital is continued. In this thriving city of 60,000 people I did not see one really fine residence, save Government House, and there are plenty of private houses in Sydney much finer and bigger than it. I know I shall be told to go out to Breakfast Creek and climb the hills north of it. Well, I went out there. I wandered about the town in search of the fashionable quarter, and there was none; I took a tramcar and travelled Woolongabba way to the five roads that lead everywhere,—including New South Wales,—and I passed from patches to rags. It was no use. I made a jaunt over to the river and the hills at the south-west, and then I stopped. There is no pride in domestic architecture in Brisbane. Plutocrats there—if there are any—put no money in brick and stone houses such as one may find in Woollahra, Darling Point, Toorak, and Windsor, and in the hills at Adelaide.

The style of residence affected by the richer class is of the bungalow order: big verandahs, Indian blinds, plenty of palm and hybiscus trees, and an occasional banyan, or fig tree, in the front garden. The poorer class have the verandahs without the trees and flowers. Nothing is more striking to the stranger, as he looks down upon the city, than the absence of trees. Yet what city in the world needs them more? It is only August now, still it is as hot as in Sydney in November. It is said that this is phenomenal weather, and I can believe it; but Sydney has had phenomenal weather too, and there is a vast difference between the two phenomena. I would advise the authorities of Brisbane to send a couple of commissioners to Jamestown, in

South Australia, to see how a waste has been transformed into a garden, and to the Bundaleer Reserve near the same place to learn what forest conservation means. Twenty-five thousand trees would make Brisbane beautiful. They would glorify its nakedness; they would give it altitude; they would bring something of moisture, comfort, and health. One gets the impression now of a town that is but half-dressed, and what it must be when mid-summer has arrived I refuse to conjecture.

I suggested that it could be made beautiful by trees. Let me give a reason for it. First, there are hills to the north, and west, and south-west—hills which have some chances of colour at sunrise and at gloaming, and which are a fine background. Then there is the river, which winds about in an extraordinary way, and is, therefore, all the more picturesque. One part of the city, including Government House, the Botanical Gardens, and the Parliament buildings, lies in the curve of a horse-shoe, and there are two large curves at Petrie's Bight at the end of Queen Street, and again at Breakfast Creek before it makes up its mind to seek the sea. Thus, many parts of the metropolis get the benefit of the pretty stream, and in years to come it will be a pleasant break in many parts of the crowded city sure to be builded in the great Queensland which is now feeling the natural force of her destiny strong within her. The stream has high banks in places, and is wide enough to be dignified in spite of its mud—mud as suggestive of permanency as that of the Missouri. But people say that the river is pellucid sometimes—in fact, often. Why should not one believe it? It is particularly muddy now owing to the recent heavy rains which flooded the valley in North Brisbane, and destroyed large sections of road. One could understand why it is that such a very large number of houses are built on piles. The inhabitants of South Brisbane suffer in the same way, and people point to marks made on their high door-steps, to show how the water crept up to drench the parlour carpet, and to provide an unmanageable bath for the nursery. These piles, capped with plates to prevent white ants from getting to the wooden super-structures, give a very unsettled appearance to the place ; in other words, an air of pilgrimage. I may be reminded of Venice, but—well, there is a difference. There is flotsam and jetsam in the front gardens here instead of gondolas.

It is a mystery to me that, built of wood as Brisbane chiefly is, those graceful forms of domestic architecture are not used which have been adopted to some extent in Adelaide. Adelaide is a model of neatness and form. Brisbane happens to be neat here and there, and chances to run into good form ; but there has been little design in the running. It must be said, however, that the wise men of the northern colony seemed to be aware of their duty, and to have some regard for dignity in the architecture of public buildings. The Parliament buildings, if not imposing, have a fine upstanding appearance, and are suggestive of what one finds everywhere in Queensland—boldness and breadth. They put to shame the miasma-making Parliament Houses of New South Wales ; they have light, air, colour, and some refinement in outline and structure. Perhaps some architects would say that they were built too bountifully ; but that is not out of harmony with Queensland. It is roomy, brawny, and big-shouldered. The new Treasury buildings are a step upwards from the Parliament buildings ; but that is to be expected ; the country is fifteen years older than it was when the places of legislation were erected. The Treasury buildings look out on the river, and tower white and cool above the jumble of buildings behind it. The Supreme Court would gladden the heart of Chief Justice Darley, and lessen the gloom that sits on the brows of Sydney barristers. The build-

PARLIAMENT BUILDINGS, BRISBANE.

ings are roomy and cool, and have something in design akin to the Parliament buildings, though arranged in a half-square instead of the oblong. The Museum is not unlike that of New South Wales. This is about the sum of state architecture of any note. The Premier and Colonial Secretary has some such place for his official habitation as would be given a lands' officer in a forlorn country district of New South Wales.

Outside of these buildings there is little to please the eye in architecture. The Queensland National Bank is a great show place, with Corinthian pillars which suggest a fashionable Baptist Church in New York, and the *Courier* building is a massive and imposing structure. Adding thereto the Mutual Provident building, the interior of the Australian United Steamship Navigation Company's structure, the Queensland Club, and hints at good architecture in one or two hotels, and there is an end of form in wood and stone and brick, in Brisbane. Standing at the north end of Queen Street, before moving down to the road that passes Petrie's Bight, one is not struck with admiration. Still, there is bustle and quick movement, and the horse-cars are well kept, and are not unwieldy. It is suggested to one what a street this might appear, by two fig-trees that, huddled between the low buildings, stretch out their green arms into the street. Poor, struggling, spited things, it would seem that the dwellers in the buildings beside them were jealous of the space they occupied. It is difficult for me to write quietly on this subject, when I remember that there is not a city in Australia that has many trees in its streets, even where those streets are wide. Let one think of some good old English towns, of cities of the south of Europe, of cities of old America and of new America, the streets of which are broken arches of green, and to what conclusion can we come but this?—that Australians have not yet learned to value beauty, nor to see that beauty has its use—to see that everything really beautiful in nature serves the mechanical and the practical as well as glorifies them? Nearly every town and village in Australia stands out staring from bare plains, brown earth, or white sand. Little wonder is it that, in the far interiors of all the colonies, children have ophthalmia. I have been in school-houses of New South Wales where 80 per cent. of the children looked out of pebbled eyelids. I have seen half-blind children leading half-blind children over glaring sand wastes to school ; to the dull walls, to the blackboard and the garish-coloured map, to windows that looked out to ghastliness and desert. I warrant, children in Jamestown, South Australia, have no ophthalmia. The trees have attracted rain, not driven it away, and people there find that there is something more in life than what is simply utilitarian.

There are more varied ways of travelling in Brisbane than in any other place in Australia—and they are all good ; let that be said of them. At the railway station, as you step out, you will find three kinds of conveyances appealing to you—the hansom cab, the four-wheeler, and the jingle, or, in vulgar parlance, chuck-me-out. The last is peculiar to Queensland. It is a two-wheeler with a body like a four-wheeler, seats for six, and drawn by a stout cob. It does not look very fashionable ; it is lumbering in appearance, and reminds one of a butcher's cart, but it isn't a bad sort when you come to know it. It is the taker-in of bag and baggage, of scrip and scrippage, and of all the household gods. I have seen family parties going to assemblies in it, and it is to be found at the door of Government House as often as not. Brisbane leads the other capitals in the matter of conveyances. It has an elastic system that suits the bachelor or the benedict, the country cousin on a shopping expedition, my lady who is off for afternoon tea or reception, the family party, or the " happy twain," —and all at reasonable rates.

The meekest cab and hackney driver is to be found in Adelaide, but he is the closest too; the most insinuating and sarcastic is the Jehu of Melbourne; the most tyrannical, exorbitant, and even abusive, is the charioteer of Sydney; and the best fellow "in the swim" is the free-and-easy driver of Brisbane. He is satisfied with 100 per cent., or even 50 per cent., more than his regular fare, and that cannot be said of my fine fellow in Sydney. (I am speaking of the class.) And now as to the Brisbane cab fares. One can travel a mile for sixpence. I never offered a Brisbane cabby sixpence for the mile; but I have offered him a shilling, and remembering my good Sydney horseman whom I summon from his stand, I feel something of a niggard; but behold, the cabby is satisfied. He touches his hat. He says, "Thank you, sir. Want to go anywhere else to-day, sir? No, sir? Well, good-day, sir." Another touch of the hat, and he is away. I tried another tack. I had to go to a Government office half a mile away. I kept cabby half an hour. Then I offered him his legal fare of 2s. He took it. The hand went to the hat; not briskly, I admit, but still it went. "Thank ye, sir." The test was good enough. "Wait a minute, cabby; here's another sixpence; you are a phenomenon." It would be libelling human nature to suggest that he was not better pleased to get twenty-five per cent. increase on his proper fare; but he would not quarrel if he only got what the law allowed him; or be wanting in politeness either. And the Queensland cabby is not a mealy-mouthed kind of party. He is like the Queenslander generally—vigorous enough to swear at a bullock team as well as to drive it.

The Brisbane horses are well kept, and travel well. They are more like the cob than the Sydney horse, and they are far ahead of the Melbourne or Adelaide cab-horse. This can be said of the cab and car horses; but the omnibus horses are below par. They rate with the horses that run on the Paddington and Newtown lines in Sydney. The omnibuses are heavy and lumbering, and are built as if for Winnipeg mud. But, if one wants to see Brisbane properly, one does so by the horse-cars and the omnibuses; and occasional glimpses are got of spots that could be made picturesque, if not beautiful. The carmen have no uniform, and they are slow; but they are obliging, and, because they have not a great deal to do, are communicative. It was a carman who said to me: "It's Parlimint that's ruining us, sir; if we could give Sir Sam'l (Sir Samuel Griffith) ten years' hard, things would get evener again. You see, he's always got some fad, and cracks things up, and we puts our bloomin' quids into it; and there you are! I put a roll into cotton, and where is it? I fell in love with sugar to a cool fifty, and just chucked it away. I put my last bob into mines, and I can't pay my calls, and now I'm flat, and nothing beads." That last simile was uttered at Breakfast Creek, where there was no public-house, or he should have seen something that did "bead."

"I ain't sayin'," he continued, "that it's all Sir Sam'l's fault. But it's his fault in the main, for he was always flauntin' about our industries, and had something new on the card for the Queenslander to make his pile. There's lots of fellers humpin' their bluey along of Sam'l—that's what there is. But he's a great chap to come over you, and he doesn't mean to, partiklar, either. It's just nature in him. Now, if you was him, sir, and standin' right here before me, I don't think but what I'd swaller everything I've said, and believe in him, and promise to vote for him. You see, he don't get excited or blow himself up like a jelly-whacker. He just yarns on quiet and a bit sarcastic and confident, and it's like a horse as knows the road—you let him have his head at night; and there's been a good deal of night for us up here in Queensland, what with drought and things goin' bung all round."

From this carman I got more sound and sage opinions, than from many other people better educated and in better positions, and much more likely to be cultivated by the stranger. I shall have something to say about the public men of Queensland elsewhere, and I shall not, therefore, enlarge here upon Sir Samuel Griffith, who, however, did not deserve this appreciation. It was from this carman that I learned the topography of Brisbane, and got directions where to go and what to see. Everywhere in the world I have found the omnibus-driver and the carman the most intelligent and observant of the workman order, next to the market-gardener. I have seldom failed to get from him that information which the writer most needs, and which will come more from the instinct of the person from whom information is sought than from the questioner. All questions that touch the labouring man at all touch him vitally, and he passes over no point of practical detail. The man who is dealing constantly in large subjects, and conducting them, often does not help you to the radical beginnings so necessary to you, and from which you proceed to your conclusions, piecing out by reason what the blunt labourer gives you from feeling and ordinary experience.

For quiet comfort, Brisbane leads the colonies in the matter of hotels. To begin with, one is struck with the fine buildings. They are of the prevailing colour of the public structures, white, not the grey dull cement-colour of the new coffee-palaces of Sydney; and they are built with arcades, and with verandahs as a part of the building, not stuck on like a lean-to. I was impressed with the uniformity of decent hotel architecture, and I was told by one of the most thoughtful and well-posted men in Queensland that it was due to the authorities, who are severe in their requirements before granting licenses. I cannot vouch for the manner in which all the hotels are kept, but I had the opportunity of dining at three of the principal establishments, and living at the Imperial, and I can testify that one is better waited on at them all than in most of the best hotels in Adelaide, Melbourne, or Sydney. The hotels in the big places appear to get beyond the power of the management, but that should not be. One has only to think of the great hotels all over the world, and then one cannot help but condemn the bad management of so many large hotels in Australia. The best Brisbane hotels are well decorated and finely upholstered. Of all the colonies New South Wales has been the most backward in this respect, until within the last year or so, and even yet it is behind Brisbane in solid comfort. Good entertainment gives dignity to the life of any city; it gives the traveller what he has a right to expect when paying high rate. It is not often that I have praised hotel entertainment in Australian cities, and I am glad to say of Brisbane what I have said here, though it may appear to do injustice to the other colonies. The gentleman before-mentioned said it was significant that, though the population of the city had increased by 15,000 in the last seven years, the number of hotels had not increased. And yet we hear a great deal said of the roping-in that Brisbane needs in her morals. Perhaps she does, but I can vouch for her apparent respectability.

I can vouch for the general air of dignity that pervades her public service, from the railway conductors up to the legislators,—and that is something.

I have walked up and down Brisbane streets by day and by night, and I have not found the larrikin. He does not appear to exist as a class. There is no "gutter toff," no "wharf rat," as an order here. The slouch-hat, the rakish jib, the drawn features are not to be seen ; nor does the young larrikiness,—that hideous outgrowth of Sydney and Melbourne civilisation—exist as a class. I repeat "as a class," because I may be challenged as to this. They do not parade the streets as they do in Sydney; they do not revel with bottles of beer in the parks as they do in Sydney; they do not hang about the arcade of the post office as they do in Sydney and Melbourne. It is a relief to see even a seeming decency and morality. It is possible,—it is probable,—that there is just as much immorality and drunkenness in Brisbane as in any of the other capitals— perhaps more—but it does not parade itself. And I repeat that the larrikin and larrikiness do not exist.

CHAPTER XIII.

QUEENSLAND IN 1889 *(Continued).*

THE QUEENSLANDER AND HIS HERITAGE.

IT is possible, if I remained in Queensland a year, I might show many sides of the Queenslander's nature of which I have no idea now; but I do not know that I should see him more broadly, or catch his general contour and force so well. The detailed knowledge might make me lose him as he appears on the horizon to the traveller, who sees, more sharply at first than ever after, what makes him distinct from the other colonists. It is strange that a mountain range, an imaginary line, or a tract of plain country should make a difference in men; but it does. It is a difference of interest, of occupation, of motive, and of social and political environment, which shapes the mental habit, the accent, and even the physical exterior. Just as I saw a divergence in the railway management as soon as I came to Wallangarra, on the Queensland border, so I see dissimilarities between the Queenslander and the New South Wales man. The difference is not so marked, of course, as that noticed when one crosses from France to Germany, from England to Scotland, from Canada to the United States; but it is as distinct as that between the Tongan and Samoan, who of colour, build, and extraction are the same, and yet are as far apart in the details of character as are an Australian native bear and a grizzly of the Rockies.

One is struck when meeting the Queenslander first by his bluffness, his freshness, his firm outdoor appearance, and his self-confidence. The last quality is noticeable enough, but it is not a stupid self-confidence. It has fine elements that redeem it. Though it is an assertion that rouses fighting elements in the beholder, it is the outcome of pride of acquirement and a sense of national achievement. Now, it may be, that there are those elsewhere in Australia—in Sydney, perhaps—who will say: "What have the Queenslanders got to 'blow' about? They haven't a third of the population that we have; their capital is only one-sixth as big as ours; they haven't our naval station; they haven't our Zigzag; they haven't our Fish River Caves; they haven't our—well, our Port Jackson, and they haven't our Sir Henry Parkes." Quite so. They have not many "show things," like New South Wales; but they have a good record for all that.

Let us see why the Queenslander, while a hearty, pushing, upstanding fellow as he is, is also self-sufficient, and being so, is not to be hot-potted for it. Where was Queensland when she was part of New South Wales? In a more unsatisfactory condition than the northern part of Queensland is now. And the same reasons for separation were urged in 1858 that are being urged in 1889: disregard of northern interests; cheap labour; sapping the north to feed the south; the tariff; and the settlement of the land. The new Queensland struggled on then, handicapped; in the words of Mr. Pickering, on Carbine the winner of the Sydney Cup, it "sobbed under its weight." The population of Queensland then was 25,000, it is now 400,000; the pastoral runs were then 1,300 in number, they are now 7,365; horses were 23,502, they are now 306,000; there were then 433,000 cattle, there are now 4,474,000 ; there were then 3,167,000 sheep, there are now 13,000,000 ; there were then 7,150 pigs, they are now 74,000. Since 1859, Queensland has given birth to the Palmer gold-field ; to Charters Towers and Cape River ; to the Hodgkinson and Mulgrave fields ; to Etherage and Woolgar ; to Gympie, Mount Morgan, Croydon, and Cloncurry ; with their grand total, up to 1888, of £20,000,000 worth of gold. The copper lodes of Peak Downs, Mount Perry, Cloncurry, and elsewhere, have had the attention of Australia since Separation Day. Where were the Stanthorpe and Wild River tin mines before 1859? There was no Queensland sugar known till 1866, and now there are 120 sugar-mills dead and living ; but of that hereafter. There was not a foot of railway thirty years ago ; now there are nearly 2,000 miles, and 9,000 miles of telegraph lines. One might dwell upon agricultural products, upon the wine industry, upon the coal industry,—which received such an impetus last year,—upon the shipping, and upon the imports and exports ; but enough has been mentioned to show that the Queenslander has some reason to be proud of his achievements, and to be entitled to plume himself, if he does so with some sort of grace.

The Queenslander does not take you about as the Melbourne man does ; he does not tell you to go and see for yourself, and thank Heaven that you have found so blessed a spot, as the Sydney man does ; he is, in city and country, much what the Western man of New South Wales is, barring the knife the latter carries against the land law. There is a uniformity in the character of the Queenslander, so far as I have seen him, in the south and in the north—from the Darling Downs to Cairns. I have yet to see the West Queenslander, the Warrego man, the Hughenden man, the man from Barcaldine; but if I find him very different from those I have seen I shall try to show the modifications. He is not likely, however, to be a distinct type, for he has been acted on by forces which tend to draw him to the general type—by, for instance, railway communication, the greatest influence on individual and national character which exists to-day. And Queensland, compelled by the configuration of the country, has pursued a different policy from the rest of the colonies in regard to her railways—a policy which I shall not enlarge on here, but which has tended to create many centres, and not to throw population on one point. Queensland is secured against centralisation; she is on the road to uniform settlement.

Looking back on his thirty years of existence as a citizen, I think the Queenslander has something of which to be proud. His territory, which towards the sun-line covers 1,300 miles, and towards the west reaches 400 miles, gives him altogether a foothold and a board of action near 700,000 miles square. Is there any fault to be found with him, because he "wisibly swells," and thinks he is the most outstepping, soundest-limbed colonist in Australia? In his speech he has more idioms than any other colonist, except the man on the Darling River, or him that hails from the Tibbooburra way. He is not unlike the American in the pungency of his criticisms on men and things. And the city man possesses the same characteristics, though not so prominently, of course, as the up-country and Northern man. There is an activity which is more full-blooded than that found in Melbourne—more natural and free. Perhaps because of its size, the activity of Melbourne strikes one as selfish, as being almost Hebraic in its prostration before the shrine of the Golden Calf. Queensland's activity is essentially Conservative, and, where it is cribbed by Radicalism, it is so through the craft of the politician, not by the genius of the people. The people as a whole are all right, and are united enough in their national feeling —more united, perhaps, than in any other colony, and without being hampered by the extreme Radicalism that finds utterance in some quarters of New South Wales. There is one topic on which they split here, and it is the topic that will make or break Queensland—the labour question. No other problem will, in the future, occupy so much attention in Queensland, in South Australia, and in Western Australia, as this; and the battle is near at hand, particularly in Queensland. The smothered excitement regarding it is shaping Queensland's character, is making the national existence more intense. From the flushed condition may come great action, which will be a great strife and then a settled peace; or there will occur a reaction which will leave one section of the community dulled in ambition, soured by failure, and unpatriotic; and will affect the general prosperity of the colony to an extent scarce dreamed of by politicians, who are used to look upon great questions as hot ploughshares to open the road to power, and not as touching the life of the people vitally.

The national character of Queensland is now fusing, as I have seen in talking with men of all classes. I began with the car-driver, and I passed to the stonemason, the small settler, the practical miner, the commercial man, the sailor, the steamship owner, the pastoralist, and, last of all, to the planter; and I find a spirit of unrest and explosive sentiment which cannot remain long as it is. And, what is more important than anything else, I have caught the feeling of men who have seen their money dwindle away, their industry totter to its fall under bad seasons, under the sharp command, Thou shalt employ no coloured labour. Without discussing the right or wrong, the wisdom or unwisdom of the last amendment to the Polynesian Act of Queensland, one faces a great problem, and sees national thought in a tense condition, and commercial venture hesitating and nervous. This is noticeable in Brisbane; it is plain at Rockhampton; it is distinct at Mackay; it is vivid at Bowen; it is excited at Townsville; it is anxious at Cairns; it is active at Cooktown; and it cannot but be active when in the south there is the adherent of the north, and in the north there is the champion of the south.

These words are written *en route*, and they are begun at one point and finished at another 500 miles away, perhaps. And so it is, that what is recorded above, has been carried in my pocket through many new districts, since it first ran from the pen. I have found men everywhere believing unreservedly in the country, whether it is a devitalised sugar district or a cargoless port. The smallest settlement on the coast thinks that its voice is potent at the capital. The hum of its little wheels is the centripetal force of the Universe. Does Mourilyan believe that it represents no figure on the national dial-plate? Does Port Douglas cease to think that it is one of the weights that regulate the political pendulum? Not a bit. Is Cairns willing to let Townsville take precedence in the anticipated Colony of North Queensland? Think it not. But there is no room for ridicule here, there is no cause for sneers. This faith, this envious faith, if you will, seems to me to be the latent strength of the land that bides its nascent time, of which all previous workings have been premature.

If I were a Queenslander I should believe in it with all my heart;—for the vast tropical rains cannot wash her out, the angry sun cannot dry her veins, the mistakes of politicians cannot destroy her; she can be smitten seven times, and even seventy times seven, and yet her forces will be climbing to the tableland of action and radiation. Bad whisky may kill her pioneers; the Chinamen may take money out of the country; the children may dwindle in the miasma of the far north, and mothers may grow wan and nerveless under the exhaust-pipes of a cruel atmosphere, but the march will not be stayed. The Queenslander will survive, and he will be robust in mind, as he will be warm in his physical vigour. The Irishman, the Scotsman, the Englishman, and the native, are distinct enough up here now, but one can see the fusion going on; the levelling down and the levelling up; the Irishman gaining directness and industrial confidence; the Scotsman gathering adaptability and warmth; the Englishman leaving off his insularity; and the native borrowing the good points of the others, and possessing also the feeling of certainty that, being of the soil, he can match them all, beat them at a bargain, and still be friends with them. One meets a good many English officers up north,—gentlefolk who have settled to the conditions of pioneering—and they show the constraining influence of the country in their habit, of speech and life. They move not neck and neck with, but in the track of the native; and give as much as they get. They have investments in land and mines. They become planters; they make a genteel yet frugal headway, and sometimes they do more. One finds fine young Englishmen—men whose family names are known in naval, military, and social circles in England —working away at the mines, on the railways, and on plantations; and doing so in such a wholesome, sturdy fashion, that one is bound to admire them; for they have neither "side" nor swagger. The Queenslander is bound to acknowledge that the young Englishman does not come here to seek a Government billet; he must admit the manliness that will handle a pick or shovel at Normanton, load a packhorse at Herberton, manage the navvies at Cairns, muster sheep on the Warrego, or ride the cattle to the stockyard on the Darling Downs.

There is one feature of Queensland life which makes the beholder apprehensive: it is the speculative spirit. There is not a township, a city, a settlement in Queensland, that has not suffered from the mining and the land-purchase fever, and particularly the former. The depression that has made the blood of enterprise in Queensland sluggish during the last two or three years, has come partly from drought, but mostly from money sunk in mines. Business men to whom I talked in Brisbane said that the fictitious value put on mining shares is the severest drain on the present financial vitality of the country. Droughts make a debilitation of commerce, and, under the first shadow of them, men begin to cut down their expenses and avoid new debts. But with speculation men pass from shadow to shadow, in the hope that haply they may retrieve what is lost, and turn back their destiny.

As an indication of the present stagnation, the manager of a great insurance company told me that, despite vigorous canvass, policies dwindled continuously during the reaction succeeding such mining booms as that associated with Mount Morgan. The difference was not so great in the number of policies as in the weight of them. Where a £5,000 policy could be got in 1886, a £1,000 policy was secured in 1888. The tide has, however, turned, and the pastoralist is venturing to breathe again, and all are beginning to feel that the shaken nerves of commerce are getting some tone from a new start. But still the strain is in the blood, and one finds men all over the country who have invested, and are still investing, in land of which they know nothing, and in mines which are chiefly on paper. I saw land in the Cairns district owned by men who bought at a venture, on a margin as it were, and who are waiting for some one to offer them a fancy price for it. They bought only to sell again, not as men do who intend to work the land and develop its resources. I saw brush land lying idle beside plantations of bananas worked by Chinamen, who are sending away thousands of bunches of fruit daily, and growing well-to-do. This brush land in the hands of real settlers would mean competence. Now it is lost to the owner, and valueless to the country. But all this is shaping the character of the Queensland people, and they will emerge from this anxious period, grown wiser. Trade and development will work through more normal avenues as time goes on, and investment will be more careful, or at least more crafty and world-wise, and that will curb the helter-skelter, speculative spirit of the masses.

I have had several opportunities of seeing the legislators of Queensland at work, and the experience has not been unpleasant. The first time I sat behind the Speaker's chair, the Assembly was discussing the financial statement. The debate had come near to its close, and the interest had flagged a good deal, but there were some forty members present, and they were all good listeners. Sir Henry Parkes is quite mistaken in his opinion that a man must have a large audience before he can speak well, for I heard some good speaking in the Queensland

Legislative Assembly, though the few members were scattered through a large building. If a man is susceptible to surroundings, he would receive nothing but pleasant sensations from the Queensland Assembly building. It is light, well-furnished, lofty, and, if a trifle too brilliant in colour inside, is not gaudy. It is a dignified structure, despite its faults in architecture, and the members seem to have borrowed some sense of reserve from it, for what the Brisbane papers call disorder in the sittings would be simply airy trifling for legislators in New South Wales. The members were rated one morning by the *Courier* for their habits of interruption, while it seemed to the beholder that they had only given the speakers opportunities to bring out new points.

Rough and ready fellows many of them were, but there was no man among them who used—and I am told there is not one that ever uses—the firebrands of disorder that have, at times, lighted New South Wales and Victoria so disadvantageously before the world. The general tone of the Assembly and the Legislative Council seemed to be one of mutual respect, if, occasionally, of bitterness and irony. I think they are good haters in the Queensland Parliament, but they are also free, open-handed haters; they are haters of the plain, not of the back-shop and alley-way; they will fight, but they will shake hands both before and after. They would dance hornpipes on the political graves of their opponents, but they would fight the battle out according to Queensberry rules. It is not a brilliant-looking gathering before us —rather a hardy, enthusiastic one. Look round. Out of the forty members nine-tenths of them are bronzed, and twenty-nine of them are bearded and whiskered. Regard the Ministerial bench. The Ministers do not look like great statesmen, but they appear men who

are fair and square in their private life, and who have
good business capacities. One would not suspect an
orator to be among them. Yes, there is one little man
with a broad white forehead, a well-lit face, and dark
hair curled about his neck and streaked with grey, who
looks as if he could speak. And, as it turns out, he can.
That is Mr. Macrossan,* Minister for Mines, and one
would stake a great deal that he has many a nugget
of fact and much power in his well-shaped head. The
Premier, Mr. Morehead, looks like a man who would shine
more as an administrator than a leader. He would be
too outspoken, too impatient of ordinary political methods
to use them. He would just as lief tell a man to follow
Nebuchadnezzar in the matter of verdure as not. He
is a man of the soil, and not of the workshop or
counting-house; and that is what strikes one in connection with all his colleagues, with the exception of Mr.
Macrossan. No one would suspect Mr. Morehead of
oratory. He has not the carriage, the direct force of eye
and feature, of a speaker. He would have all the vitality,
all the simple hatred or liking, all the one-idea habit of
the man who is a worker rather than a thinker. But I
err in saying that none of that Ministry looks the speaker
and the statesman. There comes in one from the Legislative Council who commands attention at once. The
stranger could not but be impressed favourably by Sir
Thomas McIlwraith; his enemy must acknowledge the
force of his presence, his supporters must feel his power
of leadership. He has a fine bearing, and seems never so
much in place as when sitting on the Ministerial Bench,
or when leaning over the railing in the Council Chamber,
and watching some debate in progress. He carries with
him a dignity that would make an impression in any

---

* Mr. Macrossan has since died.

Chamber, and that must affect favourably the daily habit of the Queensland Assembly. Opposite him sits the man most *en évidence* in Queensland,—Sir Samuel Griffith.* To the man ignorant of the history of Queensland, he is one to be first picked out in the Assembly next to Sir Thomas McIlwraith. He looks a man well pulled together mentally, as one who would not let his thoughts run away with him, who would never grow enthusiastic in tone, who would produce no oratorical effects. He looks every inch a counsel, a trained advocate, who sees every weak point in his opponent's armour, who also sees the weak points in his own, and would throw up defences therefor. He could be direct when necessary, or allusive if need be ; he would not permit an emotion to interfere with his judgment. He would have no attacks of rhetoric, no fulness of debate in the head. He seems in most regards a leader ; he is undoubtedly the ablest man in Queensland, but not the most inspiring. But beside him there sits a man who, like Mr. Macrossan, should be "clever on his feet" ; he should be eloquent, and of much ingenuity and originality. That is Mr. Hodgkinson, an ex-Minister ; and on the other side of Sir Samuel Griffith is Mr. Hargrave, who has a way of putting things that carries weight. These were the impressions I received the first evening I visited the Assembly, and I had them verified the next evening when I heard the discussion on the Western Australia question.

I write these later words at the foot of a great mountain range, in the land of the cassowary and beside the home of the alligator. As I look out of the window at my left there towers a peak that loses its head among the

---

* Sir Samuel Griffith is now (1892) the Premier of Queensland.

PINNACLE ROCK.   [*Page* 245.

rolling clouds ; as I turn to the open door at my right, another summit, wrapped in purple haze, lifts its giant shoulders from the plains ; almost at my feet the Barron River winds, clear and cool, over its rocky bed. I stop a moment and listen. There is the sound of great hammers on the anvils, the *puff-puff* of a locomotive toiling up the steep, the gurgle of the laughing-jackass, the drone of the locusts, the silver rustle of the long grass, and the sighing of the pines. And now there is a *boom! boom!* and a tremendous roll of sound far up the gorge. What is that? Not Heinrich Hudson and his mystic comrades with their ninepins among the hills? No, this is not the Catskills, this is no Sleepy Hollow, nor land of Rip Van Winkle. That was only the sound of dynamite, of breaking rocks, of the cracking shell of the mountain side. Go to the door ; look out. See a cloud of yellow dust leaping skywards, and growing up, and growing thinner, till it is lost among deep coverts of the primeval forest, or whirled away into the ether. Sweep a half-circle with the eye. Mark how nine hundred, a thousand feet up the steep mountain side, great slices of green have been cut away, leaving a dull red cicatrice, over which no verdure will ever throw a pitiful mantle. Down these mountain sides, where, until a few years ago, only the cassowary and the blackfellow ran, there are trundling the boulders that were century-mossed when the Pharaohs reigned in Egypt. Here, as elsewhere, civilisation is drawing its steel belts and bars clear over the mountain tops ; is making the giant hills the servants of the plain. There goes an engine now with a troop of cars behind it. It has come from Cairns, and it will wind up the gorge to Tunnel Number Ten. The track, 100 yards away at my left, 3 feet 6 inches wide, is the Cairns-Herberton Railway, by name, but what it is by nature takes time and thought to say.

Are there feats in engineering to be performed? They are here. Here are curves and reverse-curves on bridges, in tunnels, and in the open. Here are paths for the march of the iron horse for mile after mile, cut out of the hard rocks, and looking like shelves, as they really are, and made to hold no more than such trains as that which is now crawling round the face of the cliff. You may, if you please, sit on the edge of a freight-car here and there, and your feet will hang over a gorge 1,000 feet deep; you shall see nothing at all beneath you, for the car is wider than the track, and you are hung in space, the ripe sun above you, and the jagged rocks and the unfathomed waterpools below. This line, in places, is taken along the side of a gorge where the foot of the chamois would scarce have found a hold. And, if you please, you shall ride with me along ledges just wide enough for your horse to stand, and, one leg against the mountain-side, you shall drop a stone over sheer cliffs to the dark defiles hundreds of feet below. Let New South Wales never mention her Zigzag more; for here is a greater thing,—so much greater, that those English tourists who, in days to come, landing at Normanton from the British-India steamers, and crossing the gold-plains and the vast mineral beds to Herberton, and over this range of mountains, shall say when they see the Zigzag, Is it only this you brought me out to see?

There are six iron lattice-girder bridges on the three-fourths circle of that gorge, within a distance of 9 miles as the crow flies; within $15\frac{1}{4}$ miles of railway line. There are within that distance nearly 60 wooden bridges, and 14 tunnels varying from 200 feet to 594 feet in length. There are 174 curves from where I am to the present point of completion. The foundations for the bridges are set sometimes in the solid rock 15 feet below the surface, and sometimes in earth and stone 50 feet. You shall ride your horse on a path two feet wide between a dark depth of that 50 feet grave made for the piles of a bridge, and a yawning chasm of 900 feet and a bed of boulders. Well is it for you that you bestride a sure-footed horse, my friend. A snake gliding from a rift in the spur, a brown pigeon whirring from the soft leaves of the satin-wood tree, a boulder shooting down the range, and a timid horse shying, might toss you to immortality on one side, or a maimed mortality on the other. I know of nothing like this railway in the world for eccentricity —an eccentricity having its base on the apparently impossible, and which seems to be constantly avoiding what it must ultimately do.

A couple of days ago, entering Trinity Bay aboard the steamer *Palmer*, in which I had come from Townsville, the route of the line was pointed out to me. The mountains run parallel with the sea line. Herberton lies to the south-west of Cairns. What does the railway do? Does it move westward straight across the range, or south-westward? Nothing so ordinary. It turns its back on Herberton and the south, and careers off to the north-west for miles, first round a monster hill, standing in the middle of the plain between the main range and the sea; then it glides over sandy flats, and alongside mangrove and pandanus swamps to the base of the lofty mounds which aspire from 1,000 feet to 4,000 feet above the level of the Pacific. It is not a monotonous journey over that first 8¾ miles to the mountains, for one sees many small settlements making breaks in the jungle fastnesses,—the houses of selectors with their 160 acres under cultivation, fields of maize, a few banana plantations, and small railway stations built as New South Wales would never build them—simply, and at little cost: Edge Hill, Stratford, Richmond, Red Lynch, and lastly, Kamerunga.

I warrant that the new Commissioners for Railways, when they visit this scene of operations, this "plunge" of the colony, will not see the line as I have seen it these two days, or as I shall see it to-night and to-morrow. They will not sit on barrels of cement with an engine in front dropping sparks and belching smoke like Vesuvius, and be carried like so much dead freight with the concrete and timber up the hills. They will have things made easy for them; the carriages will be spick and span, and everything will have a holiday attire. For that they need not be thankful; they would see more if they roughed it from Kamerunga north-west till they came to the point, 1,100 feet high, where the line begins to think of seeking its real destination, instead of pursuing the policy of Paddy's pig. After deliberately playing at hide-and-seek with itself through the mountain gorges; after making curves like giant horse-shoes; after doubling back on itself several times to a place nearly opposite where it started; after jibbing with all its might and main, the mad thing finally makes a bolt in the right direction, and swings lazily along a fine tableland, where are great storehouses of timber and realms for agriculture. It moves down to the plains towards Herberton, till it is stopped again by another range, which it will have to climb before it enters the mining district, and sweeps away to Cloncurry to join the railway from Normanton being built to meet it.

Yesterday afternoon I started up the main gorge on

the ballast train, accompanied by Mr. G. A. Hobler, one
of the most hardy and courteous officers, under Mr.
Annett, the able chief-engineer of the Queensland railways; and it was not long before I began to understand
what this undertaking for the opening up of northern
Queensland means. But, while man's ingenuity held you
on one hand, Nature, in sumptuous attire, brooded over
you on the other. The wild banana lifted up its wide
fronds twenty-five feet in the air; the fig-tree shot down
innumerable roots from a hundred feet into the earth,
making for itself palisades of strength, and buttresses
like the wings to a majestic stage in a forest of Arden.
The wild pumpkin trailed its yellow blossoms in the
wealth of grass; the pools along the way were pano-
plied with glorious water-lilies; and ferns rivalled the
pawpaw and the slender palm in height. The fruit
hung thick upon some pawpaw trees, but, while mouths
watered, tongues could not taste; there was not time.
And what fruits they are! One has not tasted the best
that Nature gives till a breakfast has been made off the
grenadilla, a bulky elder brother of the passion-fruit; or
the pawpaw, a direct relative of the musk-melon. The
prettiest thing that one can see is the palm—as straight,
yet as willowy as a lily—reaching up to touch the pale
green leaves of the acacia-cedar, or to pay its compliments
to the sound and royal kauri pine. And while you are
filled with the pleasure of it, there will startle your
senses a view of the ocean miles away; and, between you
and it, the camps of the navvies, the noiseless villages,
and the thick swamp where the death-adder and black
snake hide, and where the fire-fly flashes in the gloom;
then, from such sensations you will be roused by the
agonised engines and the grinding of the wheels upon
the rails. You are making a great curve now called the

Horseshoe Bend, and you begin to go back towards the point you started from; you are going round a gorge; you are compassing about $3\frac{1}{2}$ miles to get started on your journey, and so, lost again in views of trees overgrown by the passion-vine, with the ripe fruit hanging down and never to be picked; of sturdy hickories; of cool arched coverts growing away into darkness; you soon forget that you have come round a five-chain curve, and that you will travel over 98 more of such curves in this second section of 15 miles.

I only know of one railway more astonishing than this, and that is the line owned by Spreckles & Co., on the island of Maui, in the Hawaiian group. I have often wondered that no terrible fatality was ever recorded from there. The exact curve I have forgotten, but I should think it is nine chains. The line goes round a gully, and its peculiar feature is a slight fall to the curve and a heavy ascent beyond it. This necessitates fast motion round the curve in order to climb the ascent, and when one stops to think how easily a locomotive or a carriage jumps the rail on a dead level with a sharp curve, the significance of the suggested danger can be understood. There is a sheer fall of many hundred feet for an erring train, but the management have had the luck of Mephistopheles. I only hope that there will be such luck for the Cairns-Herberton line.

The grades are not nearly so heavy as on the line over the Blue Mountains. The steepest is only one in fifty, and the prevailing grade is one in sixty, so that there is no need for any apprehension on that account, nor necessity for a zigzag. The anxiety of the engineer, as I have shown, comes from other quarters. He has to consider the possibilities of landslips; to settle whether a tunnel or a cutting would be best; to take into account whether he shall go round a gully or bridge it, and if he builds a tunnel, what curves he shall be able to make in it. There is now under consideration of the Government whether a tunnel, the longest yet projected for the line, shall be built at a spot where it is found difficult to get a solid foundation for the line. This tunnel will have a reverse curve, the exact angle of which I have forgotten.

These tunnels are splendidly built. Cement only is used, and they are as clean and solid-looking as if they were cut out of the solid rock. The contractor has a ballast-pit in the bed of the river, and from it he gets all his stone. A crusher is used, and the sand, cement, and stone are carried up the range. Italians are employed principally in the tunnels, and the navvies generally are of the lands of Umberto and John Dillon. Yes, the Irish flourish here, as the Scotch do at Townsville. I have seen many a railway camp in my time, but never an honester, fresher, and more orderly-looking class of men than those working on the Cairns-Herberton line. There are several public-houses at Kamerunga and Red Lynch, and there are three or four up the range; but I could not imagine that the clear-faced boys and men whom I saw knock down many cheques at them. I was told also, by those who should know, that the camp was a model one. No better evidence of that can be given than the fact that there have only been two or three accidents since construction began. You may see, if you move over the line, navvies tied to trees and held by ropes as they work on the face of the cliffs, and men cannot do that sort of thing and be heavy drinkers. I got the first knowledge of the nationality and class of men employed from seeing the Italian flag blowing on a pinnacle of rock—Stonehenge again. How did it get there? The rock presented few places where even the foot of a cat might get a purchase; and yet, somehow, the son of Italy climbed to its peak, and planted the flag, and watched it wave over the gorge, where now for many a day it has flapped in the breeze. Why Italians are chiefly employed I could not discover.

Passing through a cutting, one suddenly emerges on a rocky platform to see the Barron River winding down to the sea, or a pretty creek falling in a series of pools, over the hillside, to the elder stream. One of the most delightful of creeks is to be found after entering Barron Gorge. It was on my second day's journey that I saw it,—for these last few lines are written hundreds of miles away from Cairns and all that is thereabouts,—and the impression left upon the mind is refreshing. We had ridden from a cloud of red dust, and out of the heat of the scrub fires past Camp Over Creek, where were to be found corrugated iron pubs. and shops—primitive places enough—bearing the announcement that there were to be found "the Travellers' Home," and bargains in boots and shoes. Over it is to be an iron bridge, from which one will look into pools of uncalculated depth and into the luxurious forest. It is a forest that tires one, perhaps. It is too heavy for the simple nature of the northerner. It makes too great a call upon the senses. There is not in it the wholesome vigour of the forests under the Great Bear, but there is indolence and the poppy of forgetfulness and inanition. One could not think of Caroline Norton writing her *Irish Emigrant's Lament* in them. It is, after all, a relief to turn from the full ripeness of the tropic hills and valleys to the might of civilisation beside it—to the iron girders and the huge hickory piles, to the pick and the shovel, and the belt of steel, which is the path of civilisation. When waiting for my train the other evening I looked up the gorge round which I had travelled. The sun was drawing its gold mantle across its breast; the mountains were wrapped in violet; the cool air swept down the steep; and thinking, as I dwelt upon the scene, of what a strange mingling of the wonderful in nature and in science was being balanced in those hills, there seemed to start up from one side of the gorge a figure like to the statue of Captain Cook in Hyde Park, Sydney, but wearing a commander's hat, and pointing straight to the route of the railway round the half-circle of the gorge. There it stood, distinctly outlined against the sky. I called the attention of my companion to it. It was as apparent to his eye as to my own. The master-spirit of railways was pointing the way to the surveyor and the engineer. To a superstitious man that sign would mean much; and though it does not appear in the records, perhaps it had something to do with deciding the route of the line. Men are turned by slighter things than a tree in the shape of a human form. But there, at any rate, it stands, pointing and for ever pointing; and the work is going on, to the benefit of the land, or to financial confusion,—or worse.

The line will cost between £40,000 and £50,000 a mile, and, it is prophesied, over the fifty; but that remains to be seen. One hears from men of judgment ominous remarks about the line. When one stops to think of the great rains that occur in northern Queensland, the full force of the apprehensions may be understood. Sometimes 20 inches fall in one night, and in one week there has been as much rain as New South Wales would have in five years. There is a boulder with a great load of earth upon it. Then comes a heavy rain; the weight increases, the boulder breaks away, the line is blocked, and the rest is in the minds of us all. After the highest point is reached at the Barron Falls, the trouble is at an end, and nothing unpleasant need be anticipated; but there is not now a general sense of security in the minds of many connected with the line. The Government seemed determined to push on with it, and no doubt rightly so; for it is possible to make the line safe by increased expense in tunnels. To give up the work now, as has been suggested, would be folly. The line may make northern Queensland. The western country has tremendous resources, but no country can be developed where the only means of carriage is by packhorses. All the tin is brought so from Herberton to Cairns,—an industry can only struggle at that rate. There is no road on which waggons or drays might travel over the mountains, and there can be none. The Government built a road, but it is far too steep in parts. The railway is the only hope, and it is a hope which is not allowed to languish. There are 1,200 men, over 200 horses and mules, and 300 bullocks now working on the line, and the scene is as busy a one as will greet the eye anywhere. At the present rate the line ought to be finished to within nine miles of Herberton, the point where the other range begins, in a year and a half; and by that time its safety could be pretty thoroughly tested, for heavy rains are as sure this year as the course of the sun. Speed the day, says every man in the north; and the Herberton miner is eager to excitability. It costs him £20 a ton to send his ore to England to be treated, and he groans at that. He has told me of the copper and silver and gold and tin that he has waiting for development, and he pins his faith to the railway. When one sees the slow packhorses toiling over the range with their little load of tin, and meets them on the way back laden with groceries and goods, one is inclined to justify this expensive line, especially since it has been proved beyond peradventure that it will open up a really rich mineral district, and be an outlet for great resources.

CHAPTER XIV.

QUEENSLAND IN 1889 (*Continued*).

CAIRNS—THE BARRON FALLS—THE CAIRNS-
HERBERTON RAILWAY.

IN travelling along the Queensland coast one is struck by the likeness between its harbours and the harbours of many of the islands of the South Seas. Townsville harbour looked not unlike that of Honolulu, though its hills are not so volcanic, nor its sea so delicately coloured. Cardwell was much like a Samoan or Tongan port, though the profusion of palms was not so great, nor were the houses so white in the sun; and one missed the bronzed natives in their *lava-lavas*. One misses, too, any tendency to make the most of nature. It is soon, perhaps, to expect it; but towns that aspire to be capitals of new colonies should try to attain to some standing in the things that make for dignity. But no. Townsville has treeless streets, and Cairns is, I am told, either always standing with its feet in the water or slumbering in its dust. But Cairns is beautifully situated, and it is soon also to have a harbour up which the largest ship can sail. Meanwhile, as at Rockhampton and at Townsville, the traveller has to tranship to a tender. But that is not so bad, when everything is done with such despatch and care as marks the Australian United Steamship Navigation Company's service. I shall henceforth abbreviate this to A. U. S. N. Co.) There is no feeling more pleasant than to wake up in a new and beautiful place; and that has been my experience several times on this journey. I awoke one morning, looked out of my porthole, saw mountains to the right of me, to the left of me, in front of me, the broad sea behind me, and a quiet town fringing the shore, perspiring already in the early sun,—and that was Cairns.

I should not say that the town itself was beautiful, but it might be made so. I should not say that it has all the characteristics of a model municipality, but it has the latent qualifications to become that. It makes one shudder to see the hotels doing "a land office business" at eight o'clock in the morning; to watch men staggering up the streets before the sun has drunk the miasma from "the rheumy and unpurged air." Cairns, I should think, has one hotel for every store and shop in the place, and it does not let them languish. Not that the town is in the least rowdyish. I have seen no open rowdyism in any place in the North. It seems to be just a steady devotion to the hot and rebellious stuff that wastes no time in killing. All the liquor places in Cairns had an air of decency about them, but they were doing their work just the same,—doing it in a climate that in itself is devitalising and nerve-destroying. To understand what the climate is, just take a map and look where Sydney is, and think of its heat. Then move up the coast 1,500 miles, multiplying the heat as you go till after you come to Cairns. Look where the equator is, and think again. Think that in this wintertime the thermometer is registering 90° in the shade at ten o'clock in the morning, and 100° at noon. Then picture to yourself hills above, the sea beyond, and corrugated iron and wood and dust about you,—and you are at

Cairns in the winter time. But let not the reader conclude that this place is beyond the limits of civilisation, beyond the region of refinement. I have never been in any out-of-the-way place in the world, where culture and the instincts of the gentle life were not found. Cairns is no exception. Placed as it is, where men have come to make money rather than to make homes, still one finds a few homes there, and pleasant ones too ; and the instincts and habits of a metropolitan life hid away in a cottage on the seashore covered with bourgainvillea, or in the hot precincts of a rice plantation. The first night I was at Cairns there was an assembly, and at it ranged in airy measure the youth and beauty of the place. The hall was prettily decorated with great palm leaves, splendid ferns, and pretty flags. The traveller and writer must not, therefore, be hasty, and say that Cairns is a place of dust and sin. I can count the fingers of my hand twice over before I have exhausted the list of the intelligent and cultured folk that I met at Cairns.

Rome was not built in a day, neither can a place in northern Queensland be erected in the same time. Cairns is very young yet. Seven years ago, land in the principal street could be bought for £5 a foot; now it is worth £50 a foot. Ten years ago Cairns was a bush. Seven miles out of Cairns ten acres of swamp land were sold by the Government the other day for £4,000. These cannot be said to be fictitious values, as any one would say, who stops to consider that the town must be the shipping place for a splendid district behind it,—for Herberton with its tin and silver, for the agricultural and timber land lying between, and for the splendid sugar, rice, and fruit country about the town itself. I should not be afraid to invest money in land at Cairns. Its promise is great, its happy destiny is sure, so far as commercial prosperity goes. Rockhampton, Townsville, Cairns, Cooktown—these are the great ports of the future ; and not the least of them is Cooktown with its natural advantages and its background of resources.

Yet Cairns proper does not impress one with its vigour ; one must go to Kamerunga for that. One does not see the squatter driving into town, the stockman with his cattle, nor the driver with his pack-horses. The pack-horses that come with their heavy loads over the mountains leave their freight at Kamerunga, and only now and then the small selector is seen getting needful things in the stores at Cairns. I only saw one drove of cattle on the tramp, and that was in the mountains on the Thornborough road. They had just crossed the highest point in the range beyond the Barron Falls, and were coming down to Kamerunga. They had, 200 of them, come 150 miles, and they looked worn enough, though they had reached splendid feed and plenty of mountain water. But they were indications of a life beyond the hills which is yet to justify all the hopes of the pioneer, and the enthusiastic politician. I had hoped, while at Cairns, to get out to Hambledon, Messrs. Swallow & Derham's plantation, but at the last it could only be done by hard riding; and after three days of mountain climbing and riding, it was too big a contract for a bushman even, and I was scarcely seasoned yet. But from Cairns to Mackay, and from Mackay to Cairns, I heard of this plantation,—of the sturdy men who worked it, and of the magnificent land of which it was the centre. " The best district in all Queensland," said Mr. Bates, a hearty journalist of Cairns ; " The country of the boundless hope," said Mr. Cran, an old planter of Townsville. At Hambledon, not only is sugar-cane cultivated, but the fruit industry is fostered, and a tinning establishment is in full swing.

I had to choose between seeing Hambledon and inspecting Mr. Tom Behan's rice plantation. I chose the latter, for I should see plenty of sugar in my travels, and there is only one district like that of Stratford, where Mr. Behan has been the real pioneer in rice-milling, if we except the Chinamen with their dollies.

But why is it that in some of the streets of Cairns, and even in the principal street, one sees the grass growing, and gets the impression of a swift decay? Chiefly because the town is like Hilo in the Sandwich Islands, a place where it rains every morning. At Cairns it rains much for nine months in the year, and then it rains a little for three months, and begins again. Did that quiet fellow at Cairns tell the truth when he said that there are lily-pools in parts of the main street for weeks at a time in the summer? I do not know; I only know that everybody said that there were pools which held their own for months in that street of two chains in width, and lay there, the Dark One between them and the deep sea. I use the term "Dark One" designedly, for let us think how much that is demoniacal lies in those great pools. Can we wonder that doctors say no family will ever go to the third generation in Cairns? The dread miasma will play its part till the great swamps are dried up, and the streets of the town are kept clear by drainage extraordinary. But this might be said of all the places that I have visited. I thought Broken Hill was bad enough last year, but every town in northern Queensland can beat Broken Hill in the race of odours, hands down. Cairns looks longingly to the day, now very near, when vessels will come straight to her wharfs independent of tender or lighter; and then, with her railway and a good steam communication, she will fight her fight bravely enough, one hopes. What the saving will be to the steamship

companies, by good harbours at such places as Townsville
and Cairns, may be gathered from the fact that it costs
the A. U. S. N. Company £10,000 a year for lighters,
etc., at Townsville. The little town of Bowen has
been progressive enough to run out a jetty three-
fourths of a mile long into the sea, and small ships
can come straight to her wharfs at any time.

It was my wish to visit the schools of Cairns, but time
would not permit. I did visit, however, the School of
Art, and I am afraid it did not impress me favourably.
I have never seen a worse one, and I give it importance
because it appears to me that the greater the temptation to,
and the prevalency of, those evils which beset new places
in hot climates, the more strenuous should be the efforts
of the few who have the welfare of the community at
heart, to provide the saving clauses in the contract of
social life. Is there no parson at Cairns, no officer of
the Government, no teacher who cares enough for his
kind to keep in order and existence a scheme of refinement such as a School of Art affords? The utter
desolation of this place in Cairns suggests more than all
the reports that ever were written, or all the rhetoric of
the politicians; but in saying this one must say, too,
that the journalists of Cairns are men who do their best
to raise the tone of the community, and strengthen its
moral courage,—and Heaven knows it is needed in a
place which in rain and shine has (to use a northern
phrase) a terrible thirst upon it. I should be afraid to
set down the figures that show the drink bill of some of
these northern ports. It is appalling. Yet you can stay
at hotels in Cairns that are as quiet and orderly, and
as well kept, as some of the big Sydney hotels.

Perhaps it would be expected that I should write of
the Barron Falls before anything else in the Cairns

country. We have read, elsewhere, descriptions of these falls,--descriptions which were cheap and glowing editions of the *Cataract of Lodore*. We have been startled by whirling phrases concerning "Our Own Niagara," and have been blinded with such incantations as "The womb of uncreated night" and "Fathomless voids," until I, with others, had felt that in making a pilgrimage to this place of wonder and mystery, we should take our shoes from off our feet and go thereto on bended knees. Well, I know a man who went thereto in just such covering as Kammehammeha the First wore when he bounded down the Pali, or as that in which a New Guinea native meets his Governor now; but he went that way because it was raining so hard and he was so hot that every ounce of clothing was as a pound of flesh. I saw the falls with Mr. G. A. Hobler. I shall not soon forget the morning we started. The sun was hot, but a cool air blew down the range, and boot-and-saddle was declared before nine o'clock, I having come out from Cairns by the seven o'clock train. For four hours it was a continuous climb, and then it was two hours of descent, and the deed was done; the railway was seen in all its completion and incompletion, and the Barron Falls were ours for ever. A little while in the open, and then we began to climb the range. Trees covered with vines like mantles, and long trailing stems swinging therefrom, like endless whips or snakes, and—— "Look out," said my companion, "don't touch that lawyer-vine; it will tear you properly, and then not let you go." Too late; my fingers touched it, and the vine had the best of it. The thorns upon the vine are like barbed spears, and they would, in the language of the Yankee, tear the hide off a crocodile. "That is the enemy of the surveyor," said Mr. Hobler. "It made slow work for those who did the

BARRON FALLS, QUEENSLAND.

trial survey ; it, and the stinging plant, and the snakes. There," said he, " is the stinging plant ; it will kill hares and dogs if they but touch it, and it is most poisonous to man. I was stung by one, and the experience was not a pleasant one, I can tell you. A touch of it, then comes a stinging pain in the muscles, a lump rises on the body under the arm, one cannot sleep at nights, and when the hand is put in cold water there is great pain. It lasts a matter of weeks, but it is an experience. Now just try it ; really it is most interesting." " I am too busy," I replied. " That is all very right for an engineer who is paid by his country, well or ill ; but for me, Mr. District Engineer, I have not time." There is a pea in the Darling district in New South Wales which, it is declared, will drive horses mad, but I cannot vouch for that. The stinging plant is, however, the terror of the mountaineer in the Cairns country.

The yellow hybiscus flower greets one everywhere along the line, and an occasional orchid shows its yellow and white blooms far up a tree. Again the bushman's information was at play, and my comrade told me that, parched with thirst, the leaves of the hybiscus and of the rosella plant had kept him alive in a waterless district. What was that you passed just then—that mound ? A grave. The grave of a belated wanderer—just such graves as one sees in the barren west of New South Wales— lonely, sorrowful things—things over which the dingoes troop, and the black snake glides. Who was he that lies buried here ? God knows. Was it bad whisky that killed him ?—was it some of the poison that is sold at the bush pub., and that has as much tobacco and turpentine, as much kerosene and diluted methylated spirit in it as alcohol ? *Quien sabe?* He lies where he was found, forgotten, unknown. *Telle est la vie ;* and *Telle est la mort*, too.

Enough of that—it is life, not death, we come to see; and there is the sound of the axe and the hammer. It is a little house being erected in a covert of palms, and ferns, and acacia wood, two fresh-faced Irish lads making for themselves a home. On, on, up an ascent so steep that we get off our horses and let them climb, while we climb ourselves after them to a ledge of rock; then on again, until at last—stand still and look at it!—you are at the entrance to the Barron Gorge. It is a pretty sight, and this is the beginning of the thing which we came out to see. Ride on a half-hour or more, and then you stop to listen, for you hear the falls. There is no roar, there is no deep moaning sound such as comes from Niagara, but just the diapason of a tumbling mountain torrent. Along steep slopes, down through shrub, tired with the weight of its own luxuriance, out into the open upon a jutting rock—and there are the Barron Falls!

They are beautiful—only that; not stupendous, not exciting, not awe-inspiring—not at all. I have seen just such falls in many places in the world, and they remained without much more than a mere local reputation, and they will remain so while the earth stands. But these falls have been called this, and that, and the other, till men like myself have burned to see them. If any business man were responsible for such statements as have been made regarding the Barron Falls, I should say that he swindled me. It is as immoral to write a fancy description of a place, as it is to exhibit a painted Ayrshire as a sacred bull. The Barron Falls are not falls at all. They are a series of cascades, covering a mile and a half. The height from the top of the cascades to the bed of the river is 1,000 feet. In no place is there a sheer fall as there is at Katoomba in New South Wales, and though a great body of water must come down the

incline in flood time, it is what lumbermen in timber
districts would call a huge shoot or slide. One can imagine
a hundred mountain streams pouring into the Barron
River, rushing to the edge of that incline, and starting
over it with volcanic force,—of that first long, clean pillar
stretching down till it broke against the boulders—but
this is not Niagara. There is not a great lake behind ;
there is not a sheer precipice to make a fall. And, slide
though it is, it can never be used for a slide, though
owners of timber land in the Cairns-Herberton district
thought that the cedar logs could come over those whirling, mammoth rapids. But they would be shreds of logs
by the time they reached the bed of the river. I can
think of all the might of flood time in that gorge, and
yet I am convinced, yet I insist, that it is not right to call
this a Niagara. It would be just as fair to draw a picture
of the River Darling in flood time, with the country
inundated for scores of miles round, with the trees growing out of the great watery waste in the pale moonlight,
and by day the plains a carpet of lovely flowers, and
say, This is the Darling country. It is the Darling
country only by chance, not by general condition.

But there is joy at the Barron Falls. Distinctly so.
Lovely streams tumble in a wide river bed, and over
big boulders—big even at a distance of a thousand feet
from us. There are pools of depth that man knows
not, and that the centuries have hollowed, the one set
above the other ;—wells like basaltic pillars, hollow
steps to a pyramid, and connecting with each other
by such a rope of water as that falling from the
mountain side, a hundred feet or more, into the first one.
There are overhanging rocks and rugged bulwarks,
the cold walls of stone showing the water-mark high
up, and the hills on either side massed with their living

green. There is all that; and in the long gorge there are unexpected caves, and granite alcoves, and grottoes of green, and the tireless hills that swell in an endless summer towards the heaven, and are always greener for the rain and riper for the sun. The visitor will spend longer time in travelling through that gorge, along that river, and in those hills than at the Falls themselves, except—the saving clause again—at flood time.

There have come to my mind a hundred times while travelling in Northern Queensland, snatches of a poem which was one of my reading lessons when a lad at school. It was called *The Lake of the Dismal Swamp*, and it began, "They made her a grave so cold and damp for a soul so warm and true." One comes continually upon dismal swamps in this land of the alligator. The mangrove tree grows into the mangrove tree, for miles upon the shore of sea and river, and makes a shade that reeks with a poisonous breath and deathly damp. In these noisome places the black snake glides, and reptiles feed on reptiles. Beware of the mangrove swamp. There lurk fever and death. One never hears in them the song of bird or the voices of children. Still, still, and deadly. And next to the mangrove swamp, the jungle growth, the crowding bush, while picturesque, is forbidding in what it suggests. But swamp and jungle and brush are falling before the tread of the white man and by the hand of the Chinkie, and one sees in the Cairns district land reclaimed from desolation, and made to smile like the Garden of the Lord. Where were the gloomy tangled growths of centuries, there are rice plantations, there are thousands of acres of bananas. There flourish the pawpaw and the thick vines of the grenadilla, the lime, the nutmeg, and the pepper tree; there bends the golden corn, and there rises to meet it the verdant potato vine. The north and the south meet and join hands in a luxurious growth. And yet this land at the foot of the range was considered worthless a few years ago. The Chinaman did not think so. He rented it at 1s. an acre for five years, cleared it himself, and is handing it over at the end of his time capable of producing splendid crops, while he has grown wealthy—wealthy for a Chinaman.

My eyes were opened properly when I went to Stratford to visit Mr. Tom Behan's rice mill. The plantations cannot be seen from the railway. They are across the river, and hidden by a hedge of scrub. I had gone down in the early morning to Kamerunga to join Mr. Hobler, and give a last look at the great railway, and get some technical information; and I worked my way back to Stratford on the hand-car, or trolly, for four miles. The enjoyment of the scenery was well worth the labour. Now we crossed some bright stream, such as Freshwater Creek, stretching away into coolness; then we bridged a great pond of lilies, from which Iolanthe and fifty thousand fairies might have come, a lily for every one of them; and all along there drooped such graceful ferns, there trailed such vines, there swam before the sight such butterflies, there ran down the air such long *roulades* from wandering mountain songsters, that we seemed twice the men we were an hour before. Honest toil in the face of Nature at her best is the finest tonic in the world.

Arrived at Stratford no time was lost. We ascended a hill first, and got a view of the Barron River and of the plantations beyond it, and saw how the country was being taken up and worked in every part. "Every foot of that land," said Mr. Tom Behan,—they call him "Tom" without the "Mr."—sweeping a half-circle with his hand, "is selected, and has a future of prosperity if properly handled; if men would be content to be pioneers, and work as pioneers, instead of handing over the country entirely to the Chinkies to sweat money from it, while waiting for chances to sell. There are people in the south," he continued, "who own land here, and who, doing nothing with it, grow profane over it because it does not bring them fancy prices." That must be the experience of every new district and country. The speculator goes hand in hand with the pioneer. The pioneer bears the burden and heat of the day, and makes his country; the speculator sometimes gets a fortune through fictitious values, sometimes through the unearned increment, and often he loses what he has, because he has bought at fictitious prices, and must sell at normal values. The Cairns district is, however, pretty safe, because there is limit to occupation and there are many holders. Men, therefore, are hopeful.

Mr. Behan's rice mill is on the banks of the Barron River, about five miles from Cairns; the railway runs within 200 yards of it, and it is the centre of settlement. The river is navigable, and vessels drawing 15 feet of water can come alongside the wharf. Mr. Behan began in a small way with his mill, but he floated the enterprise into a company, and extensive alterations are being made, and new machinery is being erected. He is confident that the Queensland rice growers can compete with China rice; and with the penny-on-the-pound tariff he feels safe. In 1887 the total yield of rice for the colony was 18,856 bushels. Of this 4,790 bushels were grown in the Cairns district, while Port Douglas furnished 10,724 bushels. But the average yield was higher in Cairns than anywhere else. There, 50 bushels per acre were grown, while Cooktown came after with 37.33 bushels, and Port Douglas with 36·73 bushels. One could soon understand why the yield of rice in the Cairns district should be so great. The land was reeking with wealth. Here was the scrub land and the cleared land side by side, and the latter looked as if it had been under the hand of the farmer for a quarter of a century. The Chinaman (and the selector) has planted as he has cleared, and the ancient jungle and nineteenth-century gardens and orchards are side by side. Crop after crop of fruit can be produced in the year. The land is rich with a long-time fulness, and it will be many a day before exhaustion occurs, or before rotation of crops will be necessary. Fields of bananas spread out before us. We pass through lanes of cocoanut palms; we see the husked maize spread out upon the ground; but with two exceptions the only men we met were Chinamen, and there were plenty of them. Chinese shops were dotted here and there, and Chinese farmers met us at their doors, and gave us to eat of the grenadilla, and to drink of such tea as I would were to be found in every place. And as for rice, well, the best *chef* in the best club in Australia might learn how to cook it from the opium-smokers of the Cairns plantations. Chinese farmers might be counted by many hundreds in this district. It is a pity that the white man will not do as does the small Scotch farmer in Montana and Ontario—clear the country himself, and work it to its fullest. This is said with all respect for the many farmers in Queensland who are fighting their way to competence. Tobacco, it seems, can never be an industry in northern Queensland, because of the great expense attendant upon picking and curing; but there are rice, and fruit, and maize, and sweet potatoes, and nutmeg, and pepper; and these should make any country rich if properly developed into industries. It needs no prophet to foretell the future of Cairns.

CHAPTER XV.

QUEENSLAND IN 1889 (*Continued*).

THE HINCHINBROOK CHANNEL—TOWNSVILLE—
CHARTERS TOWERS.

QUEENSLAND has no mountain scenery so unique, so accessible, so generally beautiful as that of the Blue Mountains in New South Wales; but she possesses a coast scenery that no other colony in Australasia, save New Zealand, can equal. And for six months in the year it may be viewed with certain comfort and enjoyment. I have been travelling on the Queensland coast for three weeks now, and the sea has been often like a mill pond, and never so disturbed that the poorest sailor, the greatest victim to *mal de mer*, would find it necessary to go below. Nearly all the coast sailing from Brisbane north is done inside the Barrier Reef, and, with that wall of coral to protect the vessels, no one need fear the possible unpleasant experiences that mark the journey from Sydney to Brisbane. I have had a good many water trips in my time, and I have never had one so generally enjoyable as this, though I have tried voyaging, as the bushman says, all kinds. I have travelled on this journey by four steamers so far, and shall be on two more before I get to Brisbane again; but it has been all ease and comfort. No luggage missing, no worry about time, but a handful of hours of bad weather, and not a wish to be on dry land again. I am firm in my belief that the Queensland coast will become very soon a route for excursions. On the three vessels, *Barcoo, Elamang*, and *Maranoa*, there were invalids and others taking the round trip from Melbourne, and one could see them day by day sitting on deck in the genial sun, and getting colour and seasoning again. That is the beginning, and I can foresee to what it will come. Many a fagged and battered individual will find his Pool of Siloam in this channel over 1,000 miles long, between Brisbane and Cooktown—a channel that is walled by the undersea coral hills on one side, and the diversified coast boundaries on the other.

The Rhine is historical, is dignified ; the Hudson is splendid ; Lake Superior has a stupendous grandeur ; the South Channel, New Zealand, is silencing in its charm ; and the Thousand Islands and Lachine Rapids in the River St. Lawrence are eloquently varied ; but having seen Whitsunday Passage and Hinchinbrook Channel, having caught the glamour and radiance of Queensland seascapes, and sunsets, and the bluff beauty of the headlands, one finds all one's enthusiasm at play again. I say this with thought of Bulli the Beautiful, of Kiama, in New South Wales ; of the Huon Valley in Tasmania ; the wonder of Mount Cook in New Zealand ; and the Gippsland Lakes. But Bulli and Kiama cannot be seen with certain comfort by sea, and this coast has had made for it one long breakwater, inside of which, within the season, there is peace. No one, of course, would take the journey for pleasure in the time when, at Cairns or Cooktown, twenty-four inches of rain fall in a day. This statement is no exaggeration. The rainfall at Cairns is between ten and twelve feet in a year. Think of that, Monsieur the squatter of the Darling! A foot, two feet, of rain in a day would even satisfy Broken Hill.

One has seldom seen a coast so well lighted as that of Queensland. When a light dips another makes its appearance, and we sail from beacon to beacon. Yet I have talked with commanders, such as Captain Lake and Captain Stewart, who can remember the time when there was not a light from Moreton Bay to Cooktown, and, indeed, not one at Moreton Bay. Now there is always "a candle in the window." And attractive enough it is. There is no need to grow diffusive over north Australian sunsets; there are as good "down south"; but it may be a satisfaction to the prospective traveller to be told that he or she can spend many a pleasant moment with horizons before the eye that are never to be forgotten. Upon a background of the most delicate amber there grows the soft carmine, fading into violet, all margined by the blue of the eye of Aphrodite. Upon this sea of colour, growing into a measureless distance, there float purple clouds like islands; to the far right there climbs the dusky heaven, and to the left the rocky hills uprise, swathed in a tawny glory. On the left hand of the sun, as it dies with its face to the world, there turns the beacon-light like a gigantic firefly from outside worlds. But one must see such things; one cannot describe them. One must see Whitsunday Passage and Hinchinbrook Channel to get an idea of the most novel type of Australian scenery. The former lies between Bowen and Mackay; the latter between Townsville and Cairns. It has been my misfortune to see the former twice by night, or partly by moonlight, while the latter I saw by day. The Johnstone River scenery is also beautiful; but that could only be dimly known as we wound through its narrow channel, almost touching the thick and sensuous tropical foliage, on our way to Geraldton.

What is Whitsunday Passage like? It is a quiet sea between walls of verdure on one side and bold hills on the other. To seaward island after island rises; now a pretty beach comes white-banded towards you, or a score of channels glide into one another, as if seeking way into the mighty main again. A solitary hut with a lonely light flickering from the hillside; a tall palm outlined against the sky; a rugged spur in its passive menace to the toilers of the sea; a thousand quiet nooks; numberless surprises of water and land —this is what one counts when Whitsunday Passage is cleared: and yet it is not these things in particular which impress one, but the general outlines, the long contour of beauty. And when Bowen is reached at midnight, and the songs have died away in the saloon, and the vessel draws alongside the wharf, one only has a feeling of having had a quiet night, of having touched with nerves aglow the beauty of a world, which life's turmoil too commonly drives from the mind. When, afterwards, you listen to the woes that a Chamber of Commerce exhales in solemn deputation, you have enough grace of nature left to be patient, and learn, and even question: and you turn out upon the long pier to discuss the prospects of the meat-chilling establishment—now closed—being opened again, and this excellent venture of the A.U.S.N. Company being made to pay by a co-operative contract with the farmers of the district; to hearken to the tales of Bowen's past glory, her claims upon the country, and her rage at the abolition of Polynesian labour.

But I saw one end of Whitsunday Passage in the

early morning also, and it brought me to Mackay the second time with pleasant sensations,—sensations which became somewhat dulled by the languor and commercial depression of the place. But Whitsunday Passage was only a foretaste of what was provided for the traveller in Hinchinbrook Channel. It was not promising to leave at Townsville that best of coasting steamers, the *Barcoo*, as satisfactory in its appointments, as excellent in its service as a liner, and to take passage in the little boat, the *Palmer*, for Cairns, in order to see Ingham, Dungeness, Cardwell, Mourilyan, and Geraldton, and all that they promised in products and scenery. There was no need for regret, however, for there was good food, good sleeping accommodation, and an attentive steward. Looking out from Cleveland Bay at Townsville in the evening, past Magnetic Island, Hinchinbrook Island could be seen sixty miles away in a pink and opal atmosphere. Thitherwards our watery path lay. With a couple of planters on board we steamed up to the mouth of the Ross River, and out to sea, leaving the lights of the city behind, and soon losing Castle Hill in the darkness. When I awoke in the morning we were at Dungeness, and we had already struck the reef of beauty. All the Queensland ports, as I said elsewhere, have a South Sea Island appearance, and most so have Dungeness, Cardwell, Cairns, and Townsville. Dungeness does not bear close inspection. From the sea the mangrove swamps, in their pale green, are a pleasant fringe to the shore. There are palms, and a pretty curve to the sandy beach, but once on land the illusion vanishes. It feels like a place of death ; the chill of the swamp meeting the hot sunshine, the forsaken habitations, the forlorn hotel, and the general air of desolation, are scarce relieved by the fine scenery that one discovers in crossing the sandy fork on which these buildings stand, and coming upon the mountains and the sea beyond.

Nothing in this north surprises one more than the brief nomenclature and the ignorance concerning trees and plants. There are a great many fine peaks and bluffs, and many a striking inlet along the coast, which have no name. There are flowers and trees and vines which one meets everywhere, and yet they are nameless, or, rather, those who see them every day have no names for them. There is a vine bearing a yellow flower, something like a fuchsia blossom, and I have asked people its name from Brisbane to Cairns, and from Cairns back again to Rockhampton, and no one could tell me what it is called. And yet this vine and flower is the commonest in Queensland; it climbs up thousands of dwellings. I found much the same thing in the interior of New South Wales. The commonest shrubs and flowers had never been christened. Neither map nor man can help you in regard to many points on the coast, nor any person assist you regarding the flora. I looked on three maps before I could find the Herbert River that flows into the sea at Dungeness. I looked on several before I could find the Barrier Reef properly outlined, and with Flinders Passage south-east of Townsville marked. I talked with commercial travellers who had been up and down the coast many times; with planters and selectors and merchants who had travelled it for years; and such places as Hyacinth Shoal, Cape Upstart, and Cape Bowling Green, between Bowen and Townsville; and the names of the pretty islands beyond Hinchinbrook, such as Gould Island, Family Islands, and Duck Island, were known only as objects, not as things having the dignity of names.

There was a time when Dungeness appeared to have a future, but the fates seem against it now, and it is nothing more than an export and import station for the planters on the Herbert River and the Victoria Sugar Company. It lies there in its sand and mangrove isolation, good enough to look at from the sea, but weary to behold from where it stands. It is, however, soon forgotten in the glories of the Channel, which I can compare to nothing in scenery save the Thousand Isles in the River St. Lawrence, so full of beautiful variety is it. Here falls a stream down the mountain-side; there crowd up to the bare summits of strong hills thick legions of trees, and gorge and gully come and go. On the coast at the right a green, cultivated piece of land lies in quiet promise on a hillside, and now a tobacco-planter's place, now a lonely selector's clearing, tells of the work of the pioneer. And hard work it is, and with no certain return. A few ardent men have put money into land at £1 an acre, and have erected improvements at considerable cost; and to-day the land would not bring 6s. an acre. Still they hope on, believing, as all Queenslanders do, in the future of their country, and thinking of their children, and of the profit which, they say, is sure to come some day. There is enough to think on, in the questions of agricultural development and the land question generally, as one's eye is feasting on a fascinating scenery, until Cardwell is reached. It is high noon then, and we are ninety miles from Townsville. You shall look long before you find a more charming spot than Cardwell. The cocoanut palm, the candlenut palm, the banana, and the fig-tree, make a fine foreground for the low houses with their broad verandahs, which lie in noiseless streets; and the coast range, rising here to 4,000 feet, is such a background as makes a tropical scene after one's own heart. And so all day we plough our way past islands and high-wooded shores, till in the dusk we enter the narrow passage of Mourilyan harbour. It is not 150 feet in width, and there are precipitous walls on either side, while in the centre of the channel ahead is an angry-looking rock. We are going straight for it, we shall—no, we shall not hit it; we pass it by with a contemptuous nearness, and draw alongside the wharf, where the motley group of wharf labourers wait—Kanakas, Chinamen, Javanese, and white men.

Again we steam away, and, in the dusk, wind over the bar of the Johnstone River, and pass through exquisite depths of green to Geraldton. And you will hear at Geraldton of fortunes that are to be made in mines; of nugget-finding; and of foolish bonuses by Government to prospectors of mines. If you stroll to the hotel on the hill, kept by John Bourke, a seven-years' pioneer, you shall be enlightened on the capacities of the district. He will tell you how the place has flashed into prominence, and is sure that the surface-mining, which has sent out £6,000 in gold, will send out sixty times that ere long. He will show you town allotments worth from £200 to £300 an acre, and discourse to you of the agricultural possibilities of the district; but neither he, nor any one else, will get far beyond sugar and mining. And the one industry is depressed, and the other is uncertain. But there reaches up towards Herberton 1,400 square miles of sugar land, upon which there is an annual rainfall of nearly 10½ feet, and there is every indication, that whatever may be done in the Cairns district with rice and fruit may be done in the Johnstone River country. We wind back to the sea again in the still night, and when the morning comes we are at Cairns; and of Cairns I have written.

Townsville has character. It is a place which strikes one as having a history. The very approach to the place is suggestive. There is an island immediately in front of the town, and it commands two entrances to Cleveland Bay. Did old Robert Towns, whose name is known to every one in New South Wales—did he, in 1863, have an eye to a time when Townsville should be a capital, and would need a vantage-point for defence? If so, his dream was not a wild one. For as sure as the sun shines on Castle Hill and the wind blows dust through Flinders Street, so sure will there yet be a colony of North Queensland, and its capital will be Townsville. Once you put your foot on the A.U.S.N. Company's wharf, and greet a man from Townsville, you see that he is negotiating for a near destiny, and is doing so with an air of confidence which not even vexed questions such as coloured labour can destroy. Drive to your hotel, then walk round Melton Hill into the business part of the town, and you feel the ambitious future of this northern Australian city pressing upon you. It is not that the town is so large—it has only 11,000 inhabitants; not that it has an imposing look—there are no splendid public buildings; not that it possesses public men of exceptional calibre—they are more earnest and intelligent than outstanding: it is because the place is a natural commercial centre, and is at the beginning of its greatness; because the climate and natural conditions have gone to make a man that may be called a North Queenslander; because Brisbane is far away, and the gravitation of the public sentiment of the north, despite occasional jealousy—only accidental, after all—is towards this spot, which is far enough north to say, I am tropical, and far enough south to say, I am temperate, and finally, to say, I am so favoured naturally that through me there flow the products of all the zones and the resources of all the continent. It tells its beads of fortune over, and it says thanksgiving for ore from Charters Towers and Ravenswood; for wool from Hughenden and the Burdekin Downs; for agricultural produce from the Burdekin; for tin and silver; and for "the Malay Peninsulas" (mining shares in Malaya), which

A STREET IN TOWNSVILLE.

men speak of in Flinders Street with excited breath. The south can make up its mind that Separation is inevitable. The sentiment is too deep in the north ever to be rooted out now. Pick up the card of a merchant in the north, and you will find on it not "Queensland," but "North Queensland." Use a sheet of club paper, and it bears the "N. Q." Every newspaper prints it; every man heads his correspondence with it; and there is a separate almanac compiled for "North Queensland," thus ignoring Pugh.

You will find "Separation" shops and "Separation" hotels. It is a thing to conjure with, and if one's sense of reckoning is good for anything it will conjure into existence a northern colony.

But meanwhile Townsville toils on through a heat in summer that ranges toward 105°, and that runs between 70° and 80° in winter time, while, in idle moments, it gives a dig at Charters Towers, its dusty inland rival. Complain of the heat at Townsville,—you are told to try Charters Towers, and you will see what *is* a burning fiery furnace. Casually refer to the multiplied and variegated odours of the place, and you are requested to sniff Charters Towers from a poppet-head. Go to Charters Towers, and the resident will tell you confidentially that he couldn't exist in Townsville "for the dirty heat, and he wouldn't live there for the smells—could cut 'em, so help me! you could; and count 'em, too; label 'em, so help me! survey off the atmosphere into selections, —— me if you couldn't!" I have tried both places, and they are both right—quite right. Sitting on the verandah of the Queen's Hotel, an hour after I arrived in Townsville, and seeing a gentleman walking about the beach as if in search of something, I asked the citizen to whom I was talking if the pedestrian were prospecting. "No," he said, "that is the Mayor looking for smells." It was true; his Worship was out with thoughts of sewage in his mind. Townsville suffers from that curse, that demon of so many Australian cities—bad drainage; but the place is only twenty-three years old, and Sydney, for instance, is one hundred. With good drainage and plenty of trees Townsville would be endurable; it might be pleasant, for the citizens know how to build, and how to dress for the climate;—fine wide verandahs, houses set high on piles; plenty of windows, broad-brimmed white hats, and white clothing—these things mark the sense of the people of Townsville and of Queensland. It would please some architects one knows, to see the banks and public buildings of Townsville, built in refreshing white, with colonnades and arcades, and looking like places for human beings in a hot climate, and not like gaols for lost spirits.

But Townsville is dull just now, despite the natural vigour of its inhabitants. Money is "tight," and the banks have called up really good overdrafts, to some disturbance of trade and much dissatisfaction. But it is estimated that the worst is over, and it is predicted that by October money will again be plentiful; for sugar, to the extent of about 3,000 tons, will be coming in from the Pioneer, Seaforth, and other plantations on the Lower Burdekin, and wool from the Hughenden district; and since sugar and wool are both up in price, there is joy in the capital of North Queensland—(by courtesy). Last year was a bad one all round. The long drought had disheartened and straitened the squatters, and sapped almost all the courage of the planters. But a variety of causes will pull the town up to activity again, and should the Malay Peninsulas turn out well there will be plenty of money going. They will, however, have to succeed better than most mining shares do, or Townsville will come a cropper after all. We have only to think of Mount Morgan, in its relation to Rockhampton and Brisbane, to understand that these places are, in the words of the Northerner, suffering a recovery, like a man who has been out late at night. They are waking carefully, and sad enough heads they carry. Townsville should rather stick to its "home-made stuff," and let Malay Peninsulas, which are supposed to represent anything from 50 to 100 ounces to the ton, be consigned to

Singapore, the nearest victim; else the seven banks that have branches behind Castle Hill may have extra work to do next year in winding up estates.

In appearance, Townsville, if dusty to a degree, is "fetching." The streets are wide and of excellent make, and there is no sign of dilapidation, while, at the same time, there is no sign of excessive newness. Castle Hill, called so, I suppose, from its supposed resemblance to Castle Hill, Edinburgh—and from a point northward it looks somewhat like it—gives the place relief and dignity, as it rises almost sheer from the sea 1,000 feet. The harbour is a delight to the eye, but it would be a greater delight to the heart of the citizen if it were a better haven for ships. Dredging is now going on, as at Cairns, and a breakwater is being built which will enable small vessels to come up to the wharves. The breakwater runs out for quite a mile and is excellently constructed, forming a deep channel, which is protected from high winds.

There is a superior tone to Townsville, felt at once on entering the place. The people, if not "swagger," are as severe in all that pertains to the formal and the conventional as at Brisbane or anywhere else. And rightly so. The farther away a community is from metropolitan convention, the more necessity there is for adherence to social form. To know what a people are, I would ask to see their institutes, their churches, and their social gatherings. I had an opportunity to spend a half-hour in a Townsville ball-room, and I am satisfied that there the social convention does as much to keep young men straight as sermons. I can point to two or three places on the coast where the social life does not raise its head, where it is all in the country with the planter; and, to kill time, the young men simply loaf and invoke his swart and potent Majesty from a place hotter than Cooktown. They succeed often enough in doing that, and in blotting out their own record as well.

In no place where I have been have I found men more anxious to do one kindness, more eager to aid one in studying conditions, than at Townsville. Personally, I am much indebted to Mayor Parkes, a vigorous, high-spirited citizen ; to Mr. J. G. Macdonald, F.R.G.S., an excellent officer and a courteous gentleman ; to Mr. Laing, to Mr. Macintosh, to Mr. Dodd Clarke, and to the members generally of the Gordon Club, for that attention and kindness which is so grateful to a visitor. With Messrs. Laing, Macintosh, and Mr. James Munro of Brisbane, I visited Acacia Vale, a beautiful garden about three miles from Townsville. No better place could have been chosen to discover what might be accomplished in the matter of fruit and trees and flowers at this centre. There are ten acres under cultivation, and the gardens have been in existence for about seven years. Mr. Gulliver, the owner, began with vegetables to get the land in order, and, that done, passed to fruit and flowers. This year there will be a fine yield of fruit—oranges, strawberries, grapes, custard-apples, pomegranates, pine-apples, guavas, pawpaws, and grenadillas. Thus side by side grow the fruits of the torrid and the temperate zones. Rare tropical plants and trees are to be found at Acacia Vale, and it holds the place of an experimental garden in the district. Mr. Gulliver pins his faith to Chinamen, irrigation, hard work, and care. But at Townsville, as at Cairns, Mackay, the Herbert River, the Johnstone River, and elsewhere, no one is quite certain as to what will or will not succeed in agriculture.

The Townsville country is not remarkable for its

agricultural land; but on Houghton River and Alligator Creek there is soil adapted for farming and dairying purposes. Under the Crown Lands Act of 1884, there were 136 agricultural farms selected, but they have since become absorbed in grazing runs. Out of all these farms there are only 50 acres under cultivation. There are only about 450 acres of land altogether under cultivation in the Townsville district, exclusive of sugar-cane cultivation, which covers 2,240 acres at the Burdekin delta. It would appear that the district will never be properly developed in the matter of agriculture, till it is decided through experimental farming—(by practical experts)—what can or cannot be grown to advantage, and how it is to be grown. The evidence of those who have already experimented, goes to show that irrigation works are indispensable. With these things public men will have to charge their understanding souls; and, if they will not do so in the South, the day of separation will be hastened, and the North, now becoming the feeder of the South, will walk upon its own stilts. As testimony to the permanence of this agitation, I might mention the fact that the day of my departure from Townsville was a public holiday devoted to holding a Separation demonstration. And this, as a matter of course—a thing, to the sentiment and judgment of the people, as fitting as Independence Day is to the Americans. Let not Brisbane shut its eyes. Townsville is wide awake, and just as soon as some conflicting elements in the North are harmonised, a long-accumulating force will secure from the Imperial authorities a new constitution, and what is North Queensland now by courtesy will be so then in fact.

One can get to Charters Towers, the notorious mining

town, by three trains in the day. I took that which leaves Townsville at 5.30 p.m. and gets to the Towers at 10.45 p.m. The country one passes through is not striking. It is just bush land with grass, cactus, aloe, fern, and eucalyptus. Some good bits of pastoral country appear here and there, and there is a small settlement at many places on the line, but it does not seem a district of great possibilities. A fine range of hills is climbed, but they are just what one crosses in a score of places in New South Wales or Victoria. Powder Magazine, Woodstock, Reid River, Houghton Valley, Ravenswood Junction, and Macrossan Bridge are merely stopping-places; they represent no settlement of any extent. The 82 miles travelled could be slept over without much loss, unless one was counting, with a prospector's eye, on the possibilities of minerals in the hills and the sudden outcrops.

But Charters Towers reached, what shall you see? You shall see a mining town that suggests a developed Broken Hill,—developed commercially. I can imagine that Charters Towers, two or three years after Messrs. Hugh Mossman, C. E. Clarke, and J. Fraser discovered it, was much like Broken Hill. The outcrop at Broken Hill is a massive thing; it is one long and scraggy mountain wall, with a wide plain of scrub behind it, and a lonely, barren land stretching to the horizon. The outcrop at Charters Towers is not so prominent, but it, too, is in a stricken waste; its very look begets a thirst. And what place more thirsty than Charters Towers? Men told me with pride and feeling—men who seemed to think that they were deserving of the applause and remark of their fellow-men—that they had taken an oath to drink nothing before eleven o'clock in the morning. I know men who vow to drink nothing before eleven o'clock in the evening; yet they make a tolerable record for all that. Broken Hill was thirsty, but Charters Towers needs what a facetious lawyer termed constant liquidation,—and it gets it. When I was there the thermometer was only about 85°, and the coppers were hot. How flaming they must be when the heat strikes down upon the treeless place at 100° one does not care to calculate. If one must estimate morality according to the intensity of the climate, then I imagine Charters Towers should stand about half way between Rockhampton and Cooktown. In the latter place there are over twenty-five hotels or saloons,—or whatever they may be called,—and they do not seem to be more than enough to meet the needs of a very dry population. I think it would be a difficult task for a man to wear the blue ribbon in Charters Towers, though the Salvation Army try hard enough to get the people to do it.

It is remarkable that of all the mining fields which I visited the newest is the most sedate—I mean Mount Morgan. It was like a quiet manufacturing village while I was there. In the hotel at which I stayed I only saw a half-dozen men at the bar during the day, and one woman, who, as she put the tin pail on the counter, said, "Another half-gallon for the ould man." City people have an idea that a mining town is a place where everybody is like a character in Bret Harte's tales, and where vigilance committees abound. Such characters exist always in mining towns, and vigilance committees are necessary perhaps in the first rush; but a field soon become settled much like any other town, preserving, however, a certain *naïf* individuality quite its own. A mining town is composed of all nationalities, all social castes, all kinds of people. It is a point to which all the nations of the world gravitate; where custom rubs against custom, and where men are, as a rule, freer and broader in their opinions than in other settlements of the same size elsewhere. The cosmopolitan nature of the social mass causes this. But one must get rid of the idea of finding life exactly as it appears in story books. The unwatchful observer will not find anything unique, the outside of things is so near allied to the life in other centres. But on a gold field there gather men who, unlike that hero in *A Night Off,* have a past. I have never yet visited a mining town for ever so short a time, without carrying away with me a note-book liberally inscribed with ideas got from new types, and fresh outlines of character caught from men with whom I had come in contact. I have no need to turn up my note-book to find what interesting men and ideas I met with at Charters Towers, at Gympie, and at Mount Morgan. They are all fresh in my memory—sayings and doings and all. But Charters Towers I must regard as the most characteristic place, though Gympie is the ideal of a mining town that has outgrown its youth; and Mount Morgan is the most romantic, the most idyllic. It would be possible for me to write some true things of these places, which men would say were apocryphal, imaginative—tales, however, that would make people think more of human nature, of manhood. I have in my mind some men I met when at Charters Towers who have histories,—who, rather, make history. But why hint at these things, why use Hamlet's There be, an if they would?

Let me tell one or two stories. Do you wish to find Dow of Bret Harte's *Dow's Flat?* Then stand with me on the poppet-head of the Day Dawn Freehold, and look down the dusty roads towards the line of poppet-heads and chimneys at our right. You see a splendid pair of horses and a buggy coming up the street, and in the buggy a man, bronzed and sturdy, and perhaps unduly flushed, and driving like mad. Well, his name is Craven. He it was that in the face of opposition, of sneers, of abuse from English directors, of desertion by Australian directors, worked on and on at the Brilliant Mine, day in day out, week in week out, month in month out, with, as he remarked to me, "the hull d——d universe of luck agin me." Charters Towers sneered: "Craven is a bloomin' fool," but he worked on. Men said he was a long way off the reef. Couldn't he see the way it veered from the outcrop? He was simply wasting time drilling away so far off the gold-line. But he worked on. "I had an idea," he said to me, " and it was in my head like a maggot, and it stayed there, and—do you see that flag flying from the poppet-head of the Brilliant Mine?"

Yes, for one fine morning of this year Craven struck it rich—so rich that he has made the fortunes of the few shareholders who stood by him, and made his own fortune too. And the Australians who went back on him, the Sydney gentlemen who cramped him and cornered him and denied him, are out in the cold. And the flag is flying on the Brilliant Mine, and five ounces to the ton is Craven's reward. He worked on. And let me ask if my story put into verse by Bret Harte would not be as good as the tale of Dow's Flat put into verse by Bret Harte?

Now if you will look through the gold returns of last year from Charters Towers you will find that the Brilliant Mine does not appear. Craven's luck hadn't come to him then, and he was simply the manager of a wild-cat mine. That wild-cat mine has given a lift to Charters Towers; has started fresh mining enterprise; has made men hopeful; has immortalised Dick Craven. There are mines more "swagger" than it is—with finer machinery and all that, but none with better stone. I have a piece of the quartz beside me as I write, and there are beautiful specks and lines of gold in it. The mine stands there lonely between two great groups of mines—the Day Dawns on one side, and the Queens on the other—and is their connecting link.

The Day Dawn Freehold, on which, as we supposed, we are standing at this minute, is not so very far from it, and there are those who prophesy as great things for it as for the Brilliant. It was my good fortune to go down the Freehold, thanks to the good offices of a man whom everybody in Charters Towers called "Dad." Some doubts were thrown out as to my being able to get down this promising mine, as the directors are very strict in their regulations; but I had friends at court. Dad managed it for me. I should imagine that he could manage most things. A fellow who has been through the American Civil War, followed Stanley's track across Africa, shivered with fever in tropical lands, and who will start off on a 700 miles' prospecting tour all alone in the wilds, generally has some stuff in him. And Dad is guilty of that. I have beside me a rough picture of a mountain which is several hundred miles from Charters Towers. It is not a picture that would pass muster in an Art Society, but I would not part with it for one of Whistler's sketches for all that, from what I know of the man that drew it,—and I know more than I set down here. I could quote an extract from Bret Harte, and lay a story I have in my mind alongside it, but that would not be fair to the brave fellow who is now, I doubt not, travelling towards that mountain, which, as he says, may be a Mount Morgan. "There's one chance in a thousand of its being a mountain of gold," he remarked to me, "and I'm after that chance." I hope he *may* find a mountain of gold.

I have heard many tales of bravery in my travels up here. On the Cairns-Herberton railway I was told of two men who, at the risk of their lives, saved a wounded fellow-workman from being blown up by dynamite. This is the scene :—Three men have arranged for a blast of dynamite. Two men walk away while one lights the fuse. The fuse being lit, the navvy throws the lighted match aside. It falls in a keg of gunpowder, and he is blown up. He falls, lacerated and burnt, just across the hole where the dynamite is. His comrades see his danger, run forward, and drag him away just in time. They go on with their work as if nothing had happened. A thousand feet below ground at Gympie I was told a tale which deepens one's belief in the soundness of human nature in this selfish age ; which shows us that the heroic is as lively in the world as ever it was.

John Bradshaw and William Gilbert were ascending a shaft, after having lighted the dynamite fuses. Some distance up Gilbert fell off the bucket. Bradshaw immediately signalled to have the engine reversed, was lowered to the bottom, and withdrew the burning fuses in the nick of time to save his comrade from certain death. John Bradshaw, I am glad to say, received a silver medal from the Royal Humane Society for his noble act. Now I wonder how much nobler was Flynn, Flynn of Virginia, of whom Bret Harte tells,—

> "Didn't know Flynn?
> Well, that *is* queer;
> Why, it's a sin
> To think of Tom Flynn.
> Tom with his cheer,
> Tom without fear.
> Stranger, look 'yar !
>
> ' Thar in the drift,
> Back to the wall,

>   He held the timbers
>   Ready to fall;
>   Then in the darkness
>   I heard him call,
>   'Run for your life's sake:
>   Run for your wife's sake!
>   Don't wait for me.'
>   And that was all
>   Heard in the din,
>   Heard of Tom Flynn,
>   Flynn of Virginia."

Now sometimes I find it hard to turn from the novelist's view of these mining towns and miners to the purely practical outlook on the fields—if indeed we can ever dissociate human character from practical outcomes. It is important to know that from Charters Towers in 1888 there was £136,801 worth of gold taken out, that about £245,000 worth of machinery was at work, that over 1,700 miners laboured in the dark places, and that 1,000 men toiled above ground after gold; but it is just as important to know the character of the toilers and the conditions under which they earn their bread. Of what interest is a world without a human being in it? —what concerns a mountain full of gold if a man is not there to drive his pick gold-wards? If it were not for such men as Craven we should have no Brilliant mines. If it were not for such men as Hugh Mossman we should have no Charters Towers. I had hoped to meet Hugh Mossman while at the Tors, but I found that he had gone to England. It is five years since I first met the veteran miner in San Francisco. His is a name to conjure with in the north. Seventeen years ago three men, who had been engaged in alluvial mining at what was called the Seventy Mile, saw some peaks in the distance, and they set out to explore the country round. In the granite and syenite area, now known as Charters Towers, they found gold. At Mount Morgan gold was found at the top of a mountain, and, at the Towers, near the foot of a hill 300 feet high. Where the kangaroo ran on a No Man's Land there are now near 12,000 people—to be found in Charters Towers, Queenton, and Millchester. Now a railway pierces the country beyond the Tors for 182 miles, and the heart of a glorious pastoral district is reached. Out Winton way there is some of the finest land in Australia. And thus it is that such seaports as Townsville are destined to become great places, having behind them fine agricultural land, where wool and sugar and all kinds of tropical fruits and produce can be grown, and where the mineral wealth, if not inexhaustible, is sufficient not to give this generation, or that to come, any concern. Within the 1,700 square miles of land in the Charters Towers gold-field there is a wealth, the edge of which the prospector and miner has, apparently, only been able to touch.

The Tors is a busy place, the busiest of the mining centres. While I was there an agricultural show and fair was held, and the town was full of selectors and squatters from the West, from Hughenden, and from Winton way. Because of that, the place was much livelier than ordinary. In the streets the watering-carts kept down the dust, and people tried to wash it down inside the public-houses. To see the Tors properly one must climb to a poppet-head, and sweep a circle with the eye. I did that at the Daydawn Freehold mine and at the Daydawn School Reserve. The whole field lay stretched out around me. Here were the shafts, and there the crushing-mills; there were tall chimneys, and long clouds of smoke rising from them. And, looking round the circle of the horizon, one knew that within the space there were about 140 steam-engines at work, that 340 stamps were pounding away all day, and that through 350 pans the gold was finding its way, to be melted at last into such bars as I saw in one of the banks of the place, some of which were worth £10,000. The poppet-heads seemed innumerable. One gets tired of their array. One finds one's self listening to details with a jaded feeling, and wondering about the names of the mines themselves. Fantastic many of them are, suggestive others. One is named because of some near or far-off association in the mind of the namer; some are christened, as it were, from the font of a haphazard nomenclature. But here I send them out in pairs; and very pretty combinations they make. There is the Rise and Shine and the Moonstone; Lady Maria and Mossman's Mystery; Sisters and Old Warrior; Lubra and Martin Lyons; Bonnie Dundee and Gladstone; Forget-Me-Not and Marian Campbell; Sun-Burst and North Star; Old Identity and Disraeli; Peabody and Golden Crown; Mountain Maid and Lord Nelson; Victoria and Havelock; Donnybrook and Sunlight; Empress of the North and Consolidated Queen. And away down there, on the edge of the field, Mary and Flora. Who were Mary and Flora? I hope they may strike it rich.

It is not from poppet-heads; it is not from the seven banks, from the eight churches, from the three State schools with their 2,500 children; from the School of Arts with its 2,500 volumes; from the tidy hospital, the brass bands, the well-stocked shops, the airy hotels, the public halls, the newspapers, the agricultural shows, the fire brigade, the court-house or the water-works, that one gets the impression of solidity in Charters Towers—not from all, or any, of these. But come with me before we go, to a few of the crushing-mills, and I promise a feeling of solidity. Because the Defiance Mill is near, enter it, and see its 20 stamps at work; move on to the Bonnie Dundee, and behold its 15 stamps dropping, dropping; enter the No. 2 Queen, with its 25 stamps thundering; seek Dick Craven's Enterprise, and hear 1,112 tons falling on the breaking rock; go out to the Burdekin, and watch its 60 stamps crushing the heart out of the rock of a granite country; think of the £136,801 that these stamps made possible to the community last year, and then you have an idea of the solidity of Charters Towers. And last, but not least, go to the Pyrites works, where the chlorination process is carried on, and get a glimpse of what has made Mount Morgan a paying gold-field; for without it shares, instead of being between £7 and £8 now, would be £2 or £3. Go away with these stamps thundering in your ears, and you will find all your after-testimony regarding the place made to their accompaniment.

CHAPTER XVI.

QUEENSLAND IN 1889 (*Continued*).

Mackay—Rockhampton—Mount Morgan—Mary- borough—Gympie.

I HAD heard of Mackay as I passed north to work down. I had met on the *Barcoo* one of the planters, —Mr. Edward Long, of Habana Plantation,—and had discussed the state of affairs with him, and by the time I had reached there on my way back I was prepared to see, with some sort of understanding, the district as it appeared, not merely on the surface, but in its actual working condition. Five years ago Mackay was in its glory. It was in its golden prime. It was the planter's paradise. Fine buildings were put up, money flowed freely, a railway had been erected to run into the interior 30 or 40 miles, and labouring man, merchant, artisan, and planter, were spending halcyon days and working hard at the same time. But Babylon is fallen.

One fine morning the *Barcoo* anchored off Flat Top Island, which is seven miles from the town, and we learned that we should have to wait for many hours before we could get up the river, as the tide was running out. What was to be done meanwhile? I thought of writing while the engines were quiet; others were discussing shark-fishing off Flat Top, or oyster-getting.

But my luck has seldom deserted me in travelling, and I have had reason many times to be thankful for it on this journey. Everybody may not be a Phineas Fogg, and so be able to buy up a steamer or a herd of elephants; and the next best thing is luck and friends in need. I do not believe one traveller out of fifty could have seen all that I have seen since I left Sydney. It has been, however, nothing but luck, and the hand of a magician. While thinking upon this failure of my calculations, I saw a sail-boat beside the steamer, and some one whispered in my ear, "Come with me, and we shall get to Mackay in an hour and a half. Have your luggage sent down." Good Bishop Canna, of Rockhampton, was on board, and I would have given a donation to his hospital if he had pronounced the benediction over this man of resources. But the bishop only smiled us away with a cheery *bon voyage* as our sails caught the wind, and we were off for Mackay, tearing through the water like a racehorse. It is not unalloyed pleasure to get the best of your fellow-passengers so; still it is inevitable sometimes. But this trip was to have its variety. We were coming to a sandy bar over which the waves were rolling in great white heaps, and breaking in a fashion likely to startle the timid. "Look out!" said a voice behind. Too late. The wave was over us, and we were washed with brine. It was not a hot morning either. "Come under my plaidie," said my friend, as he lifted up the old tarpaulin jacket. It was a necessary precaution, for crossing that angry bar in low water is not to be done with garments on that will not stand salt water.

Mackay has the worst harbour along the coast. The passage of the river is a most tortuous one, and it is always changing, owing to the movement in the body of the sand, and the futile attempts that have been made to create a channel by means of walls and breakwaters. The water requires to rise eight feet in order to cover the bar of which I have spoken; but when the tide is in, there are about fourteen feet of water in the channel. Like the Fitzroy River, the Pioneer River is very uninteresting, and if it had not been for the smack of excitement in it, the short voyage that morning would have been a stupid one. As one rounds the last bend in the river, the first thing that strikes one is the new bridge, and a fine one it is. Then comes a glimpse of the public buildings, the Post Office, the Court House, and the Customs Office; and away to the right a beautiful grove of palms, the most beautiful I have seen in Australasia. We draw alongside a wharf almost deserted, having passed a fine wharf not only deserted but dismal, and we stand in Mackay the Depressed. The streets are almost empty. There is one cab plying in the place—of 3,000 inhabitants—and it does not do a booming business. We go to the Cambridge Club Hotel —the planters' hotel—and solitude reigns there. It was the crack hostelry of the place, but its day declined with the decline of Mackay prosperity, and only the reflecting rays of the better days relieve its business gloom. There is plenty of room in it, plenty of air, plenty of light, and one can be well entertained; but the planters no more meet there in joyous conclave, the cannikin clinks no longer, and, like the rest of the town, it bides the better day.

A stroll through the place is not cheering. The shops are innocent of customers, and the banks are empty. A talk with the business men is not cheering. They think of better times past, and are not very hopeful for the future, for the planters are spending, as they are making, but little money, and the humbler classes are feeling the pinch of declining capital, retrenchment, and drought. Yet the drought was really only for one year. Consider what a drought is in the north of this colony. If a South Australian gets twelve inches of rain in a year he is abundantly blessed; if a New South Wales squatter out the Darling way gets six inches or seven inches he is happy; if a Mount Browne man gets four inches he is on the way to immortal peace; but not so the Mackay or the Bundaberg man. A Mackay squatter complains of last year's drought. "What was the rainfall?" you ask. "Thirty-six inches," he replies. "What should you have had?" He answers, "Oh, about fifty inches." Think of it. He has one year's drought, and he is full of lament. The squatter has five years', sometimes, and his sheep die by the tens of thousands, and we are surprised if he grows irritable about his rents. It must be said for the sugar-planter, however, that a failure of the sugar crop for one year means more to him than a year's drought to a squatter. The latter has, as a rule, food enough to carry him over a couple of bad years, and he can afford to wait. But the planter has a host of men about him; he has mills going at great expense, and he cannot reduce the movement of his great machinery to the level of his production for the year. The result is that he must either close his mills, and allow his crops to stand uncut, or run them at a loss.

I met many of the planters of Mackay, and visited several of the plantations, among which were Tekowai, Alexandra, Branscombe, Nebia, Habana, Nindaroo, and the River Estate Mill, besides driving through such plantations as Meadow Lands, and Victoria, and visiting the Racecourse Central Mill. It was a splendid country through which I passed. Every mile of the way, one was impressed with the rich soil and the air of thorough cultivation which pervaded the estates. This season is a comparatively good one. Mackay will send out about 15,000 tons of sugar, which is double what was sent out last year. Rain came in time. The price of sugar is up and the country is smiling, though the planters are still keeping the purse-strings tight and avoiding expense. They have need to do so. Some poor fellows have gone to the banks, and have said, " It is no use. I can't go on. You squeeze me as soon as I get a good season ; you take from me chances of pulling myself together again, so I shall get out and give you everything." That has been the case at Mackay and at Maryborough. Perhaps in some cases the planters have expended too much money in machinery and buildings, and encumbered themselves at the start, but misfortunes which drive men to abandon their estates are to be regretted.

And in some cases it is not through too heavy investment. For instance, Mr. Davidson, of Branscombe, is looked upon as one of the best, the most successful of planters in the Mackay district. Yet, the mill at Nebia has been closed, and valuable machinery lies there unused, and a large sum of money—certainly not less than £10,000—has been sunk. No,—low prices, drought, and restrictions have played a mighty part in reducing Mackay to its present condition, and in making the sugar industry stand shivering between elimination and a new life. And it may be said here that the co-operative scheme suggested by the Government has not proved a greater success than the large plantation system that has its hold on the country. The Government proposed to erect central mills, the farmers taking shares in them, and giving mortgages on their land to the amount of the capital expended. At Mackay two mills of the kind have been erected, but neither has proved a success as yet. Perhaps if I give the substance of a talk I had with Mr. Davidson, the manager of Alexandra, Tekowai, Peri, the Palms, and Branscombe, of whom I have before written, my readers will be able to see the question from the standpoint of the planter, while it may be taken as conveying the opinions of the planters generally.

Mr. Davidson is one of the most cultivated and clear-headed men that I have met in my travels. He was not inexperienced. He had been in all the great sugar centres of the world, the Southern States of America, the Sandwich Islands, Egypt, the West Indies, Mauritius, and Penang, and has had nearly twenty-five years at sugar-growing. He manages over 8,242 acres of cane land, but less than 3,000 acres are under cane now. There was a time when on his plantation there were 4,500 acres under cane cultivation. Last year only about 2,000 acres were cut, and some of that was poor enough. Of the five estates only the Palms and Tekowai are at work. Think what that shows. There are thirty thousand pounds' worth of machinery lying idle.

"Yes, it means a great loss," said Mr. Davidson, " when you consider the amount of capital that is locked up in idle machinery in the sugar districts now. The regular estimated decrease in value is 10 per cent. when at work. We are heavily handicapped in the struggle here. Five years of bad seasons and Government restrictions have dealt hardly with us." "Now, what would you propose, Mr. Davidson, as the way out of the difficulty?" I asked. "Well, above all things, the continuance of Kanaka labour—in other words, the extension of the Polynesian Act, and reciprocity with all the other colonies. Why," said he, "we have to compete with countries where coloured labour is employed altogether in the manufacture of sugar. It was only just now

that I heard there are 5,000 tons of sugar on the way
here from Java. We have to compete then with black
labour; with Mauritius, and Natal, and elsewhere; and it
is madness to expect us to do it unless we are put upon
the same footing in regard to the price paid for labour.
It costs us now 12s. a week for the Kanaka. The
coolies of the Mauritius are only paid 6d. per day, the
Natalese 3d. per day, the Javanese 4d. per day, and the
Chinamen 3d. per day. It is all very well to cry 'Queensland for the white man!' but how shall Queensland be
retained for the white man, if natural conditions are
defied and the industry for which she is well adapted is
crushed out because of a sentiment, which is, after all,
only a cry, and not a principle? There is hope, also,
from irrigation, but that means great expense, and irrigation schemes are not put into motion in a day. To be
of value up here they must be on a vast scale, and they
can never be attempted by the planters. Irrigation is
untried, and is only a possible relief. There is a sure
relief in intercolonial reciprocity, and the continuance of
Kanaka labour at reasonable cost. Sugar must be the
backbone of this tropical country. Other things may be
cultivated, but they must be side issues—supplementary
products, as it were. Kill sugar and you go far to paralyse
the heart of the north; and what is to take its place? That
it is on the verge of destruction you can see. Why, instead of buckling the straps tighter on us, the Government
should give us greater freedom. We have never abused
our privileges; we have worked within all prescribed
limitations, and would still do so if we were allowed. I
tell you frankly, as I doubt not other planters have told
you, that we cannot carry on our plantations with white
labour alone. We shall have to close." "How many
Kanakas do you employ?" I inquired. "Last year I

employed 320 Kanakas and 80 white men," he replied, "and a few Chinese, but the last not regularly. I once employed many more, but the bad seasons have squeezed out labour. The Europeans do all the machine work and all the skilled labour."

On looking over my notes taken from conversations with Mr. Long and Mr. Robertson, of Habana; Mr. Paget, of Nindaroo; and Mr. Turner of Goondi on the Johnstone River, I find a remarkable similarity of statement. They all agree that Europeans would not do the field labour outside of ploughing, and that black labour was a necessity. Messrs. Long and Robertson are old planters, and have been most progressive and broad in their system and their ideas. They have encouraged small farmers on their estates, and there are now nine of them contributing to their mill. These farmers find, though they started with an idea of growing cane by white labour, that they would have to employ coloured labour, and they accordingly did so. Wherever cane has been grown at a profit, Kanaka labour has been employed, with white men to do the skilled work. Thus, it is maintained by the planters, the Kanaka, necessary as he is to the conditions of North Queensland, opens up avenues of skilled labour for the European, and makes population and commerce possible where otherwise there would be complete stagnation.

The only hours that the sea has been uneasy since I left Sydney, were those that immediately preceded my arrival at Rockhampton by the steady-going steamer *Maranoa*, of the A. U. S. N. Company. The Rockhampton people agree in saying that this perturbed condition is an unusual thing during the winter months. "Why, you could go outside in an outrigger most of the season,"

said a member of the Central Queensland Rowing Club.
Since people generally state the same thing, we may
conclude that the trip to Cooktown from Brisbane is,
as I have found it during my many weeks' journeying,
with the exception of one day, a passage down a sleepy
bay. I did not see Rockhampton on my way north.
I have worked down to it by many stages, but, thanks to
the excellent steam service of the A. U. S. N. Company, an
easy and an interesting one. Rockhampton is a bustling,
self-confident place; but could excessive modesty be expected of it, when its Customs receipts for the first half of
this year exceed those of Brisbane? The Rockhampton
Chamber of Commerce feels its importance, and considers
that it should be as strong at the capital as the Brisbane
Chamber of Commerce. One can see no great evil in the
jealousy and the ambition of these central and northern
towns. This aggressive emulation bespeaks an activity
and an independence that bode well for the future.
There is no *laissez faire* north of Brisbane, and one can
feel the muscles of the north working like a young giant
from head to foot in the pioneer struggle. Despite the
blows that Rockhampton has had through a mania for
Mount Morgan shares, the soundest business men say
that the depression is only for a moment; that the reaction to healthy life has begun, that a bigger business is
being done this year than was done in 1887 or 1888, and
that, before a year has gone, the losers by mining shares
will have fought their way to a normal commercial
strength again. The squatters, as far back as March,
said: "We have had enough rain for this year already.
We do not care if there does not fall another drop. We
are safe." They say now that they will have the biggest
wool-clip that they have had for years, and they are
spending money as, I fear, the planters of Mackay and

Bundaberg will not be able to spend it for some time to come, unless there is a vast change in the doings of Parliament, and in the attitude of the miners who are so bitterly opposed to Kanaka labour. West of this place, far back to Barcaldine, 350 miles away, and beyond that again for hundreds of miles, there is some of the best pastoral land on the continent,—land though that requires irrigation to make it agricultural. And one can see from the railway line, as one travels westward, land irrigated by Chinamen for gardens here and there. The worst has happened for Rockhampton so far as Mount Morgan is concerned; the best is to come, for things have settled down to a legitimate state, and Mount Morgan is now the quiet, orderly, and prosperous station of a great mining industry.

Rockhampton suffers, as does Brisbane, from its position. It cannot boast the admirable harbour of Townsville. The large ships anchor 40 miles away in Keppel Bay, and passengers and freight are brought in by tenders. When the tide is right the journey up is slow enough—four hours generally; when it is not quite right it may take six or seven hours; and, if there is low water in the river, there may be half a day to wait before a move citywards is made. A more uninteresting journey could scarcely be made than that up the River Fitzroy. Mangrove swamp, low shores, and dull bush-land mark the passage. Fortunately the tender service is better than might be expected, and meals are provided free of charge by the A. U. S. N. Company, or else the hours spent *en route* might be detestable. I have learned, since I came here, a good deal about the continual efforts that have been made to get a railway constructed to Port Alma, a spot on the river about ten miles from the town where the largest ocean vessels could anchor and discharge their cargoes. The general convenience, the economy that would be secured by such a course, is plainly to be seen ; but it appears there is a feeling among the working men and some landowners in the town, that this railway would tend to lessen the importance of Rockhampton as a shipping port ; and they vote against it. Still it must come, even as there must come a similar railway at Mackay, where the same harbour conditions exist.

To see Rockhampton properly, one must go to the hill called The Range, on which stands the hospital, and look northward. There lies the city on a plain, level as your outstretched palm; there winds the river, ever rising or falling ; and there stand the hills, with their caps of cloud, abruptly beyond the river, and like a wall to the town. You will see to the eastward of the city, and some distance up the range, a cluster of houses. Beneath them, and beside the river, is the settlement of Lake's Creek, and a meat-preserving establishment started some years ago with huge capital, and struggling along now at an annual loss. It seems hard for some capitalists here to learn that, in this line, they cannot compete in London with America and the Argentine Republic. The Americas are a week from London ; Australia is six weeks away. The only success made in this direction in the Southern Pacific has been with New Zealand mutton. It appears to stand alone in its success. In Rockhampton at present, there are those who look with some hope to the establishment of the Canadian Pacific mail service as a means of helping Rockhampton along. This, I fear, is a vain hope.

If I were asked the chiefest charm of Queensland, I should put it in these two words,—orderliness and cleanliness. From the moment I crossed the border I felt the charm, and I can honestly say that I have not been in a town where I have not been instantly struck with the apparent dominance of these two characteristics. I have missed verdure and foliage, but never these other two things. In a settlement of navvies, in a young mining town, in the scrub country, in outskirts of cities and towns, this unwavering feature of Queensland life has met my eye. And not mine alone, but that of every traveller with whom I have talked. You see in some places streets, dusty perhaps, but clear of rubbish of all kinds. You see door-yards innocent of grass it may be, but swept and garnished after some fashion. In justice, too, let it be said that the Queenslander loves flowers. He does not know their names—he calls most things bourgainvillea—but he trains them about his doorsteps, and runs vines up his verandahs, and upon the iron roofs. It is as common as the sun to see houses almost buried in the orange flower and the bourgainvillea, and every house has its verandahs; and kept—you should see it. It is the living room of the house—the open living room—screened by Indian blinds and netting, made inviting by cane and canvas chairs, hammocks, and couches. It is altogether comforting. Even the poorest have their rude elegances of the sort, and life is always out of doors, always close to nature. See the trim blinds to the windows, fresh and well kept; mark the domestic pride that holds good all over the colony. I believe that Queensland is cleanlier, domestically, than Victoria or New South Wales, partly because it is difficult to secure good sanitary conditions in large centres like Sydney and Melbourne and their environs, where settlement is so rapid, and also because Queenslanders live so much more in the open. Kitchens in Queensland are detached from the houses, carpets and wall paper are little used, and

A TELEGRAPH MESSENGER.

curtains are of the lightest material, or else wooden and Indian blinds are used.

Rockhampton lies there in the morning light, as fresh as if it had had its bath and a rub down with *eau de cologne*. The streets are wide and well cared for, and the shops are bright and tasteful in their arrangements. Some of the fruit shops here are models of delicate and graceful display; and the book stores are as good as any in Sydney. I referred elsewhere to the prevalence of arcades and colonnades in Queensland towns, but in looking at Rockhampton I cannot help emphasising it —they are so common here, and particularly in connection with all Government and municipal buildings and banks. And I cannot abstain from making a note of what splendid buildings the Queensland National Bank Company have erected throughout Queensland— they are at least models of pleasingly bold architecture, having all the freedom and comfort that would be given some southern town in Europe. Sometimes these buildings seem out of proportion to the apparent prosperity of the towns in which they are, as, for example, in Mackay; but it is another evidence of the confidence there is in the future of the colony, and of the many centres that dot the Queensland coast.

From this rational manner of living, from the disuse of customs of dress and architecture, and domestic habit, which belong to climates different from theirs, the Queenslanders are becoming the most unconventional, the most simple, and the most forceful of the colonists. The whole life is different from that of the other colonies, and I believe that this will be the greatest colony of the group, and that the people will have characteristics at once the most striking and the most national, of the peoples of the southern hemisphere.

Viewed from the purely figurative standpoint, the colony seems to me like a great sheet of paper which has not yet been blurred in the drawings made upon it. There does not seem necessity for many erasures. Only bold outlines have been sketched, but they are in the right direction, and are in conformity with the character of the paper; the great problems will be worked out with Herculean power; there will be little confusion in the issues.

The traveller in Queensland is asked at every point, Have you seen Mount Morgan? And to acknowledge that he has not, is to call forth expression of solemn astonishment on the part of the questioner. But you will do so before you leave? is the earnest interrogation that succeeds; and only an assent will relieve the mind of the Queenslander. Mount Morgan is the great show place of the Northern colony. To see it is to have done the first duty of man. Having seen it, the general question then is from every cordial citizen, Well, what do you think of it? What did you think of it? What *could* you think of it? I was fortunate enough to have met the Hon. William Patterson, the Colonial Treasurer —who is a large shareholder in the mine—at Brisbane; and at Rockhampton I met Mr. Wesley Hall, one of the chief owners, who gave me a magic passport, which opened up to me Mount Morgan and all things that appertained thereto.

How shall you get to Mount Morgan? You will take train at seven o'clock in the morning at Rockhampton, run out to Labra, a distance of ten miles, and then coach it over a road that has shaken the enthusiasm out of many a man for another fifteen miles. Yet the drive is an interesting and pleasant one if taken in fine weather.

There are passengers who have been known to object to
opening gates, and letting down slip-rails on the way, to
utter unearthly language when climbing the Razorback
(a very steep hill about two-thirds of the distance out),
and who have been ready to take their affidavit that the
horrible jolting disarranged their systems, so that the
lover, in protest, laid his hand upon the sphere of
the liver instead of the heart, and the bilious man fixed
the seat of his troubles in his lungs. But these people
must not be entirely believed, for there are, if I remember rightly, four pubs (as they are called) on the way to
Mount Morgan, and there is nothing like bush "aroma-
tics" to heighten the imagination. The day of these
pubs, however, is gone. *Ichabod* is written over their
portals, and the owners thereof feed but imperfectly on
the coach passengers who seek the mountain of gold.
But on such a morning as I went to Mount Morgan,
there was no need of pub or of landlord. The Engineer
who was with me smoked on through the spring air with
a robust relish, the Melbourne alderman opened his note
book (that note-book which appeared wherever its owner
was seen), and uttered some fresh calculation, and, through
its mysterious contents, instructed the Engineer on the
building of railways; while Sonny—called so by his father,
the alderman—just breathed the crisp, sweet air, and
watched for new plants and trees, on which he was an
authority. A little of everything was Sonny, and a little
of everything was his father. Whether it was in the
chlorination works at Mount Morgan or in the sugar
regions of Bundaberg, the Alderman and Sonny were
equally at home—the one opened his note-book, the
other disgorged his memory, and the Engineer and I
were nowhere. So much discounted were we, that we
determined to carry a pocket encyclopædia henceforth.

Nothing is so strong in argument as a note-book pulled out at a critical moment, with facts and figures to parade before the face of your antagonist. Whether the figures are right or wrong the effect is tremendous,—unless your adversary also happens to be master of the same methods.

Here a lonely selector earned a meagre subsistence; there a Chinaman dug a living, and something over, from the soil; and yonder was a miner looking for another Mount Morgan. And we bowled through the bush, and over the hill, through clumps of fern and grass-tree, catching the glint from the hard surface of the gum leaves and the yellow glare of the wattle flower as we passed. Even the Alderman paused when Lindsay Gordon's words came up,—

> "In the Spring, when the wattle gold trembles
>   'Twixt shadow and shine,
> When each dew-laden air-draught resembles
>   A long draught of wine:
> When the sky-line's blue burnished resistance
> Makes deeper the dreamiest distance,
> Some song in all hearts hath existence—
>   Such songs have been mine."

While resting for a moment at the Half-way House, we saw a trap drawn by four horses coming pell-mell down the hill under armed guard. They did not slacken pace a second, but darted past us as if all Australia were at their heels. Bushrangers and that sort of thing rushed through one's mind. What was it? Sonny knew, and the alderman did not need his note-book. "The gold escort," they both cried, and with a laugh and a *Coach O!* the armed guard darted by.

But at length the morning drew towards noon, Difficulty Hill, and every other hill and difficulty, were passed, and suddenly there lay beneath us the great mining

Gold Escort on March.

settlement, and at our right the mountain of gold. Looking down on the town and away to the hill, it is just as well to stop and consider what the place is, what once it was, through what freak of fortune or stubborn industry it came to be what it is, and who they were who made known to the world a phenomenon that verifies the dreams of the poet and the trick of the novelist's fancy. Into this region which an amateur pastoralist would fancy, shut in by hills, and watered by such creeks as the Mundia and Dairy, and the River Dee, came, many years ago, one Donald Gordon, and took up 640 acres of land. Gordon had cattle and sheep in his mind— these only. For years he slaved, rounded up his cattle and mustered his few sheep, but never keeping ahead of bad luck. The droughts were too much for him, and so, with millions of wealth over his head and under his feet, he passed from bad to worse, until, forced to give up the life of the pastoralist, he took to mining, the last resort of indigent souls. But even at it he was not to find the ease and comfort for which he strove, for which he toiled and sweated. Then there struck through his brain vaguely, the thought that this dark rugged mountain had a destiny : but it was not for him to share in that destiny. It might almost seem as if the thing itself had tried to speak to him, while he could not understand its language. He pointed out this hill that troubled his mind to Frederick Morgan, an old miner, who understood the vocabulary of the earth better, and Morgan bought of Donald Gordon his undiscovered fortune for £640,—that is, 640 acres of land at £1 an acre. And afterwards the poor old pioneer used to tell of how he sold the soft pumice-like stone of the mountain to the citizens of Rockhampton for cleaning purposes,—stone that was full of gold. I knew a camp of men who ate cakes in which there was ample gold-dust, but to clean the brass handles of one's door with gold is a trifle too exasperating.

I saw the grave-like hole out of which Frederick Morgan took his first handful of gold-soil, and I have a piece of volcanic stone from the same place which has something more than traces of gold. Standing beside that hole, one is 1,200 feet above the level of the sea, and can look abroad over hundreds of square miles of bush land and small plains. On one lucky day, in those silent hills, Frederick Morgan found his fortune.

The town of Mount Morgan is one of the quietest places I ever visited, and one of the most suggestive. The streets are well enough defined, yet the place has more the appearance of a settlement than a town. There are, of course, buildings hastily thrown together in the rush, but the town is much superior in appearance to Broken Hill. There are signs of premature decay, too, in the flagging commerce, due to the over-abundance of shopkeepers, and the empty humpies of miners and workmen, who have left, now that the big boom is over. But the place is right for all that. Charters Towers was cosmopolitan in its feeling; Gympie was conservative; Mount Morgan is natural, yet romantic: it seems to have struck the happy mean of energy, and the balance of its capacities and powers. It strikes one in much the same way as would a fresh and vigorous manufacturing town which over-production had not injured, and which had not yet been blackened outwardly by smoke, and inwardly by revolt against hard conditions of labour. There is nothing mongrel about Mount Morgan; it is free from the foreign element; it is held well together by an Australian energy, and, I should say, has the best of Australian character in its development. Walking towards the Mount from the hotel, there were to be seen many evidences of thriving and sturdy life. Churches were springing up in three places, a fine School of Arts was in full swing, and the public school gave token of such a settled life as rarely comes so soon to a mining centre. And if any one doubted what the Mount Morgan climate was like, one had but to lean over the fence and watch the children. There were groups upon groups of rosy faces, and lines upon lines of healthy forms.

The yearly expenses of the mining-plant are about £250,000. There are 5,000 people in the town and district of Mount Morgan, living directly out of the mine. I was fortunate to have Mr. Roger Lisle, the mining manager, to take me to the hill and through the works. Partly walking, partly pulled up on the trucks of the cable tramway for nine hundred feet, we reached the summit, while there ran over our heads another cable on which buckets containing ore swung down the mountain to the works below. It is strange to see these boxes of ore swinging through air earthward, and from the earth mountainward. Arrived at the top, we were face to face with the mineral wonder of the nineteenth century. It is little I know of mundic lodes and freynacke strata, of thorite, silica, augite, hornblende, and trippean tufa; and so I am content to look upon the wonder, and let the scientists and would-be scientists rage on. Imagine cutting a loaf straight through, horizontally, to the back crust, and then cutting down vertically, leaving a perpendicular wall, and that is the way they are levelling Mount Morgan. Tunnels are driven in to meet shafts dug from above, and the rock and decayed stone are dropped through to trucks.

And there they are cutting the hill away, and there

all theories must await the pickaxe and the spade. Next to the Mount itself the process of chlorination is the most wonderful. It need not be detailed here. It had best be told by those who understand it more than I do. We watch the ore pass through the stone-breakers, and stamped into bits no larger than a woman's thimble; we see it move into the furnaces to dry, ere it creaks through the rollers, from whence it sifts down into wire gauges. Then comes the roasting, that all organic matter may be destroyed, and then the chlorination. Water is put with the dust till it becomes a kind of pulp; chloride of lime and sulphuric acid are added, and round and round the barrels turn for two or three hours. Next one sees the mass in vats, from which leaks out the green-coloured water, in which is the gold, passing into charcoal filters, and again the filter-beds, and the roasting in the reverberatory furnaces from which is drawn the metallic gold, three-fourths pure. Fused borax goes with this; there is more smelting in a plumbago crucible; again it is smelted and run into ingots, and—well, that is about all I know of the process of chlorination. He who would know more must go and see for himself. And with this I leave Mount Morgan behind.

There is a semi-weekly sea-service from Rockhampton to Bundaberg, but if you wish to go between these times you must take steamer to Maryborough, and go back by rail to Bundaberg. I was in this case, and was considering seriously the loss of time ensuing from such a course, when some one said to me with the voice of a good genius, "We'll see if we can't make the *Fitzroy* stop at the pilot station at Burnett Head, ten miles from Bundaberg, and let us off. I'll telegraph for a trap, and there we are, saving time and money."

What would a man say under such circumstances? What could he do but gaze and admire? As predicted, so it was. We boarded the *Fitzroy* at midnight, and steamed down the moonlit river, and when morning came we were on the Pacific again. This portion of the voyage I had made at night going up, but now there was an opportunity for enjoying the fine coast-line, and watching the soft-coloured islands rise into prominence and fade away again. It was a day to be remembered; and I repeat here, if any one wants a holiday, take the trip from Sydney to Cooktown in the months from May to October. Of course, to properly enjoy it you must not do as I am doing—turn the land inside out for information, and ride and drive, and rise from bed and go to bed at all hours. Just dismiss everything like business from your mind; let things "slide." Get aboard the *Barcoo*, or the *Maranoa*, or, better still, the *Cintra*, and do nothing more. Just drift to the land of the mango, the cinnamon, the cassowary and the alligator, and be glad. On an afternoon that might have fallen from blue Olympus, the *Fitzroy* dropped anchor at Burnett Head, a boat was put out, and my companion and I were in it, and not we alone, but half a dozen others who had learned of the design, and away we went to the shore, rowed by four sturdy sailors. Some of us were sixteen stone, some feather-weights, and one was a lady. I mention this because suddenly the boat grated on the sand, and the boatswain said, "We shall have to carry you ashore." Even so. Out went the sailors, and out went we on their backs to the shore, 150 yards away. There was a parson long and slender, there was the Melbourne alderman—he of the sixteen stone—there was his son and heir, of summers tender; there was the engineer of railways, who had been over the Cairns-Herberton railway; and—well, no matter who the rest were; we were all soon astride our coursers, who went in for a ding-dong struggle shorewards. In spite of the fact that the parson's feet ploughed the water, his steed came in by a neck ahead. A drive then through sugar country to Bundaberg, and we were set down at an excellent hotel in time for dinner.

Bundaberg is a pretty place. It has fine wide streets, a population of about 3,000 people, and is well laid out. The public buildings are fairly well built, and a new post and telegraph office is being erected. All along the line from Rockhampton down, I was struck with the excellent Schools of Arts in the towns and villages. Those of Bundaberg and Maryborough are exceptionally fine. They have excellent libraries, and periodicals from all parts of the world are on the tables. They also have good halls in connection with them,— halls that would do credit to any city. Bundaberg gives the impression of a place likely to become a city; and even on a Saturday afternoon, when it is shut up, it has an air trim and taut, and as if it were ready for work at any moment; a thing common to Queensland towns. The only exception to this that I met was Mackay, but even that seemed as if it only needed one charge from the battery of good seasons to galvanise it into life again. The small towns of Queensland, in spite of their heat and treeless condition, are not repellent, and Gympie and Maryborough are not treeless; while Bundaberg has a forest land about it, a pleasant river running through it, and is green with grass and fresh with flowers.

Mr. Phillips's hotel is a planter's resort, and I had the good fortune to meet not only a number of planters there, but also many principal citizens, some members of the Chamber of Commerce, and an irrigation enthusiast, who is trying to bring the Chaffey Brothers (of Mildura) to Bundaberg to revolutionise the district. He has many followers, and there is a company being formed composed of many of the principal planters. The promoters think that with irrigation they can defy the rainfall and secure regular crops. Meanwhile, however, the Bundaberg planters are in better heart than those of Mackay. They have not suffered up to this year so severely from drought, and they have some advantages which will favour them even in the decline of the industry. Should the planters of the north fail, labour will drift southwards, and there will be plenty of white men and Kanakas to be had at 10s. to 15s. a week "and found." Even now about Townsville and Mackay, owing to the closing of mills and plantations, Europeans can be got for 15s. a week, and board and lodging. The small farmers are throwing up their places, and are pushing into the towns, willing, let it be said, as they are some of the best men in the country,—not unemployed loafers—to do anything for bread. But that must have an end, and the Bundaberg planter should be alive to the fact that the age of cheap European labour has passed, and that, though men may take 15s. a week, they only do so until they get enough to take them into places still further south. If you want to know what wages are in any part of the colony, go to the European labourers on a plantation, or the rouseabouts on a squatter's run. They have their friends in all the colonies, and they are thoroughly posted as to the labour market and the rate of wages. It appears reasonable to conclude that the Bundaberg planter must suffer from the same causes that bring injury to the planter of the Johnstone River, the Herbert River, or Mackay.

Every plantation that I have visited in Queensland

bears tokens of thrift and endeavour. Through no shiftlessness or lack of intelligent management have planters come to grief. Mistakes they may have made, but they are mistakes that all men, all organisations, make in a young country. And experience is a costly and merciless master. If the governments of the immediate past could be punished for their mistakes, what a holocaust of politicians there would be! Now, the Queensland planter, if he has here and there invested too much capital in machinery at the start, if he has taken up too much land, if he has attempted to force development and trade, he has done so with the best intentions.

It has been my good luck to have no wet weather in Queensland, and my journeyings in the Bundaberg district were of the happiest so far as weather is concerned. As soon as one leaves the town, the sugar country is struck, and one drives or rides past such fine plantations as Fairymead and the Hermitage, owned by the Messrs. Young; Bingera, owned by Messrs. Gibson and Howes; Windermere, owned by the Nott Brothers, natives of New South Wales; Mon Repos, owned by Mr. A. P. Barton; Duncraggan, owned by the Cran Brothers and Co.; the Hummock, owned by Mr. Farquhar; and many others. The soil is red and volcanic looking. It will grow anything tropical with plenty of rain and sun, and one could understand the hopefulness of men who looked out upon their land in a good season. The Hummock plantation takes its name from a hill behind the homestead, the only hill in the district, and prized accordingly. From this hill the view is magnificent. The eye sweeps the 600 acres of the plantation under crop, and passes to another plantation and then another, the green cane waving in the morning sun. There is a straight road which runs as clean as an arrow between walls of cane ten and twelve feet high to the sea ; and, to the right, miles away, there is a wide belt of land, seven miles long, on which herds of cattle are grazing. " It is good enough," said my companion, the Manager of the A. U. S. N. Company. Good enough! It was a sight to make a man thirst for the life of the soil, in place of the life of the office, to long for open air and tilling of the earth. Impressed as I was by the Mackay district, Bundaberg struck me as still more promising. The land seemed to be richer, and the growth from it more abundant. Farmers have gone in for other cultivation than that of the sugar-cane,—lucerne, sweet potatoes, maize, grapes, cotton, English potatoes, coffee to a small extent, and even barley. Some have faith in rice-growing, but they will find, I imagine, that irrigation on a large scale will be necessary, before rice can be grown successfully anywhere south of Townsville. Rice requires feet, not inches, of rain. I received the most information from Mr. Farquhar, of the Hummock, Mr. Nott, of Windermere, and Mr. Barton, of Mon Repos, at whose places I again tasted Queensland hospitality. In spite of the bad season that is upon them, they are hopeful, if, as they say, the Government will give them a chance : if the Polynesian Labour Amendment Act is continued.

Whatever course the Parliament of Queensland pursues regarding this question, one must believe in ultimate justice to the planters, and the triumph of the good sense of the people. The great trouble is at present that the mining community is arrayed against the agricultural community. The miners have no sympathy, no feeling with the tillers of the soil. Besides, they are combined, and they have the strength of combination. But in northern Queensland it is not so much the miner himself, not so much the ordinary member of the Trades Unions who causes antagonism, but the would-be leaders or demagogues. The *bonâ-fide* leaders have been won over to see things in a certain light; but the would-be leaders, finding therein their opportunity for usurpation, straightway have stirred up trouble. There can be little doubt that the Separation movement would have been much stronger, if it had not been for rival leaders in the Trades Unions. And now let me sum up broadly the dark details of the sugar industry in Queensland. At Cairns I heard of the Weary Bay plantation, once valued at £100,000, being closed. The Hop Wah plantation at Cairns is abandoned; and the mortgage on the Pyramid plantation has been foreclosed after an expenditure of £130,000 upon it. On the Herbert River the Gairloch plantation has been closed; Hamleigh has been sold for one-tenth of its cost; and Macnorth for one-fourth of its cost. On the Burdekin Delta, one of the largest plantations has been closed. The Pandora mill and the Yeppoon plantation have gone down in the Rockhampton district. At Maryborough there is £50,000 worth of machinery lying idle, and that which is in use is worked at a loss.

Against these ominous things we can only set down the fact that, in good seasons, money was made in Mackay and Bundaberg; and that at these places, at Cairns, on the Johnston River, and in some small districts on the Logan River, plantations are holding their own. Planters declare that, given reciprocity with the other colonies, and cheap labour, they can yet succeed, because the worst is over with them so far as experience and knowledge of economical working are concerned. They are sure that they can, being granted these concessions, make the industry more than it has ever been to the

Carrying Sugar Cane.

country. This is reasonable. There is a feeling among
some thinking men of the north, that the Labour question
could be mastered by the importation of Europeans,—
Germans, for instance,—who should be given outright a
selection of land after they had cultivated it for three or
four years. They could sell their cane to the big planters
or to the central mills. This is a scheme in the right
direction ; but would it succeed ? We know where we
are, but we know not where we may be. It could be
tried, but it is not an entire solution of the difficulty.
The planters have encouraged this small settlement,
and would be glad of it. They have not taken up such
large areas of land that there is not plenty of room
yet for the selector and prospective freeholder. North
of Rockhampton, every person whom I questioned, said
that it was impossible for white men to do continued
labour in the fields. Even doing other work they found
that they must reduce their hours, because it told on
them before long. One man said to me : " You see I'm
a strong-built fellow, and I don't dislike heat, but I find
I cannot work here full pelt without suffering for it."
When I was at Cairns the weather was like that of
Sydney in December. Just add 70 per cent. to it,
and some idea may be had of the heat that rages from
Cairns down to Rockhampton in December and January.
Charge that heat with moisture from a land that receives,
at times, as much as a foot of water a day, and an idea
can be had of what white men are called upon to endure,
who are asked to do field work in northern Queensland.
The climate is dead against the white man at work in
the open, and none but those who are blindly opposed
to Kanaka labour go so far as to say that the white
man can take the place of the Polynesian or Chinaman.
But, supposing that the white man can do the field work,

will he do so? That, so far, has been answered by a decided negative. If, then, Polynesian labour is abolished, and the white man will not do field work, what will be the result? Northern Queensland will have to depend upon her mines and timber, for there is nothing else to work upon. She has not much squatting land north of Townsville, and her coast land would be practically unworked. We know well that minerals alone will not make a country rich. The heart of the north is tropical agriculture, and to it must the population look for its constant prosperity, or, rather, for its everyday commerce.

It produces sugar and rice first of all. These are to northern Queensland what wool, wine, and wheat, are to South Australia. Parts of it can be made to produce rice as satisfactorily and as abundantly as China or Japan, and as cheaply with cheap labour. What has been done with sugar we know. It is the natural home of the banana. The steamer *Maranoa*, by which I travelled from Mackay to Rockhampton, carried 5,000 bunches of bananas to Brisbane and Sydney. There is carried now by the A. U. S. N. Company every week about 6,000 bunches, to say nothing of what the busy steamers of Howard Smith & Co. carry. Two years ago there were not 600 bunches shipped per week. Banana plantations are being planted all over the north, and the trade will soon rival that with Fiji, from which the A.U.S.N. Company brings 23,000 bunches weekly. The North also will produce the cocoanut, mangoes, oranges, lemons, limes, citrons, custard apples, tamarinds, tapioca, the mangosteen, cinnamon, pine-apples, nutmeg, pepper, and tobacco. Plantations of the cocoanut palm, of pine-apples, limes, coffee, and ginger exist.

Now, is the Pacific Islander keeping the fruits of the

soil from the Queenslander, the Anglo-Saxon, and the European? Every planter who gave evidence before the Royal Commission held here in 1888 and nearly every other witness agreed in saying that the Kanakas did labour that the white man would not do, and that their employment gave work to the white man,—work which would not otherwise be given. I take one case as an example. Mr. Angus Gibson, president of the Planters' Association, Bundaberg, in his evidence before the Commission, said that the wages he paid the Kanakas amounted to £2,271, while the sum he paid the whites was £5,655, to which would be added the sums paid for medical attendance on the Kanakas, rations, buildings, etc., all of which were supplied by the white man, and amounting to £2,936; fencing, firewood, and contractors' work, amounting to £1,054; making a total paid white labour on the estate of about £9,645. Turning to another witness,—Mr. A. R. Blackmore, manager of the Hamleigh estate, in the Herbert River district—one finds that he paid in 1888 wages to Europeans to the extent of £2,160, and to Polynesians £725. And this witness further says, in reply to the question whether whites were able to do the field work, " I have never been able to get them to think of it for a moment; I have tried them repeatedly." Now these are figures and statements that are repeated over and over again by planters and others. The Polynesian is engaged, for three years under contract, through the Government, and is then returned to his own country again. He is, therefore, only a sojourner, and in his labour is restricted, according to the Amendment Act of 1884, to tropical or semi-tropical agriculture, which means " field-work in connection with the cultivation of sugar-cane, cotton, tea, rice, coffee, spices, or tropical or semi-tropical productions or fruits."

This shuts Kanakas out from the business of "engineers, engine-drivers, engine-fitters, wheelwrights, farriers, sugar-boilers, carpenters, sawyers, splitters, fencers, bullock-drivers, mechanics, grooms, or coachmen"; from "horse-driving or carting, except field work; and from domestic service." This law is broken, as the police court records show, but on the whole it is kept very well, and the Islanders are worked within the prescribed limits.

Even those who are opposed to Polynesian labour agree in saying that the Kanaka is an inoffensive and reputable sojourner in the land. His vice is tobacco, his weakness finery of an inexpensive kind, and his good qualities many. Even when brought to the country first, "a savage," he is not violent, or brutal; he is simply wild, and needs taming. He will run away, not *from* anything, but, because, like an animal, he seeks a new camping-ground. There is nothing of that latent look of malignity in his eyes, so often noticed in the gaze of the African negro,—no restrained ferocity. He is simple, childlike, and amenable to discipline, if not very quick at learning. The Polynesian is saving and industrious, is the character generally given.

Inspectors, police magistrates, planters, merchants, and disinterested people all over the colony, bear testimony to the general good conduct of the Islander. It is the white man and the Chinaman that debase him, when he *is* debased. It is impossible for one to mix among the Kanakas on an estate without being struck with their docile appearance. They have full and gentle eyes, and remind one of the Hawaiian, though not so good-looking. They have married whites in very few cases, and in many instances they bring wives with them from the New Hebrides. Little danger need be apprehended from the social standpoint. They have filled a place, and they are filling a place, in the development of Queensland, which no others have been able to fill.

I ran down from Maryborough to Gympie by train, starting at 4 o'clock in the afternoon, and getting to the gold-field at 8.15 p.m. The journey was not uninteresting. The country was better than most that I had been through, and there were signs of thrift all along the line. The timber industry has a hold, as evidenced by two sawmills that we passed. It is an unobtrusive country, and should be a prosperous one. There is good soil and timber, and, given energy and pluck, there should be a good future for this part of Queensland. Gympie at first sight pleases one. From the station we went down steep hills, then through busy streets, and then up steep hills, to the best hotel of the place, near which is the Post Office and the Court House. Gympie is full of life and vigour. At night the main street is paraded by the miners, the most orderly set of fellows that one could find, and standing a good deal on their dignity. They are well combined, and their leaders are not backward in making the most of their position. They have their own building, their secretary and responsible officers, and they assemble in solemn conclave quite as often as is necessary. Gympie altogether feels its importance, and properly so. Since 1877 it has been climbing steadily to its position, and it has honestly earned its prosperity. There labour nearly 1,400 miners; there work 65 steam-engines; and there underground mining is approaching perfection in system, as I had an opportunity of seeing in the long hours I spent in the North Phœnix mine. Some of the mines go down to a great depth. The great Monkland shaft measures 1,460 feet; the

Gympie Golden Crown, 1,228 feet; the Inglewood, 1,200 feet; and the United Smithfield, 1,160 feet. In the North Phœnix mine I went down 900 feet.

Gympie is one of the prettiest places in Australia. When I was there the many hills were green, and quiet habitations dotted their sides. The River Mary wound along its steep way, and the scores of poppet-heads rose up like outlook posts for armies. Above an immense skating-rink there floated a flag, a huge circus-tent reflected the sunlight, omnibuses plied their dusty trade in the undulating streets, and horsemen galloped away into the valleys. Yet it must not be thought that Gympie has a mountain climate; it is, in fact, only a couple of hundred feet above the level of the sea, and a few miles' travel down the river brings you to the ocean. Gympie has its watering-place, and puts on all the airs of a metropolis. It even has all the vices of a metropolis. Men trick the law in the matter of mining-leases, cut each other's throats commercially, and play at hide-and-seek with conscience and morality, just as much as they do in Brisbane or any other wicked place. Yet Gympie tries to be right; else why so many churches, else why those ten book-stores and stationers' shops in one street? Tobacco shops, brokers' shops, stationery shops, and saloons, seem the dominating characteristics of the main streets. The place outwardly is one of the most orderly to be found. And concerning the dignity of a metropolis, both Gympie and Charters Towers kept pace with Brisbane in one thing—they had their " Pies, all hot !" Nowhere in Australia, besides Queensland, have I seen the pieman—the white-hatted, white-coated, white-aproned pieman. "Pies, hot pies, pies all hot!"—this you will hear in nearly every large town in Queensland up to midnight. I talked with one in Charters Towers, and he told me that he made a good living. "Who buys?" I said. "Oh, all the Johnnies," he replied; "they all likes 'em, an' it's the fashion. Sometimes I'm called into a house where there's a party, just for the fun of the thing, as the gents think; but I has all the fun, for I sells my pies. . . . Pies, hot pies, pies all hot!"

I had a chance to see many mines, but I preferred to go down one only. The North Phœnix was my choice, chiefly because it was one of the latest, and yet was far enough advanced to be in complete working order. It began its career about the same time that Hugh Mossman "got there" at Charters Towers. The manager (George Argo) told me that since the first crushing no call has ever been made upon the shareholders. I visited the mine with Warden Selheim, whose name is known well throughout Queensland, one of the pioneers of the north as he is. The crushing mill is a splendid affair. Everything is in the most excellent order, and as clean as need be. The company owns a splendid Huntington mill, and a crushing battery of 60 heads of stampers. The ore obtained at Gympie is not very rich, being, even in the North Phœnix, only about 1 oz. 3 dwt. to the ton; but it pays well enough. I saw two of the directors while at the mine, and they were men who had been practical miners, and suddenly found themselves lifted into opulence. But that is common to all the mines of Queensland. In mining the general rule is reversed. It is the toiler who makes his fortune, not the kid-gloved speculator.

No better evidence of the prudence, and even "cuteness," with which the Phœnix mine is managed can be advanced than this. The manager asked me if I would like to see a few fine bits of ore. Of course. He opened a safe, drew out some lumps, dipped them into a basin of water, and handed them to me: lumps of ore, with thick veins of gold, like streaked marble. "How many ounces to the ton?" I said. "Anything over two thousand," was the reply. Now, why were these lumps kept in the safe, so? To show visitors like myself? Scarcely. When a bad streak was come upon, one of these lumps was put into the pile of bad stuff, and, eureka! up comes the average again, and the shareholders get their regular dividends. A wise fellow, is Manager Argo. I spent a long time below the surface, here going down in the cage, there climbing from drive to drive, up and down, and following the reef along for hundreds of yards. The timbering was splendidly done, and the machinery was of the most perfect kind. Sometimes I climbed over great piles of broken rocks, dragging a man with me,—now in damp darkness, now coming into the light of candles stuck in the wall, where the pick and drill were at work. Once, when we came to a turn, my guide stopped. "Now, that was the turning-point in the mine, raly," he said. "We lost the reef there, and plenty sold out, thinking we had run out our luck; but that was a bad job for them. We careened off here to the right, and there she blows away, sometimes thirty feet, sometimes five feet wide." And this is the way that fortunes are made and lost in mining. Next to the Phœnix, the most notable mines are the Glanmire and the Great Eastern. As at Charters Towers, the knowing ones believe in deep mining, and evidence has gone to prove that they are right. Altogether, I should say that Gympie, with its 10,000 inhabitants, with its ever-developing mines, with its good country round it, should long continue to be an ideal town in the matter of prosperity, as it is in appearance. And one thing makes for such a hope: the co-operative principle which exists there. As at Charters Towers, the mines are worked from within; foreign capital does not rule the roost, nor are the miners shut out from legitimate speculation. I believe that both these places owe their success to the extension of this principle. To give men interest in the mines in which they are working is like making a man part owner of the house he lives in,—he will take care of it.

On looking over my notes regarding the gold yield for the whole colony, I find that Charters Towers comes first, with a total yield since it started of 1,749,499 oz.; Gympie comes next, with 1,430,599 oz.; and the Palmer next, with 1,288,596 oz. And the total value of the gold taken from Queensland since the records began is £21,310,947. Now the relation of the gold yield to that of other minerals, may be gathered from the fact that the value of tin, silver, lead, coal, and copper, raised during 1888, was £381,229, while that of gold for the same time was £1,694,750, or over four times as much.

While this book is going through the press, Sir Samuel Griffith the Premier of Queensland has, one is glad to say, declared for the revival of Polynesian labour, thus performing a *volte face*.

CHAPTER XVII.

QUEENSLAND IN 1889 (*continued.*)

THE RAILWAYS—THE PASTORAL INDUSTRY.

THERE are special features of the railway lines of South Australia, Victoria, and New South Wales, which deserve commendation from the traveller's standpoint; but to Queensland must be given the palm for uniformity, considerate carefulness, and general wisdom in construction. From the national outlook, the system pursued seems to be that which most commends itself to the outsider. I take the map of Queensland, and I find that not only has the colony a series of harbours along 1,500 miles of her coast, but that she has railways running to the interior of the country, from these harbours. This means, first, prevention of centralisation; then it encourages the natural development of the country, and the establishment of commercial centres, each with a splendid area of productive country about it. Victoria, of course, has the most complete network of lines, having 22·77 miles of railway to every 1,000 square miles; next comes New Zealand with over 16, New South Wales with over 6, and Queensland with nearly 3 miles of railway to 1,000 square miles of country. But that does not mean so much when it is remembered that the area of Queensland is 668,224 square miles, as against 309,175 of New South Wales;

104,235 of New Zealand; and 87,884 of Victoria. It is easy to pierce a small colony with railways in all directions—that has been the case with Victoria. All things considered, Queensland has, according to her period of existence and population, done more in railway construction than any of the colonies; and in the matter of system has worked upon a principle which is wiser, and more prudent, than that pursued by one or two of her neighbours. Aside from the fact that it would be impossible for New South Wales to build lines in from the coast as Queensland has done, and its liability (from the configuration of the country) to centralisation, there remains to be considered the question of construction. Queensland would never have developed as quickly as she has, were it not for the cheap lines that have been built. The gauge is only 3 feet 6 inches. The cost has averaged at £6,302 per mile, or over £31 per head of the population. The railways of New South Wales have cost £13,031 per mile; of Victoria £13,115; of New Zealand £7,595; and of South Australia £6,459 per mile, or £25, £25, £22, and £31 per head of population respectively. In considering these figures, regard must of course be had to the fact that the population of Queensland, like that of South Australia, is only about one-third of that of Victoria or New South Wales.

I travelled over the southern system, over the western system out to Charleville, over the central system towards Barcaldine, over the Mackay line, over the northern system to Hughenden, and over the Cairns line as far as it has been constructed. My impressions were that the lines had been constructed in keeping with pioneer development. Everywhere the stations were of wood, cheaply yet carefully built, and thoroughly in harmony with the necessities of the country. I can point to railway stations in out-of-the-way districts of New South Wales, which have cost thousands of pounds, where one of a few hundred pounds' cost would do. For example, take that at Michelago, which is the first that comes to my mind at the moment. It is good enough for a town of 20,000 inhabitants; it is in a district bald of settlement. The old New South Wales policy can be well understood—it is construction for posterity. But is not the principle of pioneer life—temporary construction—enough to meet the needs of the time? Queensland has not only erected cheap lines of railways which meet her present needs, and will meet those of the coming generation,—she has carried the system of economy and prudence into all the ramifications of her railway organisation.

The travelling is slow on the Queensland lines. For instance, the distance from Brisbane to Wallangarra is 232 miles, and it takes over 12 hours to cover it. That is, the rate is about $19\frac{3}{8}$ miles per hour, which is not, to say the least, striking. Or again, the distance from Brisbane to Charlesville is 318 miles, and it takes 16 hours to make the journey, the rate being about 20 miles an hour. Or still again, the distance from Maryborough to Gympie is 61 miles. It takes $4\frac{1}{4}$ hours to do the journey, the rate being about $14\frac{1}{2}$ miles per hour. Of course, at this rate of travel, the wear and tear to rolling-stock is not great. The cost of maintenance of the Queensland lines is £121 4s. per mile, as against £190 per mile in New South Wales, £179 in Victoria, and £79 in South Australia. There is no loss in working any of the main lines in Queensland, but there is a list of small branch lines which represent a deficit of £15,488. The branches are the Highfields, Beauraba,

Killarney, Isis, Kilkivan, Springsure, Clermont, and Ravenswood. The only main line that was worked at a loss in 1888 was the Mackay railway, which was mulcted in the sum of £2,498. It is not hard to see why this line came short. It goes through a sugar district, and sugar was a failure last year. The branches that have black marks against them were lately built, and are for development and the future. If railways are to meet the necessities of the present, they should also be expected to play their part in advancement, and be like the plough to the soil and the axe to the oaks.

How are the lines paying? They bring altogether 2·754 per cent. on the total expenditure on lines opened to the public, and 2·485 per cent. on all lines both opened and under construction. There are eight systems opened for traffic, comprising a total of 1,931 miles of line. The total cost of construction since 1865 is £12,169,237. There are now under process of construction nineteen lines, and several others under survey.

A study of the question justifies the conclusion that, generally speaking, the railway policy of Queensland has been a wise one. The one doubtful spot in it is the Cairns-Herberton line. Still, if the line but proves safe, it will be a great thing for northern Queensland. It will open up a finer country than do the central and northern systems. At present the policy is to build branches from the existing systems, thus developing the country in great circles, as it were. The next move will be, no doubt, to connect either Hughenden with Cloncurry, the tin-mining district in the Gulf country, or else the famous Croydon gold-field with Herberton and Cairns. Following that will probably be a line running from Hughenden south, touching the termini of the southern and western and central systems,—Barcaldine and

Charleville. That done, Queensland will have a wonderful scheme of railways—wonderful in economy as in value towards development. As it is, there is little reason for the people to be dissatisfied, since the Governments have pushed ahead construction as fast as was possible in so sparsely settled a country. The policy is (by comparison) even ahead of the age and the condition of the colony.

All things considered, Queensland is well supplied with communication. The coastal service, if not perfect, is as perfect as can be under the circumstances. The A. U. S. N. Company and the Howard-Smith Company supply constant communication with the north. Much of the trade is done by the A. U. S. N. Company. It gives a service from Adelaide to Burketown in the Gulf of Carpentaria. Standing at the top of the tower on the capacious and admirably-constructed building of the company in Brisbane, I could see eight of their vessels in the harbour, including a British-India steamer. Time's changes are great. In 1842 occurred the first land sale at Moreton Bay; in 1851 the first wool ship stood out into the Pacific from what is at present the port of Brisbane. And now the harbour is alive with shipping; the land is being banded with railways; there is constant communication from the Gulf to the capital. From the passenger's standpoint, the communication is of course more pleasant in the steamers than it could be on the railways. The lines running westward are slow and somewhat rough; the accommodation afforded by the A. U. S. N. Company is excellent. On the seven steamers by which I travelled there was fruit on the table at every meal, there was afternoon tea, the cabins were comfortable, and if only the detestable custom of tipping could be abolished the service would be generally excellent. I think in no colony is tipping carried to the same extent as in Queensland, and the further north one goes the worse it is. It is the one thing continental in Queensland. I have a commination service arranged, by which the ignoble army of the tipped shall catch it worse than the Jackdaw of Rheims.

I am now fairly well educated in the matter of land conditions in Australia ; that is from the standpoint of observation and travel. No man yet, I fancy, was ever thoroughly informed on all the ramifications of the colonial land laws. They have defied the explorations of the most earnest students and politicians, and in such a case where am I ? Just in that region of present experience which has some accurate general outlines, but no good glossary of all the language of land legislation.

Under the Crown Lands Acts of 1884, the grazing farms which correspond to the New South Wales homestead leases—with the exception that the maximum area is 20,000 instead of 10,000 acres—have proved a success in most districts. There are also agricultural farms, the maximum area of which is 1,280 acres, and the minimum 320 acres. Besides these, there are the village settlements, which have proved dismal failures. Out in the Mitchell district I saw villages staked out, but there were only stakes, nothing more. It was a fatuous intelligence which said to would-be settlers, You shall have a lot in the village for your business, and a lot out of the village on which to build a house and live ; and then offered land in districts where there was no water within miles, and from which artesian supply would be either impossible or achieved at vast expense. And even if there were water, what should these villagers live on? With station property surrounding them, and barren enough in places at that,—why, it is like putting a horse to feed on a cemented tennis-court. The thousands of pounds spent in surveying these village settlements were idly spent,—were squandered,—and the country has had to pay the piper. They were like the homestead leases in the far west of New South Wales—a delusion and a worry. But altogether the feeling in Queensland regarding the land law is better than it ever was in New South Wales. Radically the Queensland land law is right; it is only incidentally that it is wrong.

One thing is most noticeable in squatting in Queensland,—there is not so much overstocking as in New South Wales and Victoria. Now the Fitzroy Downs is a far finer country than the Darling district of New South Wales, yet the land is not stocked so heavily. I can put my finger on a station of 1,200 square miles at Mitchell, where there are carried not more than 30,000 sheep and 10,000 cattle. Compare that with New South Wales, where on land that requires five, six, and even ten acres to support a sheep, the land is stocked up to the hilt, and beyond it. There is little allowance made for vicissitudes, and the result is the great losses occurring in those western districts which have filled squatters and the public with dismay. I have seen a station in New South Wales where only 30,000 sheep were saved out of 150,000. That would seldom occur in Queensland, because, in the first place, most of the worst squatting country is better than the worst squatting country of New South Wales, and the land is not stocked so heavily. There are many things I should like to review in the Queensland land law, but I can only put forward conclusions, not the processes by which I have come to the conclusions.

No one has seen Australia till he has visited the Darling Downs in Queensland, and the Darling River country in New South Wales. I have written about the latter; I have now a few words to say about the former. I shall never forget my first view of them. It was a beautiful morning, and I had had a full repast of glorious mountain scenery spread out before me. I cannot dwell long on that journey from Brisbane to Toowoomba. My space grows short in which to take my leave of Queensland. But if I had a friend to whom I wished to be kind, I should send him to the Blue Mountains first, and then across the hills from Brisbane to Toowoomba, and beyond to the vast plains. You start early in the morning, and go swiftly by those places which from the river are very pretty, and in days to come will be what the Hudson River suburbs are to New York and the Thames suburbs to London—Toowong, Taringa, Indooroopilly, Graceville, and Ipswich; and then, after a few score miles, begins the climbing to Helidon, Murphy's Creek, and Highfields. Let us pause. Did you ever see anything more exquisite than this? Vast billows of wooded land stretching out and beyond for 80 miles, and you are winding round the mountain side, where are repeated the marvels of construction, the tunnels and the curves, you saw at Cairns. On one side of a horseshoe you look across and see the way by which you came, cut through the ends of vast mounds like graves, driven through great hills, fringing deep chasms, triumphant over nature and centuries of loneliness. There hang in yellow grandeur orange orchards; there droops beside a mountain stream the willow; there hides a quiet home among the bushes, and there while you dream is Toowoomba, a quiet town, and full of possibilities. It is surrounded by small farms varying in size from 10 to 200 acres. There is "the little German vote"; there dwell the sturdy Teutons who have done wonderful pioneer work in Queensland; who have cleared the Rosewood scrub, who work as Englishmen in this country never do,—they and their wives and their children. Away down at Warwick, on the Darling Downs, where I spent some pleasant days, I saw also the houses that the Norwegians had built for themselves in the valleys, living their quiet stupid lives in a frugal and honest fashion, and hated by their English and colonial neighbours, because they make money where others lose it. The Englishman will not toil and save and struggle in this land, as do the foreigners who come to settle. The temper of the country seems against it, as well as the instinct of our race. Throughout Queensland are Germans, Norwegians, and Swedes, making a good living, and showing not only their own powers of industry and perseverance, but demonstrating also the capacities of the land.

But the Darling Downs. Leaving Toowoomba, we are upon them, and I travelled far across them; and again across the Fitzroy Downs, a distance of 483 miles, to Charlesville. Many a splendid estate was passed, and one heard frequent tales of the pioneers of the land. I had the good fortune to travel with Mr. M'Farlane, of Waroonga, on the Fitzroy Downs, whose hospitality I enjoyed, and with whom I drove behind a good pair of horses over many a score miles of country. There is no land in Australia like parts of the Darling Downs. For fifty miles west of Katoomba I travelled over stations that were simply vast farms, which could be cultivated like

a Chinese garden at Rushcutter Bay at Sydney. It
reminded one of the great farms in Colorado, Minnesota,
and in Manitoba and the north-west territory of Canada
—hundreds of square miles that could be put under
plough, if there were good seasons. There is the rub.
This land, like the land of Canaan, might flow with milk
and honey, but that the heavens are sometimes unresponsive as burnished brass, and the gates of the sky will
not open. And so, though there are some estates on the
Darling Downs which are smiling with boundless wheat
fields and reeking with fatness, there is the one thing
wanting that prevents the gold from being retorted. It is
a broad free life up there, with a climate almost superior
to any in Australia, in tone and bracing qualities. While
I was there, the heat in the middle of the day was strong,
but it was not oppressive. The air was dry and clear,
and as for the nights, they were like those of the Blue
Mountains—cold and bracing. And why not? Waroonga,
for instance, is 1,500 feet above the level of the sea, and
the atmosphere is really that of the mountains. I think
the most enticing meal I ever ate was one that Mr.
M'Farlane and myself cooked under the trees between
Roma and Waroonga—plain chops which we had carried
with us, bread and tea, and a bit of cheese; but the
relish of it! However, the horses came near to spoiling it
all, for a fine run we had after them, and if there had
not been a wire fence a couple of miles off, we might
have had to take the dusty wallaby track.

The towns in the far west of Queensland are very like
those in the Darling district of New South Wales. Dalby,
Roma, and Mitchell are sad-looking places. Each had
its day as the terminus of the railway. As soon as the
line was opened for traffic to another point, the sails of
commerce were unfurled, and those who could moved on

also. Roma and Mitchell have wide streets, and in the former place an honest attempt at dignity is being attempted by planting trees; but who are to rest in the shade of them? Look through the highways of commerce at any hour in the day, and all that a bullet could hit would be a Government officer. The New South Wales western towns compare favourably with them; Wilcannia, Wentworth, Bourke, are superior to Roma, Mitchell, and Charleville. Yet my recollections of Charleville are pleasant. I had gone there chiefly to see the artesian water supply that had been struck, and which was yielding 2,250,000 gallons of water a day. It was no easy journey there, and when I arrived I found the bore sealed up. What was to be done? Charleville was, in itself, as nothing. I might see some of the station property round it, as I did—weary sand-wastes. There was the Warrego, a bed of sand, with spots of water here and there; and I had crossed, two days before, the Maranoa at Mitchell, without the horses wetting their feet—dry as the bones of the prophets. I was used to this. I have had my fill of desert country, from the cactus and alkali scrub plains of Arizona to the Mount Browne quartz levels. There was but the old story to tell, of drought and decimated sheep. But this bore was to lift things, men said; it was to turn the land into a smiling garden. One knew better. One knew that the great sum of good coming from them would be to provide safety for the travelling of stock, and be a guarantee against a water famine in a town in dry times. Irrigation in that western country must be only in patches and small lots, and to supply individual needs. Further than that is all in the clouds. Markets and communication must come before irrigation in the great plains can be of much service.

But this bore was closed by Government order, and there was only the scaffolding and the 8-inch pipe on which a huge timber was set; and all sealed up. Well, must I go back unsatisfied after travelling the heart of the West to see this harbinger of better things? True it was, that I could see the prison of the water, I could see the great channel cut by the overflow down towards the town, a channel like that of a river, but—only that? No, I would not go back without beholding the fountain of joy, as a happy squatter, the owner of the bore at Kerribree in New South Wales, called it. And I did not. I saw the workmen gathered together; I saw Morrison and Newton, the contractors, put on their overalls and go at it like navvies, and I saw that pipe opened, and a column of water eight inches in diameter shoot up into the air like a monster catapult, carrying with it stones and bits of rock. And this water was coming up 1,375 feet, warm and pure, to seek the outer world. The thing was managed. I knew the town 10,000 miles away where these contractors' homes were, and,—well, you cannot wash nationality out of a man's veins. Sometimes the water would shoot up fifty and sixty feet into the air; sometimes it would be but a solid column up to a distance of twenty feet, and then fall over like a monster fountain spray. These men, Morrison and Newton, are doing good work in Queensland. They and their partners work under the title of the "Queensland Boring Company." They have sunk wells successfully at Cunnamulla, getting water at 1,406 feet; at Blackall with water at 1,663 feet; at Tambo at 1,002 feet; at Lansdowne Estates at 2,530 feet; at Brisbane at 1,780 feet, getting at the last-named place 10,000 gallons a day. At Blackall there are 350,000 gallons got; at Tambo 280,000 gallons; at Cunnamulla 540,000; and at

Charleville 2,250,000 gallons per day. The contractors say that the bore at Charleville is the best they have ever seen. It discharges 400 gallons in 14 seconds. The machinery is moved by the Government from place to place; but so much time is occupied in transferring it that the company have made no money by their successful work. The tubes used are made by Stewart of Glasgow, and they have been found to work perfectly. Only one accident has occurred since the company began their operations. It is not possible to over-estimate the value that these bores will be to the interior of Australia, from the standpoint of preservation of stock, which is their chief present use.

I had intended writing of the Warwick district, another long-settled and most prosperous portion of the Darling Downs; to tell of some of the magnificent country I saw there, along, and beyond, what Mr. Anthony Trollope called the sluggish Condamine; but I must leave these Queensland topics here, with pleasant thoughts of the most interesting tour I have taken in Australia, and with gratitude to so many in official and private life from the Governor and Premier down, who showed me kindness and helped me on my way. Would that I had told my tale better, and had done greater justice to a noble colony. Hail, and farewell.

[NOTE.—Much of the success of the Queensland railways is due to the ex-Secretary of Railways, Mr. F. Curnow, whose administration was marked by intelligence, carefulness, and judgment.]

CHAPTER XVIII.

WESTERN AUSTRALIA IN 1889-90.

THE VOYAGE TO ALBANY.

WHEN I left Sydney for Western Australia it was also to go from the continent altogether, to leave behind the land, the compass of whose quality and promise I had touched at nearly all points, ranging round from the Carpentaria country to the beginning of that western north which is called Kimberley.

Is it nothing to leave a land behind that has been kind to you? If it is, then there is not that in you which may be called gratitude,—not what may be called loyalty. When the ship you have chosen for your home moves out from the dock, and the line of division begins, the feeling of separation also begins, and ever broadens and deepens, until it is swallowed up in the interminableness of the ocean, where there is only sky and water and your transient dwelling-place. When you move from that quay where stood your friends waving good-byes, you left not them alone; you left the good old earth which was made for man. The sea was ever a fitful unfaithful friend. It has always seemed to resent man's attempts to master it, to bind it to his will. And yet man, in the conquest he has achieved, has suffered. Though the mighty green-backed animal is subdued, he makes his rider uneasy. No, the land was made for man, and the sea for fishes. Everything to its element. The albatross caught and brought aboard a vessel immediately gets uneasy, as does a man when he attempts to woo the sea to his needs. A certain bishop, when dying, seemed to regard his passage from this world as a thing to be lamented. His body-servant ventured to remind him that he was going to a land of happiness, but the holy father in God said, " Ah, yes, John, but England is a very good place." Let us admit all the pleasures of voyaging with its array of odours, and all that—there still remains the fact that the dry land, with its odours more distributed, and its sure-footedness, is good enough for us.

I have eaten my Christmas breakfast under many skies, and this one, in 1889, I ate on board the *Carthage* at Williamstown pier. This fact in itself is nothing, but there comes to me, with the thought, the associations connected with that morning. To see the harbour of Melbourne in the early morning is an experience. Ranged along the rail on the lower deck leaned a score of Lascars fishing; dark-visaged, slow-thoughted men, who will sit there all day in the hope of fish that are loth to respond. Yet they will fish on, and show no disappointment. Others are eating their breakfasts, squatting round a large bowl of rice and curry. A dip with slow and nerveless fingers in the rice, a spot of curry, a lazy lifting to the lips, a passionless, noiseless talking with each other, and so they spend their time on Christmas morning. Soon, crowds of boatmen throng about the ship, and out go lines without number in the still water. And now look beyond the Lascars and the fishers and the surrounding shipping; look far off. There rises the city of Melbourne. With a glass you can see all plainly—the heart of the metropolis, the range of buildings to the east, Government House, St. Kilda and beyond, all in the mist of the morning.

What thoughts does all that bring up? The days half a century gone, when Balmain and Henty pastured their flocks on this then uninhabited coast; of the time when Collins Street was a stock-yard, or part of one; and when Imperial explorers declared the country good for nothing, an impossible land; of the period when, with the merest handful of settlers, a New South Wales Governor named the place Melbourne; when other explorers like the noble Sir Thomas Mitchell, to whom the pioneers taught the way, pierced the heart of what is now Victoria, and told of what might yet be achieved; when Gippsland and the Murray River district were unknown lands: of those first ardent days in the early Fifties, when, cotemporaneous with the acquirement of a separate Government and a Constitution, there came the getting of gold also,—there befell the Great Rush of '53.

Yes, of all this and much more would you think, if you stood with me this Christmas morning on the deck of the *Carthage* of the Peninsular and Oriental Company, whose service from England to Australia is unsurpassable in comfort, elegance, great ships, and courteous officers. For here rises before us a giant city, and yet not a full-grown giant. It is only a mammoth in its infancy yet; capable even now of prodigious feats. Where stands that Art Gallery there stood a mimi fifty years ago; where the Earl of Hopetoun rides through high-columned gates, there rushed the blackfellow with his spear a generation gone; where sits the merchant prince at Toorak before his Chateau Léoville and olives, there sat a kangaroo, one man's life back. None but the Anglo-Saxon could have done that. Where has any other race built up great nations outside of their own boundaries? Consider the feebleness of the Dutch in Java; the French in India, Guiana, and Lower Canada; the Germans in Africa. Of all those nations that rivalled England, Holland, and Spain, the Portuguese alone succeeded in successful colonisation,—that is one record. But England, and the United States and Canada, and Australia and Africa,—that is another. We have the faculty for colonisation, and it is a great faculty. Are we losing it? That is a point too great to be attempted here; but even if we were losing it, we might well be satisfied, for all the fields for colonisation have been entered upon. The desert itself, and the Dark Continent, have been told off to the spoiler and the pioneer. In the natural course of things, there will be no need for new fields for English colonisation for a long time to come. We have only taken up the fringe of the continents that are ours; the broad champaign is simply touched. There is Victoria, the most fully populated of the colonies according to its size; yet Victoria is but begun. It has 1,036,119 of population; it could support seven times that. And we shall be able to put five Victorias into the splendid colony of Queensland, that land of the golden promise. Yet there will never be a Melbourne in Queensland; there can be but one Melbourne, as there can be but one Sydney, in Australia. The days of centralisation are gone, the era of decentralisation has begun; there will be more Ballarats and Newcastles and Townsvilles, and fewer Sydneys and Melbournes.

But that is neither here nor there. And even Christmas musing and moralising must have an end, and breakfast, and lunch, and dinner must be eaten, and we must "move on." Yet I should like to have had more of my brother landsmen on board the *Carthage* on that

Christmas Day, to show them with what admirable taste the sailors decorated the saloon, and what a wonderful six-storey cake we had on exhibition. All day long visitors from Williamstown and from the city came down, and all day courteous officers gave up their pleasure to give pleasure to others : a feature, as I have said, of the P. and O. Company. It was such a day as one would wish to remember—the air of September, clear, sweet—even (as æsthetic folk would say) precious. But let us pause at this, for the next day was one too to be remembered hereafter, even when inhabiting the hottest of all places of which literature speaks. It was a scorching desolating day. No man could say a thanksgiving service in such a time and place ; the Litany would be his only refuge. Melbourne people may boast of their climate, but it is a thing to be taken all round, and not by specimen days. And all day through that terrific heat I visited artists and artists' studios, and the Art Gallery, and the public buildings, and I thought, when it was all over, that I had done as much penance as should wipe off last year's sins. But we left Melbourne behind at last, and Adelaide came next (visited by me for the fourth time), with its modest architecture and mountain-framed beauty. Early in the morning we got there. Mount Lofty, 3,000 feet up, cooled its head in the white clouds, and beneath, the city put on its holiday attire. Anniversary Day, I think they called it. And already, when we landed, the people were gathering at Largs Bay for their outing on the staring sands. What a contrast are Melbourne and Adelaide to Sydney in this respect! Sydney has, within fifteen minutes of its centre, a score of wooded retreats, where there are sea, sun, and shade. What are St. Kilda and Largs Bay to Middle Harbour and Bondi ? Let us not think on it. But instead, in the scorching afternoon, see those crowds of people at Largs Bay sitting in the shade of the piers, having found the sands too much for them.

Slow, steady South Australia, one of the first, yet to be one of the last. Before Queensland, before Victoria, yet following them now. And why? Because she had no great mining settlement. It is a thing to be noted that, in Australia, settlement has followed mining. Victoria, New South Wales, and Queensland, received their first impetus from mining,—an impetus which they have never lost. South Australia has gone ahead on the basis of her agricultural and pastoral development, and now she ranks fourth in the list in population and revenue. Queensland has over £1,000,000 more revenue, and her population is 50,000 more. Yet South Australia has a day before her, though it comes but tardily. Her courage has been great, and her endurance is also great. If she only averages ten bushels of wheat to the acre, that is, after all, better in the long run, if it be consistent, than gold mining and silver mining; for the soil lasts, and the labour put into it goes on reproducing. One felt, on leaving South Australia behind, with its vast territory of 903,425 square miles, stretching from ocean to ocean, 2,000 miles between water and water—with one hand pointing towards the Orient and one towards the silent South—that there is a future for it, not to be reckoned altogether by the past. For she has left the first stages of development, and has come into the area of confident progress. And yet one must conclude, from all evidence, that South Australia, like Western Australia, is not so great in its possibilities as the colonies farther east. The line was drawn by nature rather cruelly, or else the explorer, the pioneer, and the prospector are out in their calculation. But those who have visited all the colonies with impartial eyes must, I think, come to the same conclusion. We shall think more on this as we pass into that colony which takes up nearly one-third of the continent, and is known as Western Australia.

There is further food for thought as we move onward and outward, past Yorke's Peninsula, across Spencer's Gulf, beyond Cape Wills, and into the Great Australian Bight. Full of historic memories is the long wash of water on this rocky and inhospitable coast. One naturally thinks, as I thought aboard the *Carthage*, of those devoted men who, for the cause of science, civilisation, and humanity, made paths along that weary coast from Perth on the far west to Adelaide in the centre. And first and chief of them is Eyre, the gentle, the dauntless. What explorer ever attempted so much on such little capital,—I mean, with such a small basis of resource? Foiled in his attempt to find good country beyond Lake Torrens, he turned towards the silent west, and said, I will go to Perth. And on January 25th, 1841, Eyre began his dangerous enterprise. Nine horses, six sheep, and a provision of flour for nine weeks,—these were the stores carried by him. His companions were his faithful overseer and old-time servant Baxter, two natives, and a boy called Wylie. But nature had said, *Thou Shalt Not*, for it provided water only in handfuls in that vast desert. It was a new Ilium to be conquered, and but this handful of Greeks to do it—this one Greek to do it. One hundred and forty miles and no water; six days and only three quarts of water; 150 miles and no water; 650 miles from the western coast, and but three weeks' provisions at starvation rates,—these are parts of the record telling of what that journey was. The heart of

Baxter failed him, and he wished to return; but Eyre knew only the one word *Forward!* and Baxter stood by him. But Baxter was never to reach the coast, nor yet turn back. Like many another pilgrim, he stopped half-way; he made the great compromise: for the cowardly natives murdered him and ran away, taking the bulk of the provisions with them, and Baxter was left there alone with no sod or mother earth over him, but wrapped in a blanket under the open sky. No grave could they dig in the barren rock, and they left him there alone,—

> "No useless coffin enclosed his breast,
> Nor in sheet nor in shroud we wound him,
> But he lay like a warrior taking his rest,
> With his martial cloak around him."

And only Eyre and the boy Wylie were left. But they struggled on. We know from his diary of what Eyre felt, but what of that boy Wylie? That young and faithful hero. He suffered as did his master, and he endured; he ate horse-flesh and kangaroo; he never faltered, till at Doubtful Bay they were taken on board the *Mississippi* and cared for ere they started again for Perth. After twelve months of constant hardship, Eyre and the boy Wylie entered Albany, and the tremendous task was over. And we went past that spot where he looked out on the sea, in a fashionable steamer with all the comforts of life about us, enjoying something of the fruits of his labours, and of those who went before him and came after him in the field of Australian exploration. Over that same track, twenty-nine years after, John Forrest, the indomitable West Australian explorer, travelled, and suffered anxiety, if not hardships, almost as great as Eyre. Forrest's journal shows to what danger he and his party were exposed. "This is the third day without a drop of water for the horses, which are in a frightful state," is no uncommon kind of statement to find in his journal.' "The horses, which four days ago were strong and in good condition, now appeared only skeletons—eyes sunk, nostrils dilated, and thoroughly exhausted. . . . During the last sixty hours I have only had five hours' sleep, and have been in a continual state of anxiety." We pass the cliffs from 300 to 400 feet high as we near the Hampton Range, of which John Forrest wrote as he journeyed : " Continuing for four miles, we reached the cliffs, which fell perpendicularly into the sea, and, although grand in the extreme, were terrible to look upon. After looking very cautiously over the precipice, we all ran back quite terror-stricken at the dreadful view." At both ends of the Hampton Range these cliffs extend for 100 miles or more. Looking at Mr. Forrest's chart, there is seen such remarks as these at frequent intervals : " Grassy plains," " rich grassy plains," " rich loamy soil beautifully grassed," " beautiful grassy country," " splendid feed," " grassy undulating country." This is pleasant reading. This would excite the pioneer spirit and the avarice of the land-getter. But let us pause. For here are ominous lines : "The land from Eucla to the head of the bight is entirely destitute of water," " chains of salt lakes," " rock water-holes." The last appears very many times, but from Esperance Bay to Spencer's Gulf there is not a river marked, not a stream, only " rock water-holes," etc., holding from two to thirty gallons of water.

John Henry Newman, when he first walked the streets of Rome, said, " And this is Rome—is Rome." Prince Albert Victor quotes this in his journal on his visit to Australia, and says, "And this is Australia—is Australia."[*] I may be permitted to say, as I look on this historic coast, "This is Western Australia—is Western Australia." For indeed it has been to me one of the most vivid points of interest in the southern hemisphere—interesting because men have said it is uninteresting; because it is backward; because it is held in disdain by the more successful and more populated colonies, and because it is unique in its constitutional conditions. During dinner on Christmas Day in Melbourne, a lady said to me : "Oh, you are going to Western Australia, are you? Why, people are considered rich over there if they have a £10 note, and you are looked up to if you have half a crown in pocket-money always by you. The colony is a hundred years behind the times, and a long hundred years, too." "Worse than Tasmania?" I ventured to ask; for it is the ungenerous custom to say such things of Tasmania. "Oh, much worse," was the reply.

Well, long ago I gave up putting faith in such statements, which are made without malice no doubt, but have just the piquancy of disdain about them that cuts deep. Now I am not a West Australian, and I have no axes to grind in that colony; but I shall have something to say before I am done about its so-called inconsequence. I have been to Western Australia, and I am ready to give evidence according to my experience, and not beyond it, without imagination and with sane facts. I am ready to take oath that it cost me as much to live at a hotel in Perth as it would at the

---

[*] While these pages are going through the press the death of Prince Albert Victor, the Duke of Clarence and Avondale, is announced. The deplorable occurrence has called forth the utmost sympathy from Australia, where he and Prince George were received with much enthusiasm and remembered with loyal affection.

Grosvenor in Sydney or the Langham in London. I
am prepared to attest that I paid 10s. a day at a little
place called Beverley, where the train hitches up at
night, and goes on in the morning. I am willing to
bear testimony that at Albany I was as much in
the hands of the spoiler as I ever was in the biggest
cities of the world. Rich with half a crown in your
pocket! Bring just as much money to Western Australia
as you would to London, Sydney, New York, or Paris.
You shall find that you will need it. Cabbies in Perth
are the same as cabbies elsewhere in the world, and
perhaps a little worse than they are in some places.
Now I am not, I hope, "green" in the ways of the wicked
world. I have been inveigled and despoiled in many
places in the universe, but I did not find that I was
superior to the demands and seductions of the caterers
to public needs in Western Australia. I came away
humbled in many respects, though I had not gone there
with any false pride or insistence. I merely was prepared for anything; but I am ready to be a witness to
the fact that Western Australia in many things is not
behind Tasmania, or Victoria, or England, or even an
American watering-place. Trust not that man or woman
who says you will be rich in Western Australia with £10
in your pocket.

It is near sunset time at Albany, in Western Australia.
I wander forth from the Freemasons' Hotel in search of
relaxation, and to look for all that may be worth the
seeing. Whither? Just as the smoke of my after-dinner
cigar blows. Southward, is it? Then southward shall
it be. Along a terrace that slopes to George's Sound
moves the commissioned traveller; his thoughts bent
in no direction; his mood a lazy one; his activity put

off until the morrow, when there's work to be done, people to be seen, notes to be taken, and general conditions to be spelled out. Unconsciously, as I stroll down the street, I become possessed of a feeling that I am in an atmosphere that is familiar, yet strange, too. What does it mean, this old-time scent in the nostrils, this long-gone hand upon one? When? where? I never was at Albany before. When saw I this basin of brine shut in by hills and high shore, and these stony streets that lead off among the hills into the untrodden wilds? Never before. Yet the tide of years rolls backward, and a host of recollections come—recollections that belong to the time when I scarce was big enough to wear an Eton jacket, or to be profane with my first Latin oath. I am in a haze of nebulous memories; of long-past impressions. Beyond banks and law offices I go; on to the big building on the side of the hill, which combines court, customs house, post office, telegraph office, police station, and British resident's office; and then I stand still and look round. I am not clear yet, though there is no attempt to think.

I retrace my steps as if by instinct to a little shop on the street that I have trod, and there I stand still. A moment's pause, the mists pass, the nebular becomes clear sky, half-shadows float away—I have found it. Now let them laugh who will. I tell my tale, as it pleases me to do. All this has come about because of a dozen sugar toys. I make my own impeachment—a dozen sugar toys was the keynote to all I saw and thought upon in Western Australia. Years ago—five, ten, fifteen, twenty, twenty-five—shall I go on? No. But in the region of a quiet childhood just such sugar toys entered. Sugar men and women, and dogs, and bulls of Bashan, and full-blossomed angels, used to stand in the windows of a little country town, and a little boy used to go there to look at them when he hadn't money, and when he had he entered in and was satisfied. Now the secret is plain;—that combination Government building standing on a side hill, and the sugar toys, belong equally to a slower time. This and that. The smell of the fresh air is the same, the quiet streets, the wild flowers in the fields, and the ding-dong of the church bell—it is the same, yet not the same. That belonged to an age of which it was a natural part. This is not "jump to the time"; it is a lagging behind, a languorous step in the march of progress. That place was called—well, no matter; and this is Albany.

The shop window is what Western Australia is just now. The currants piled up, the sugar men—I thought such sugar men had died the death, and that all boys, and, of course, all trade, had outgrown them—are signs of what Western Australia is. One could not see such an old-fashioned window elsewhere in Australia, nor in America, nor on the Continent—only, perhaps, in some buried, and half-forgotten, town in England. But this is Australia—is Australia: this is a land of progress. From these sugar men and dogs and things I turn to other things, to houses, people, buildings, places of labour, and general living. And I have my key. Do not despise it; it will open many a door to places of observation and speculation in Western Australia.

Let us leave this window, and move on towards the mountain whereon a flagstaff is. There is a view to be had on climbing it I make no doubt, so I go slowly up the main street, past houses built like gaols, many of them with no eaves; upright, unhomelike, bare; on, into thicket of banksia, sarsaparilla, and the places of boulders. I did not know the direct road up the hill, and so set my face towards the top and went at it. For an after-dinner jaunt it was now becoming something severe. But it was pleasant, too, for I seemed to be climbing hills that I knew a quarter of a century ago. And every step upward gave one a more commanding prospect. But I will not use the vantage until the summit is reached. Up over boulders, tumbled as if by some giant hand in an age when the world was being adjusted to the needs of all time, I go. Five hundred, a thousand, fifteen hundred feet, another mass of rock, and then— the summit! Now look round. It is worth the climbing, it is worth the time. The sun is setting. The clouds are purple on the horizon-line.

There are hills beneath, on which there is a long white gash, as though some burning plough had been driven down their sides and had made this ashy wound. But let the eye sweep to the left. Will the picture ever fade from the mind? I do not think so. The surprise was too great. We had come into the harbour in the early morning, and we had not seen the beautiful entrance. But there it was in the gathering twilight. Two great gates open, and in the centre, two lovely sentinel islands. Against one of them a fleecy cloud lay,—spray cast high up against its rocky sides. Away still further to the left, a bay, with white beach, stole in for miles, and I could count every pretty indentation and curve. But what a congregation of curves it was! And what a wonder of dramatic composition in the scene!

For behind me and that endless sea, with its rocky embrasures, there rolled away into silence the sombre plains, lit up here and there by bush fires. One, two, three, four in the half-circle, and not a house to be seen outside the town there at our feet. Yes, there is one house, there are two, perhaps more, but so small they seem lost in the lonely immensity. It might be said of this scene, as William Cullen Bryant said of his loved prairies, "They stretch in undulations far away, boundless and beautiful." From this height all the crudities, all the irregularities are softened, and we stand, as it were, outside the world, and look upon it. Beautiful, did I say? What! With thought of starving, thirsting explorers, defeated pioneers, poison land, and uninhabitable territories before us? Beautiful! This long rolling waste, it would almost seem, was only intended to be gazed at, not lived upon. But men live on it as they live in the Stony Desert in the barren west of New South Wales. See off there where lies a lake—Ten-mile Lake it is called. This side of that lake there are steam ploughs at work, and the land is being reclaimed, with what success remains to be proven.

Near to us is the town of Albany—here, just at our feet. It lies closely together; it is built with a kind of easy compactness to a certain line, and then it ends abruptly, and "the big paddock" comes. Protected on one side by Mount Melville, and on the other by Mount Clarence on which I stand, it has seemed to grow according to its natural position, and with a sense of what is required of it as a strategical point. The streets are well laid out,—seven running almost parallel between mountain and mountain, and others are leading at right angles towards the bush. But all, save one, appear only to run to the edge of the town, and then they stop short, as if afraid to venture into the wilds. That *one* goes over the side of Mount Melville, and skirts the edges of the silent waste, as if it feared to trust itself to the thirsty unknown.

Albany has such a climate as has no place else on the continent. Bracing, nerve-making, it seems as if it did not belong to Australia at all, but was a genial bit of Scotland set down here as a gift from the Old Land. And here I must record my opinion that the climate of Western Australia is altogether the best on the continent. The day I landed in Albany it was 98° in the shade, and I felt it no more than I would have felt 80° in Sydney. The day I arrived in Perth it was 106° in the shade, and I suffered from it no more than I should 85° in Sydney—less, in fact. For in the worst heat in Western Australia I felt able to work, was nerved to work; and who ever felt impelled to labour at 80° in Sydney? If any, speak, for him have I offended. As I walked down the streets of Perth that day of January I felt my moustache like fire as my lips touched it; my clothes seemed burning, too hot almost for the touch; yet there was no physical depression. And what seems more curious is the fact that, in the northern or tropical part of the colony, the atmosphere is dry; not moist and unhealthy, as in northern Queensland. There are here no tropical rains, no downpours of five inches in a day—would for the country's sake it had at present. Hot and dry is the record. Were there but water with the dry atmosphere the colony would have tremendous advantages; but it is "the thirstiest land of all the lands of thirst," as the explorers, as all miners, have found. Even as out on the Tibbooburra Road, in New South Wales, the bones of gold-seekers bleached in the sun until removed into nameless graves, so are bones bleaching now in the hot land up north known as the Kimberley district. Nature has not been prodigal of her gifts to Western Australia. Nearly as far as the eye can see about Albany the land is of little worth. And there are few who venture to turn it to account. Albany exists, as it were, like a camel in the desert. Yet it has its source of growth and sustenance in the really good land that lies up towards Beverley—good agricultural land, on which there are grown twenty bushels of wheat to the acre. It lives by the occasional squatter of the north and west, and by the incidental farmer, who finding a good bit of country here and there, seizes upon it, works it, and makes Albany his market and his commercial capital. The wonder is that Albany is so large, for indeed there seems little to support it outside of what the Government renders to it in payment of its officers' salaries. I have never heard any one speak ill of the town of Albany. It may not be handsome, but it is quaint and modest, well situated and clean. It may not possess much nervous activity, but the traveller does not care about that. It offers kind hands to the wayfarer, and a simple, unprofessional hospitality. A great city I do not think it can ever be; it has not the background of resources to make it so. Only minerals can make it a great place. A strategic point, a valuable coaling station, a fine and beautiful port, an important *entrepôt*, a sanatorium it can and will be; but beyond that all is in the womb of time—in the wild area of speculation.

The night is falling fast, and finding the road that leads to the town from the mountain-top, I stroll down in the still evening, well satisfied that I have beheld one of the most striking scenes that Australia shows. Equal to it, and exceeding it, are Govett's Leap, the Katoomba and Leura and Wentworth Falls, Bulli, and Macquarie Pass in New South Wales; Mount Wellington, at Hobart; and the Red Bluff on the Cairns range in Queensland. But this scene at Albany is unique and inspiring. On the spot where I am, Vancouver stood just one hundred years ago, and looked out on the picturesque loneliness, the beautiful barrenness; and here, too, came

D'Entrecasteaux, Captain Matthew Flinders, and Surgeon Bass, and spied out the land, and told their tale of possibilities. But not till 1860, when Major Warburton explored the coast, and 1862, when Captain Delessier was impressed with the not irreclaimable nature of the land, was anything done to settle that long irregular line of land which stretches from Cape Leeuwin to Cape Catastrophe. And when it was discovered that something could be done, it was done but slowly—what encouragement to settlement was there? For hundreds of miles there stretched sheer cliffs, and ports were impossible. It was not till 1867 that Port Eucla, about 260 miles west of Fowler's Bay, was discovered; but the Port Eucla of now is not far advanced from the Port Eucla of then. It is a good harbour for shipping; and if its use rested upon one thing alone, it would be worth the money expended on it. It was the means of saving John Forrest and his party in 1870. Were it not for the timely help given there by the steamer sent to meet him, he and his companions would in all probability be sleeping in wilds that have never been reclaimed;—for even now at Eucla there are only eight whites, and the land is only known for 100 miles back, and that land is almost waterless. Was ever such a stretch of uninhabited coast? Not to the east from Port Albany must we turn our eyes, but towards the north and west. To the space west of the 121st meridian of longitude, it would appear, lies the future of Western Australia; between the 121st and the 130th meridian bides a land over which no explorer has stretched hands of blessing. It may be that it will have the same fortunate fate as what was once known as the great American desert, but of that we cannot tell. We can but proceed on what we know, and the difference between the alkali plains of the United States and

Canada, and this vast region here defined is, that the former have water, and the latter has little or none; the one is flanked on either side by splendid land, and the other is not. No; let the prospector and pioneer speak:—

The Song of the Desert Pioneer.

I.

How shall we sing of watered plain,
    Of birds of song, and golden days?
How shall a simple gladness drain
    Through silence of these arid ways?
How shall the hand be raised to bless,
    When Nature with red fevered eyes
Breathes anger through a wilderness,
    And sets a furnace in the skies?

II.

How shall the thousand cattle feed
    Upon a waterless expanse?
How shall we plough or scatter seed
    In bondage to an awful chance?
We die with gold in handfuls thrust
    'Gainst lips that madly thirst; we rain
Down curses on the desert dust,
    And chide the heavens in our pain.

III.

What worth the altar if the fire
    Be not provided? if we stand
Like priests beside a flameless pyre,
    Our sacrifices 'neath our hand?
How can we sing where all things seem
    But half completed—where the sign
Of death o'ershadows the Divine,—
    Where life is one short anguished dream?

Is the picture too strong, too realistic? Ask the settlers who have ventured on the edge of the district east of the 123rd meridian of longitude; ask Alexander Forrest, who, in 1871, travelled out to the Hampton plains; or John Forrest, who went all the way across in 1870 and in 1875; ask Eyre through his journal, Warburton through his, and the Gregorys through theirs. All the evidence bids the settler, the investor, and the politician to put little hope in that region east of the 121st meridian and south of the 20th parallel of latitude. The space that is thus excepted from the ban is the Kimberley district. It appears to have possibilities; but of that hereafter, when we shall consider the conditions under which the colony moves on its humble way.

CHAPTER XIX.

WESTERN AUSTRALIA IN 1889-90 (*Continued*).

NORTHWARD FROM ALBANY TO PERTH.

I FANCY I should not have visited Western Australia just now, had it not been that a railway was opened up between Albany and the capital. I had but a limited time to spare, and when I found that there was no longer the long coach ride of 350 miles to take, or the old coasting journey to undergo, I determined to attempt what, under other circumstances, might have been put off till a more convenient season. Western Australia is isolated now. What that isolation was before there was a railway, can only be understood properly by those who have been in the colony. Even now the place has a far-away feeling—an antique loneliness that ranges from the quay at King George's Sound to the Cambridge Gulf. It is but a step from the hotel to the railway station at Albany, and at eight o'clock in the morning I am off to Perth by a land-grant railway. The West Australian Land Company, Limited, have constructed the line, receiving 12,000 acres of land for every mile constructed, the land to be selected within a belt of 40 miles on either side of the line, but with half the frontage to the railway reserved to the Government. This is on the plan of the Canadian Pacific Railway. The

Canadian Company received 25,000,000 acres of land and £5,000,000 for the construction. This £5,000,000 was, however, supplemented ultimately by another £1,000,000. As to the wisdom of the policy, it is not quite easy, nor is it my place here, to decide; but it can scarcely be condemned offhand, since the custom has been one that is followed by many countries. There are things to be said in its favour. It has been proven that governments are never able to utilise forces, to economise, or to manage a commercial undertaking, as does a private firm or company. Enterprise on the part of a government, if not undignified, is, at any rate, too little in accord with red-tape requirements. In land-grant railways there is the danger of monopoly; but even that, as in the case of the Canadian Pacific Railway, is often reduced to a *minimum*. The Dominion railway company sells its land at the same price as the Government, and it has made more successful efforts to secure settlement than the Government. The alternative block system prevents "picking out the eyes of the land," and as all institutions that cater for the public must ultimately bow to the will of that public, so must a railway company. Extortionate rates and poor accommodation can only exist for a time. It is now necessary for a railway company to pursue the seductive policy of ordinary commercial organisations.

As to the advantages which this West Australian railway company has gained I cannot speak. I only know that it is a very excellent service, and that the line is better constructed than the Government line from Beverley to Freemantle, with which it connects, thus completing the communication between Albany and Perth. The carriages on the Company's line are excellently kept, and the guards and conductors are attentive and good-natured. All the railway stations in the colony are connected by telephone, and business is transacted with considerable dispatch, so far as the body of officers of the line are concerned. But one must be careful not to trust too much to the subordinates. Luggage has a trick of going astray, yes, actually going astray on this —shall I call it?—backwoods line. Two of us in one compartment, who had our luggage stamped with our names in full, who saw it carefully bestowed at Albany, and taken off at Beverley, where the train stops at night, arrived at Perth, each with a bag missing. Mine came in all right, however, next day.

It might be well for the Government and the West Australian Company to consider whether a through train would not pay better in the end than the service now rendered. We start from Albany in the morning, get to Beverley by seven o'clock in the evening, and there wait till the next morning at seven o'clock, arriving in Perth at about two o'clock p.m. I started from Albany on a Saturday morning, and was obliged to spend Sunday in Beverley, getting to Perth on Monday afternoon. This quite suited me, as I wished to see the district, but I fancy it would not suit most travellers. It suits also mine hosts of the hotels in Beverley; but I do not quite see that we have any reason to be glad of that, especially when some of those hosts, as I have said, charge at the rate of 10s. a day. I could not discover the reason for the present system, except it is economy. But, if one might venture to advise a Government and a Railway Company, Limited, it could be said to them that there is such a thing as being penny-wise and pound-foolish, and that the day must come when what they hesitate to do now will be forced upon them. As it is, all mails and passengers are delayed twelve hours. The Government, I have been told, is not averse to a through-train scheme; it is the Company that objects. The reason assigned for this objection is that the Company wish the travellers by the line to see all the land *en route*, which they could not do if part of the journey were made by night. This is not the sort of thing expected of colonial business men. And, indeed, the view obtained by night or day, as we travel, would not be calculated to inspire great anticipations, or to induce investment. Over forty miles of the journey from Albany there is one long scrub, one stretch of unhappy country.

Now and then through the grass trees and the eucalypti one sees a great patch of snow, with the sun at 100° in the shade. Now we come full upon another, and skirt it.

> "Strange thought that in this angry burning land,
> My fevered eyes should sweep an icy plain."

Yes, there it was, white and cool, with tracks upon it from the hoofs of cattle and the feet of men. The yellow cabbage-tree flower is gleaming near, flanked by the white-and-green banksia, and a blossoming gum-tree is full of a regal beauty. Snow! Nothing so comforting. This is the whiteness of a salt lake, dry and deathly. Look where you will on the maps of explorers in Western Australia, and you will find the same tale—" salt lake," "chains of salt lakes." It suggests the desert and the valueless wild. The land, however, is no worse than many parts of New South Wales—it is, indeed, vastly better than much that one sees between Sydney and Bourke. The most of it looks far better than the Mount Browne district, and it can and does support life.

What kind of life that is I am not prepared to disclose.

A Chinaman Gardener.

But I enquired right and left, and not without avail. The first thing that struck me was the number of tents erected along the line and the few houses that one saw. But I answered the question to myself immediately, for in my nostrils was a well-known perfume—one that I had inhaled in other lands—the "faint, sweet smell of the sandal-tree." These tents were the homes of the sandal-wood cutters. And here were the piles of sandal-wood, hundreds of tons here, thousands of tons altogether, ready to be shipped to China for incense and for making into boxes. Thus it is, that this new southern civilisation provides the old Orient with a means for preserving its heathenism—at a cost of about £34,000 a year. What sweeter thing is there than the incense of fresh perfumed woods rising up in the pure air of morning? I doubt not that the incense of Kyphi was pleasant to the nostrils of the old Egyptians; but one English rose would be worth it all. The antique worlds are welcome to their decoctions of rosin wine, juniper berries, aromatic bark, mastic, grapes, and honey. One whiff of a buckwheat field, one waft from a pine tree, one puff from the sandal in the open, is worth all the perfumes of Arabia, all the spicy altar fires of the Land of the Sacred Crocodile. For the Chinaman lives on rotten fish and eggs and a pinch of rice; and the Egyptian fed on onions and garlic, while the priests waxed fat, and the sacred drones drew off the life and vigour of the land, for the sake of power and their own fat larders.

These Western Australians have food to eat that the wretched Egyptian never knew of, or the Chinaman either until he came among us. It is better to live on damper in the wilds of West Australia, than to have eaten papyrus pith and lotus seeds in the shadow of the Temple of Ammon. It is better to ride in a second-class carriage on a gauge of 3 feet 6 inches through the poison land of this new colony, than to be the ruthless soldier, bloody with his toil, dragging captives behind the chariot of a Rameses, or the slave that bent beneath the blows of a follower of Osiris. Better even to get drunk as an Anglo-Saxon in the shade of this miserable public on the line, on liquor bought with hard-earned pence, than to swill from beakers of wine dispensed on some gala day, by a chief or king who wished to return thanks for booty to licentious Sechet. And yet these knots of drunken loafers about the railway stations and sidings are a sorry sight : the blear-eyed sandal-wood cutter, with his arm over the shoulder of a blackfellow, inducing him to have another " roll in "; drunken fathers and drunken sons arm-in-arm in this social infamy; overhead, the sky like burning metal ; beneath, the desolate reaches of this Australian scrub. But not quite desolation. Here is a patch of cultivated ground ; there runs a narrow road that leads to a small sheep station, and near by sits an honest selector on his horse. It is not so bad that it might not be worse.

But I must speak frankly, though it displease, and say that the average of intelligence among the lower classes of Western Australia, so far as I could see them, seemed very low. I talked with people in the carriages and at the railway station ; I watched them, and if observation goes for anything, I should say that there is a type of citizen in Western Australia which gives one little hope, for nearly all the people will soon be voters. Isolation, belated progress, narrow life, and no political or social teaching, have done their work, and torpid brain and low intelligence in the lower orders are the result. An old Government officer said to me that Western Australia was a place where a man might, without any difficulty, "get a clean shirt and a bellyful," and that, therefore, having neither to work hard nor to think hard, he had degenerated, and was hardly prepared for enlarged political conditions. Of this political element I shall have something to say hereafter. I must not touch the question here. But when we consider the low capacities of certain classes in Western Australia, we cannot wonder that the colony has gone its way with halting feet. Indeed, a ball and chain would seem to be upon the leg of progress there. This, I know, is an allusion that might be easily misunderstood, and misconstrued. I mean nothing more than that the world will say, as it has said, that Western Australia has lagged behind because she has had the convict element there somewhat recently, and her enlightenment can, therefore, come but slowly. Is it so?

Undoubtedly the convict element still exists in the colony. It makes itself felt; but that it is at present responsible for the slow progress of the country, is a thing to be discussed, and I fancy it wise to touch upon it here, for much depends upon it. Those who are best qualified to judge, say that the convict element has not been so great a bar to the inward progress of the colony as in other colonies, where the "lag" has occasionally attained to considerable social and political eminence. I am told that in Western Australia no convict has ever risen from the ruck, and that socially the evil influence is not felt. But all West Australians admit that convict settlement was a mistake. It might have been prevented, but the colony was so hard-up that, when the English Government sent out a batch of convicts to Freemantle in 1850, no objection was raised by the people; chiefly because they coveted the revival in trade it would give to the struggling, and even suffering, population ;—suffering, because there were no markets for produce, and trade was then, as it is largely now, one of exchange and barter, not sale and purchase. English gentlemen with large families came out and invested heavily, stocked farms, built houses, surrounded themselves with all the graces of civilised and refined life, and set to work to make homes and fortunes in an out-of-the-way and unrecognised colony. Strange tales are told of people camping with pianos and *bric-à-brac* under trees in lonely valleys ; of those who lived in their carriages for weeks ; of young gentlemen who went out on bush-prospecting tours in the costume of an English squire,—and all that. But in the Fifties their hearts had sunk, and men and women hailed anything that would give them a little life and commercial movement. It was a sorry yielding to exigency, a pitiful capitulation. Better to have starved as free colonists afar from the penal shame of England, than to have lent an assenting voice to a convict settlement in Western Australia. The West Australians have bitterly repented the act since, for come what will—come the pride of success and the glory of achievement, come wealth or honour, or anything soever—the unpleasant legend is engraven on all records, and remembered by every colonist, and every Englishman. It is of little use to leave out the fact from the Year Book of Western Australia ; the history of the place can only be read in the light which convict settlement lends, and the fact should be calmly faced, as it is in the other colonies that were once penal—Tasmania, New South Wales, and Queensland. But Western Australia, unlike the others, was a consenting party to the deed of penal commission. As Sir Malcolm Fraser, the present Administrator and Colonial Secretary, said in a speech made recently, " In

1850 the colony sold itself into bondage." It sold, too, on a basis of non-redemption.

It is not an uncommon thing to hear a man (I fear, with exaggeration) say, "I know nearly every man, woman, and child in the colony." The thirty-nine immigrant ships, in 1829, brought passengers to the number of 1,125, and money to the amount of £144,277; and yet in seventy years there are only forty times as many people. Compare Victoria, New South Wales, Queensland, and South Australia with it. Does it not appear that there are causes underlying convict settlement and everything else, to keep the colony back? That must in the nature of things strike one, and these causes I shall, later on, attempt to show in some detail, having already touched upon them. Along this 350 miles of railway line, there are only three places of any size at all—Beverley, York, and Guildford. Some of the stations are simply in the bush, backed by a public, and flanked by the tents of sandal-wood cutters. Here and there is a saw-mill; here and there a settler's home; now and then a fine bit of cultivation; and between York and Perth occasional vineyards, and a few fine farms. But the great body of the land is solitary or neglected. The two refreshment-rooms on the line, exclusive of the hotels at Beverley, York, and elsewhere, are at any rate clean and orderly. One was sure of a good bit of "boiled," and a pudding of modest, but healthy, quality. At Chidlow's Well I bought figs for twopence a dozen—beautiful ripe figs, grown on the plot of ground near the railway station. There is land in Western Australia that will grow anything, from hardy apples to the tropical banana. As for wine, I tasted some that would compare with the best made by Costella, Lindeman, or Hardy in the other colonies. The following fruits may be, and are, grown in the colony with success: grapes, apples, oranges, lemons, pears, figs, peaches, apricots, Cape gooseberries, plums, loquats, bananas, quinces, strawberries, melons, mulberries, pomegranates, gooseberries, cherries, currants, almonds, medlars, guavas, and olives. All of these, bananas included, will grow in the southern part of the colony, and there is no reason why fruit should not become as successful an industry in Western Australia as it is in Tasmania. But as yet the people do not even grow fruit and vegetables for their own use. There is splendid potato land all along the railway line, yet there are only about 2,000 tons of potatoes grown in the colony. The rest consumed are brought from New Zealand and elsewhere. There is plenty of land that will grow anything, and there is little in the southern part of the colony on which a Scotchman, a Swede, or a German could not make a living, excepting, of course, the poison land. And as for the last-named, I met three squatters from the Geraldton way, all of whom had coped successfully with the poison plant, and had eradicated it. About half way from Albany to Beverley there is splendid land.

Seldom in my life have I been more wearied, than when I got into Beverley on one Saturday night at seven o'clock. All day in a close compartment with four other passengers, I had come under the burning sun. The hospitality to be met with at the Settlers' Arms, Beverley, is not ostentatious, but it is wholesome, and grateful enough to a tired man. Remembrances of some weary nights spent in bush taverns and on the open plains of the other colonies, made this modest habitation princely by comparison. Yet this was not the Far West of Western Australia, but near the very centre of her life; to be placed in relation to Perth as Bathurst is to

Sydney. Beverley is a collection of a couple of dozen houses, three of which are hotels, and one a parsonage. The prevailing tint of the place is red ; not that rose tint that one finds at Jeypore, not that inexpressible and tender colour which makes the great Indian city a very paradise to the eye, but the dull red of the ironstone, the dreary and Typhonian red of a Maine barn ;— for Beverley, like most other towns in Western Australia, is built of red brick, made from the very soil on which the houses are built. Old-fashioned enough these towns and villages look ; and in the conjugation of progress to be spoken of as in the past tense. We drive through lonely streets to the old-fashioned hotel, and are given the luxury of a bath : next, a meal of ham and eggs, destructive prawns,—as some of the party found,—mutton, and plenty of milk and good tea, and then a smoke and rest outside, under the warm and misty moon.

I cannot soon forget that night's quiet ; the wheat-field from which the grain had been stripped in front of us ; the long dusty road at either hand ; the little orchard of mulberry and apple trees near by, and the slow monotone of the old settler at my side. He had trod this very road, bare-footed, driving oxen thirty years ago, and now he is a mill-owner, and the possessor of valuable land. Many a tale did I get from this self-made man as we travelled, for he was a good smoker, and while he smoked he talked. He was full of memories of the days when soap was eightpence a pound, and flour sixpence a pound, and when such boys as he had with him went many a night to bed hungry, because there were not enough sixpences in the house to get the necessary amount of flour. " In them days," he said, " we had little to eat and much to do, and we never knew when we'd starve to death ; and as for the women folk —God knows it was rough on 'em !

Many a mother of us chaps went out to work like a nigger; for there ain't none can work like a good mother with a family of children, is there, sir?" I assented to that proposition. I had seen women in new countries like this, with lustreless eyes and empty breasts, with sunken cheeks and lined faces, with life drawn from them, as it were, by some great exhaust-machine. I thought of those I had noticed along the line that day with staring and meaningless eyes, and children— the offspring of such—with inane and effortless faces, doomed to be hewers of wood and drawers of water throughout their lives. I recalled the conversation of one of these women with this very man beside me, as she sat with her two children in our compartment. She held the child, heedlessly, carelessly, as it half slept, its head hanging over her arm unsupported, its mouth open; and the boy of five stared in front of him and said nothing, too stupid to be mischievous. Here was a woman who had lived at least thirty-five years, yet she was but a child, and talked as a child. Thus,—

"I never was to Albany before. Albany they say is goin' ahead. I dunno. I have an uncle lives up Goolga way. I ain't seen him for fourteen years. Maybe he's forgot me. I dunno. There's a good bit of change since I was down this way. I never see the ocean before. Lord serve! You know Jim Davis; he be uncle to us —he. We won't see him this time, will we, Teddy— you?" And Teddy roused himself from his five years' stupor, kicked his heels over against the seat for reply, and then was stupid and silent again. The woman's lips never closed over her yellow teeth, the eyes never lighted, the mouth never smiled, the cheeks only creased when mirth came—if it could be called mirth!

"Did you hear Mr. Crane had his arm broke—he?

No? Well, his wife got a telegraph from him last night, and some one said his arm was broke." The settler assured her he had seen Mrs. Crane that morning, and she had said nothing about it.

"Well, she got a telegraph; one of my cousins seen the boy hand it to her. My cousin missed the train last week going down to Wagin Lake—he! This train goes shaky like, don't it? Lord serve!" So she wandered on through these shreds and patches of senseless thought—she whose life had been bounded by a circle of a hundred miles, and who had brought children into the world, a child herself in all save growth and function—nothing more.

I would not be so unfair as to say this is a type of the poorer class of West Australian, but I do say that I saw a good number of such, and, travelling, one meets all kinds of people, and is able to strike the average somewhere. I have seen just the same type in the interior of the other colonies, only it was far away from the centre, and this was near. In justice, though, I must say that a year ago this was not in one sense near to the centre, because there was no railway. I only show these things, because it will give an idea of how primitive, how slow, how nerveless is the life in this colony, even while it is bidding for a more active, freer, and healthier future.

It was pleasant to wake up in the morning and feel the simple life of an agricultural district about you; to go into the garden, and pick and eat mulberries until hands and faces were stained, out of sheer childishness, and for the sake of memory; then to wander into the district, and talk to the farmers and selectors, and learn how little they hoped for, how barren were their ambitions; and to return, feeling that the most you had learned was, that the land would grow twenty bushels of wheat to the acre, and that fruit would succeed if it were cared for, and encouraged. But who grows fruit in this fine district? Very few indeed. The spirit of agriculture is not, it would seem, properly in the people. They choose rather to cut sandal-wood, and earn a passing and precarious livelihood, than to make homes and cultivate farms. A humble living is easily made in Western Australia, and that seems to satisfy the many. This sandal-wood industry, after all, does more harm than good. It draws off the selector from his selection, and the small farmer from his homestead, and the country suffers in the long run.

On Monday morning we were off through the hardly-waked little town to the railway station, and crept on over a pretty rough line past Mokine, Clockine, Chidlow's Well, where we had dinner; Sawyers Valley, where there was a saw-mill; Midland Junction, Guildford, and then Perth. York is about 21 miles from Beverley, and is situated in a fine agricultural district. It has some good buildings, but its high stone walls give the place a prison-like aspect. Guildford has the same failing, though the latter place has an English appearance. Quiet stone churches, vine-covered homes, pretty valleys, the Swan River winding by, and the little farms about, make a picture more like an English village than may be found anywhere else in Australasia, save Tasmania. One of the largest landowners along the line is Mr. J. H. Monger of York. He has a fine residence, and is a central figure in the district, as are Mr. Samuel Hamersley and Dr. A. R. Waylen at Guildford. The latter has a large vineyard, and has been one of the most successful vinegrowers in the colony. The Hamersleys are one of the oldest and most respected families in the colony.

Haliburton, their freehold estate of 20,000 acres, is one of the best farms in the colony.

The first sight of the Swan River, near Guildford, is not very impressive, but the stream rises, until at Perth it is no longer a river, but a large lake three or four miles wide. The Darling Range of hills gives relief to Guildford and the surrounding country. The Blackwood Range, in the south, has several fine peaks not far from Albany ; but the highest peak in all the colony is not quite 3,000 feet. The appearance of the colony generally is flat and little diversified. It has nothing like the Australian Alps or the Blue Mountains.

CHAPTER XX.

WESTERN AUSTRALIA IN 1889-90 *(Continued).*

PERTH, THE CAPITAL—FREEMANTLE—MINERALS AND LANDS.

PERTH is not inviting at first sight, but it improves on acquaintance. There is nothing of "bounce" about it; it is built for use, and that use is an humble one. Architecture? Look at the Roman Catholic bishop's palace, it is like a remnant of past glory—Corinthian pillars and portico, balconies and broad front; but come near it, how forlorn and dilapidated it looks! The floor of the portico is rotten and full of huge cracks, the pillars are discoloured and unstable-looking, and when you knock at the door, a feeling of loneliness comes upon you, for the sounds appear to re-echo through empty rooms. The cathedral hard by seems just as careworn and spiritless. Is this a sign of Perth the progressive? Is this an evidence of the energy of the colony that is applying for responsible government? Let us not be unjust. First impressions may be wrong. The bishop who lives in that palace is one of the most hardworking, self-sacrificing, and genuine men in Australia; as witness the Subiaco Boys' School, the Perth Girls' School, the Roman Catholic Girls' Orphanage, the Roman Catholic Boys' Orphanage, and Bishop Salvado's native mission at New Norcia. There is a good work going on under the bishop's guidance. We must not judge the meat of the nut by the shell.

Look again. There is the Town Hall of red brick, with a bold clock tower, and as bold but plain a front— built by convict labour. In it are the Municipal Offices and Law Chambers. There is behind it, and attached to

POSTAL AND TELEGRAPH OFFICE, PERTH.

it, a one-storey building. That is the Parliament building, a shy and pious-looking structure. The architecture is nothing, but there the rulers meet, and there is turned the heavy wheel of State. And the place is equal to the needs of a colony yet in its swaddling-clothes. There is beside this hall of legislation an antique place which looks still more pious. It is that which once was a cathedral, but now forsaken for the more sumptuous building beside. Enter this new cathedral. It shows progress. Its large surpliced choir well trained, its "advanced ritual," its "high ambitions," its "lively faith," all tell of vigour and other things. And the refined and devoted Bishop Parry carries goodness with him wherever he goes. Another look about : there is a rather formidable building at the end of St. George's Terrace—situated, as the Treasury Buildings are, at the head of Collins Street, Melbourne. It was an old barracks; now it is devoted to the more peaceful purpose of education. There is a small but important-looking building " set on an hill " ; that is the Hospital. There are a few bank buildings, stately and well builded, and one or two private residences of external repute, but the catalogue is limited.

Is that all ? Have we exhausted Perth, its architecture, its beauty, its suggestiveness? Come down with me across St. George's Terrace, straight to the water's edge. Few cities are granted a nobler sheet of water at their doors ; saving Sydney no city in Australia has such a pretty foreground. The Brisbane River does not bear the same beautiful relation to Brisbane as the Swan River does to Perth. Who could have thought that the insignificant stream at Guildford could open into this glorious expanse of water two or three miles wide ? It is, in fact, a bay curving round a picturesque shore, flanking the hill Ann Eliza, and running away in stately fashion to Freemantle, called, as it travels, by such names as Fresh Water Bay, Rocky Bay, etc. Let us walk along the esplanade, past the yacht-club's house, past the rowing-club's house, by snug homes, until we come to this dilapidated building with pillars, belonging to past generations. The early West Australians must have had a mania for pillared architecture, for many of the old buildings, public and private, have these ancient porticoes. But this old building, what could it have been? It is now the Supreme Court building; it was once a commissariat store; and it looks only like that now.

One step further, and we pass into the Botanical Gardens, which are not equal to those of any of the other colonies, but give a promise of a future. Let us move beyond. In front of them are the new Government buildings, in which are the Treasury, the Lands, the Attorney-General's, and other offices. The building is not completed. It is a very plain structure—too plain. A little more taste could have been displayed without the expenditure of any more money. One can hardly understand why a colony, the heat of which is as great in summer as that of Ceylon,—and greater,—should neglect to erect buildings with colonnades. Brisbane has not failed in that respect, and places like Townsville and Rockhampton have not forgotten that they are in tropical regions.

But we have saved the best to the last, for now we see through the trees a turreted building, with colonnades and bold and pleasing front; a stately, yet home-like residence; such a house as a wealthy country gentleman in England would build, and situated in luxuriant foliage: broad gravel walks, verdant lawns, rare and beautiful trees, well-kept gardens with a number of flowers in them, and a little orchard, the fruit of which, I had the opportunity of discovering, was delicious. Nothing in Western Australia struck one more pleasantly than this unpretending, yet admirably builded, vice-regal residence. At the present time, the duties of Governor are performed by Sir Malcolm Fraser, the Colonial Secretary. While

I was in Perth, more people crossed the threshold of Government House than had done so for many a day, for with the departure of Sir Frederick Broome, the late Governor, went also a great deal of the bitterness and anxiety of faction, which had its origin in the strife between Chief-Justice Onslow and the Governor. The colony was divided between the two contending parties, and the community is so small, that the agitation unsettled social relations to an extent hard to be understood by outsiders. I could feel the embers smouldering under my feet while there ;—I was on the after-swell of the storm.

One night, in the interstices of talks on political subjects and spying out the land, I joined a party to go crab-fishing. It was amusing sport. With a line, a bit of meat, and a hand-net, we captured the blue-and-brown-backs by the dozen, and in the dark afterwards we had the pleasure of eating the fruits of our labours boiled. To me the most enjoyable part of the excursion was the sail over the bay to Sandy Point. The best view of the city is obtained from it. The town rises from the shore with enough trees to give relief and colour. And on the shore itself are a couple of breweries, suggestive of aids to the ascent of Mount Ann Eliza, 300 feet up, where a fine prospect may be had. A small building among the gums and bamboos is pointed out as an alms-house, where indigent and helpless West Australians resort. The Freemantle Road, which runs round Mount Eliza, is one of the prettiest town and suburban drives of which I know in Australia. Any afternoon one can see traps and riding parties on this road, the one fashionable resort in Western Australia—more fashionable even than the cathedral or the old convict prison at Freemantle. There are places on this Swan

River, near to Perth, where delightful summer hotels could be established ; but such things are, I fear, a long way off. Perth does not need them yet, or, if she needs them, she cannot afford them. The most popular exercise, in the capital, next to riding, is yachting. Any fine afternoon and evening the broad stream is, like Elizabeth Bay at Sydney, dotted with yachts, some of them large and well built.

Perth has all the instincts and practices of a metropolitan life. The Weld Club is as fine an institution in its way as the Australian Club in Sydney, and the people one meets uphold the dignity of the life of a metropolis. There is as gracious and gentle a life in this Western capital as would be found in some good old cathedral city in England. And one meets here, also, more gentlemen of the very old school than in any other place in Australia. I say the very old school, because some of them are a type of what has become very much modernised in the other colonies, and even in England. You will be met by the invitation to take a pinch of snuff from a gold snuff-box ; you will come into an area of old-time after-dinner conversation ; you will imagine yourself sometimes in the days of William IV., or of the First Gentleman in Europe.

There is little wealth in the colony. I do not suppose there is a man in Perth worth £100,000, and perhaps there are not four in the colony who could sign a cheque for that amount. Maybe the people are just as well off as they are, but it cuts hard in some directions. The poor are poorer than they are elsewhere, and though the rich are not so rich as they are in Sydney or Melbourne, they fare no worse in reality. The anxiety of life occurs up to the point of procuring necessities, and it is in that region that the humble people in poor communities suffer; for though living is, on the whole, cheap, the opportunities of earning a living are few. So is it that one may see in this colony serious economy side by side with all the cost, as with all the expenditure, of modern metropolitan life. And here I might touch on a point to which I intend referring later. There is an idea among many West Australians that their colony is poor, and that it never can be rich, and there are, therefore, those who are afraid of immigration, and regard the incoming of strangers as prejudicial to their interests. Madness merely.

Business in Perth and Freemantle is dull now. One sees few people in the shops, and few people from the townships trading in the city. Freemantle is much the same, though the shipping element, which is not large, lends an air of activity to a portion of the place. 255 vessels with 249,813 tonnage entered this port, and, 185 vessels with 214,824 tonnage cleared, in 1887. Freemantle is eleven miles from Perth. It has not a good harbour. The entrance is wide, but the water is low. A scheme has been proposed to cut a canal through the narrow neck of land that divides Rocky Bay—an enlargement of the Swan River a few miles above Freemantle —from the sea; but to this the people of the port town are opposed, and quite naturally, because it would cease then to be a port, and Perth would get the benefit of the change. It is probable that, instead of this, an attempt will be made to build breakwaters and to dredge. It seems their only hope, and at best it will be an expensive undertaking.

It is a marvellously pretty journey from Perth to Freemantle. I took it one afternoon in a steam launch as the guest of the Hon. John Forrest. There were present Sir Malcolm Fraser (the Administrator), Sir Samuel

Griffith (of Queensland), the Hon. Septimus Burt, and others. We had an excellent opportunity for seeing the beauties of the river. We passed some fine homesteads and some beautiful gardens, fronted by groves of bamboo or banana, and saw some exquisite bits of shore and wooded upland. It was my second visit to Freemantle ; I saw it both from sea and land. It is not an impressive-looking place. A hard mass of white stone on a barren shore is the first impression, and it is one that remains. There are two things next that strike one—a building of considerable pretensions to architectural comeliness to the left among the trees,—the few trees that are to be seen,—and another high on the hill; a bare ominous building which would hold, one would think, 1,500 prisoners. The first is a lunatic asylum ; the second is the Freemantle Prison—the noted prison where dwelt some of the greatest rascals unhung, where lived, too, many who endured shame and ignominy far beyond their deserts. Some of these criminals were sent out for small offences,—

> "A rabbit or a loaf of bread
> To keep starvation back a day,
> The price of some poor varlet's head,
> And shame for him and his alway:
> Children that yet had scarcely quit
> The haven of their mother's breast
> Were driven white-faced with the rest
> To penal shame. . . . ."

I went through this prison soon after I arrived in the colony, accompanied by Mr. Forrest, who was some years ago comptroller of it, and who was able to tell me many interesting, if painful, things of the old days— "of the old days," because convict transportation is past, and there is now only a handful of life-prisoners left in the immense structure; with many good handfuls of ticket-of-leave men, who have found their way back within the walls where they had long served their Queen ; some in irons, some in strait-jackets, some in dark cells. Irons? What cared they for irons! I was told of one convict who could run up and down a ladder like a squirrel, with forty pounds hanging to his legs. This great white building is such a monument as Western Australia would, if it could, tumble into a mass of forgotten ruins. But that may not be ; and it is still used as a gaol and for those who are yet Imperial prisoners. But its glory is departed—for there is glory even in a prison. The superintendent takes as much pride in a full prison, as a theatrical manager does in a full house on the last night of a run. I asked the superintendent of the prison at Freemantle how things were—a mere, How goes it ? and he said, in a tone that was touched with regret, " Oh, very dull, sir, indeed ; hardly enough to keep things going." Every man to his business.

I cannot say that the journey through this big penitentiary was a very pleasant one, in spite of the fact that the gaoler showed with an honest pride everything, from the new ovens to the joyful working of the gallows. We were shut in a dark cell ; we were bade to look on the irons, on the strait-jackets, and were taken to the spot where the floggings were administered. As for the prisoners, one never saw a more depraved-looking lot. There are no inhabitants of high places gone wrong among them ; just chiefly old offenders of such a cast of countenance as would do for pictures of Bill Sykes.

I was shown the cell from which the bushranger Hughes escaped some time ago, and after having listened to tales of such men as the clerical Beresford, who was sent here years back, and who before he died became a rouseabout of a camp, I walked about the glaring streets of the town,—for there was not a cab to be had. I think the white sands of the Sahara could not be more trying than the streets of Freemantle. The limestone reflects the sunlight with intensity, and forces one to shut one's eyes when walking the streets. But I must say that, with the thermometer at 108°, I did not feel the heat more than I felt it in Sydney at 85°. I should not like, for all that, to be compelled to live in Freemantle. It is a dreary place, even with its sprinkling of gentlefolk, and its orderly and not inactive population. I met a remarkable man there—a doctor of much force of character and refinement. His leg had been amputated once, and he found, owing to renewed trouble, that it must be amputated higher up. He asked brother surgeons to do it. They objected, and said that it would kill him; that it must not be done. He laughed at them, and cut it off himself. It is a remarkable case of pluck and nerve.

Altogether, I should sum up the towns of Western Australia as cleanly and healthy in their life; anxious rather than acutely ambitious; cautious rather than fervent; agricultural than manufacturing: not suggestive of great things to come; not speculative, and yet not timid socially: temperate, and well grounded in the faith of a larger hope, founded on long-developing political aspirations. They have the foundation for a sound superstructure—we shall see what we shall see. But I hope I may be pardoned by this hospitable and kindly colony if I say that the population may be divided into those who buzz in their little world, and neither see anything beyond it, nor permit anything from without to come in, and influence them to new thoughts and possibilities; and those who have felt the outside world, who have learned the alphabet of progress and enlightenment, and who know how to institute comparisons, to their own benefit and the advancement of the land in which they live. And the sum of it all is, that the onward and steady tread of the latter will encourage and lead the hesitating step of the former to the more lively political, commercial, and social existence.

I did not find it altogether easy to get a grasp of the conditions of the soil in Western Australia, though the land laws appear to me to be comparatively free from the entanglements and inequalities that so encumber the land laws of New South Wales and other colonies. The West Australian can speak positively of only a small portion of the colony; of the rest he speculates,— that is all. The man who knows the most of land conditions in the colony is the Hon. John Forrest, the Surveyor-General and Commissioner for Lands. He has travelled over more of the country than any other man, and his right to speak authoritatively needs no support from me. In many long talks I had with him I gathered that he considered at least one-half the colony as capable of little development; about one-third as calculated to permit of considerable occupation; and by comparison but a fraction as adapted for advanced cultivation. These proportions, actually, he did not give me, but on going over the lines he drew on a map for me I conclude these divisions to be in accord with his ideas.

All the evidence goes to show that the growth of settlement must always be slow. Had the land been generally better, the settlement would have been greater. It is not due alone to convict transportation that the colony stands where it does. Men do not hesitate to put money into good things because there are penal stations about; as witness even wretched New Caledonia, where Englishmen have become planters and miners, and have so far sunk their past predisposition and training as to become French citizens. There is a deeper cause than the social-leper plea. It is to be found in the very moderate attractions that the land offers for pastoral occupation and agricultural uses. I have talked with men who have owned squatting land in the colony, and with those who went to buy squatting land; they have all said, So long as there are such good chances to be had in the other colonies, Western Australia must take a back seat. There is reason in that. There is plenty of good land in Queensland and New South Wales, there are markets, and there are opportunities for investment which are not visible yet in this far-away province. No doubt the opportunities have been under-estimated, owing to extraordinary movements elsewhere, but they have not been sufficiently conspicuous to attract a speculative attention, save in two instances—the Kimberley gold-fields rush and the Perth and Suburbs Land Investment,—and of the latter the less said the better.

Strange to say, New South Wales, though farthest away, contributed most to the excitement connected with these two things. Kimberley was a disappointment, and the land speculation was an injurious boom. Kimberley may yet prove a source of wealth to the colony, as may Pilbarra, Nullagine, Yilgarn, the Green Bushes tin-fields, in the south-west corner ; and Kendinup between Albany and Perth. If it should come to pass that the opinions of the Government geologist are correct, there may be that done for the colony, which pastoral occupation and agriculture have not been able to do. At Kimberley, surface mining was a comparative failure, because the miners went there hoping for rich alluvial mining, but found only shallow deposits. Mining is still going on, but it is good old-fashioned reefing, for which machinery is being set up, and into which careful money is being put. Want of water, however, is a serious drawback, and it has done as much as anything else to retard mining development. There are about 800 men employed at Kimberley, Pilbarra, and Yilgarn; there might be three times that number if there were good water to be had. As I said elsewhere, considerable sums of money are being expended at Kimberley in boring for water, but as yet the efforts have not been very successful.

It is strange that nearly all mining efforts have been failures in Western Australia. Lead and copper were found on the Lower Murchison and in the Champion Bay district, but though smelting works were erected in the hope of securing the ten thousand pounds which the Government offered for the first 10,000 tons of lead smelted, they have gone to the wall. In forty years the exportation of copper from the colony has been 7,917 tons, and of lead 31,105 tons. The Irwin River district seems likely to be a source of wealth in the future. Copper and coal have been found there, the coal being in 6-feet and 8-feet seams. There is coal also in the Kimberley district, and probably in many parts of the carboniferous formation along the coast. Coal was also found as far back as 1845 by Mr. Gregory on the Fitzgerald and Phillips Rivers, east of Albany. But this may, after all, mean little or much. The coal found as yet is of indifferent quality. This prevents any excited anticipation, because none but excellent and plentiful coal could compete with that of New South Wales. The Queensland coal is not bad, but it cannot compare with that from Lithgow, Bulli, and elsewhere. Even if the West Australian coal were as good as that of Queensland it would not encourage outside capital. It will be seen that I am not presenting a rosy picture of the colony, but that, I am sure, is not what the public want, if rosiness is synonymous with exaggeration. West Australians will, no doubt, thank me for trying to be fair to the outside public as well as to themselves. I cannot find that there is anything on which to base fervid apostrophes. I have turned to the remarks made at different times by the most prominent men who have lived in the colony, and I find them all cautious in nature, even when delivered in England before the Royal Colonial Institute, or on the platform before a geographical or science association. I refer to such men as Sir William C. F. Robinson, Sir Frederick Napier Broome, Mr. Alfred Hensman the ex-Attorney-General, and the Hon. John Forrest.

With mineral development, as I pointed out in another chapter, has come the rapid settlement of three of the other colonies, and, if it should chance that Western Australia has mineral fields such as Turon or Bendigo, Gympie or Charters Towers, Mount Bischoff or Broken Hill, and if, at the same time, water is found easily, we shall expect to see a proportionate rapidity in increase in the population of this province. What more can be said? Even among the knowing ones of Perth there is doubt and uncertainty. Mines may look well to-day and assays may be encouraging, but, like the thousand wild-cat mines that followed Broken Hill and Sunny Corner in New South Wales, they may be in a month or two remembered only by those who have loved and lost. And speaking about Broken Hill—at the next table from where I am writing on the *Victoria* (that magnificent steamer of the magnificent P. and O. Company), in the Indian Ocean, there sits one of the original proprietors of the great silver mountain, Mr. James. A few years ago he was almost penniless and entirely unknown; now he knows not what to do to fill his time or how to spend his money, and he cannot make that use of his notoriety that he might have done had his early opportunities been better. I watched him buying Indian curiosities and fabrics at Kandy in the heart of Ceylon the other day, and I could stake the patrimony I ought to have had, that he was buying simply for the sake of chucking his money away, as the larrikin would say. Western Australia has no James. Would that she had! The total return of gold for Western Australia for 1889 was not over 50,000 ounces, and perhaps it was less. This is but an atom in the heap of Australian gold exportation. But it may be that all the hopes of the most enthusiastic West Australians will be realised, and that there is only capital needed to work the reefs already discovered. That is all in the area of speculation, however, because there has been no deep mining; in no place has over 100 feet or so been reached. Yet we will not quarrel with the prophecies of them that say, " If it be not now, yet it will come."

But when this is said, one can confidently affirm that there are good chances for prudent investment in the colony. The land conditions are easy, and there is enough good land untouched to absorb profitably the capital of the industrious pioneer and genuine capitalist. Where I have appeared to depreciate the possibilities of this vast colony, it must be remembered that I have in mind its comparison with the sister colonies; its hitherto slow progress, its unequal conditions, and such unfortunate circumstances as good land without water and water without good land near it. In no colony is this so apparent as here. I take up Mr. Forrest's *Notes and Statistics respecting the Six Land Divisions of Western Australia*, and I find his commendations set most carefully forth, sufficiently so to warrant my not I hope, unappreciative, if not flattering, opinions. Of the South-West Division, which is the best of the colony, he says : " In its natural state it takes about ten acres to keep a sheep, but with clearing and improving it will keep a sheep to two acres, and in choice places a sheep to one acre." Yet it must be remembered that in this division there are only 24,514 square miles leased for pastoral purposes out of 67,000 square miles. Of the North-West Divison, he says, "It is a rich pastoral division consisting of well-grassed plains. . . . It is fairly well watered. . . . It is capable in the best portions, when fenced in, of carrying a sheep to two acres." In this division 32,678 square miles are leased out of 81,000 square miles. In the Gascoyne Division 52,065 square miles are taken up out of 133,000 square miles ; in the Kimberley Division 24,131 out of 144,000 square miles ; in the Eucla Division, 12,101 out of 59,000 square miles ; and in the Eastern Division 23,384 out of 576,000 square miles. That is, out of 1,000,000 square miles of land only 172,859 are taken up for pastoral purposes. From this pastoral land, there were 8,475,240 pounds of wool exported in 1888. Compare this with the 224,295,209 pounds of wool exported from New South Wales in 1887. One may say, therefore, that, by comparison, Western Australia does not show a great deal for its age and its opportunities.

That there were opportunities may be gathered from the fact that, from 1829 to 1850, land was given to the settlers, according to the value of the property they brought into the colony, subject to certain required improvements; and up to 1850 1,137,177 acres had been granted under this regulation. One would think that such easy conditions should produce much settlement, and be the means of making plenty of rich men in the colony. There are not many rich men, however, and there is but limited settlement. What are we to think?—Only this, I fancy, that there are some hindrances to wealth-making in this colony. Neither by hook nor by crook did men grow rich; and that there were hook and crook, some old settlers, to whom I talked, assert. One of the ancient dodges was this: two or three men got land from the Government all on the same personal property. For instance, A would go with £1,000 on Monday, and the Government would give him land according to this amount shown; B would take this very sum on Tuesday (lent him by A), and get property according to its value; C would take that same £1,000 on Wednesday, and also be given land according to its value. Really a pretty trick. I cannot of course vouch for it; it is given as I received it; but stranger things than that have happened in the doings of Governments. According to Mr. Forrest, Lord Glenelg, the Secretary of State in 1837, wrote: "I will not attempt to deny the difficulty which I experience in dealing with the subject of the grants of lands, owing to the embarrassments created by the erroneous system under which the colony was settled, and particularly from the improvident manner in which land was granted to individual settlers."

Since 1850, however, all that is changed. Up to that date 121,682 acres had been sold. Between 1850 and 1888 555,244 acres were sold, thus making a total sale of 676,926 acres since the founding of the colony, as against 1,137,177 acres of land given away. It will be seen, however, that the evil was done in the early days. In this connection it must also be noted that 3,000,000 acres of land have been given to the West Australian Land Company, in consideration of the construction and working of the railway from Beverley to Albany. But this is not all. There is to be considered the £600,000 of money put into this railway by the company; there is the provision for prompt communication with future markets; and there is the direct benefit to government lands from the improvements and settlement of the company's lands. So far as I can see,—and I have gone through the schedules carefully,—the days of land-grabbing in Western Australia are over. Since 1850 there have only been given away 53,936 acres of land, and nearly 24,000 acres of this are in consideration of short railway lines, built at the rate of 2,000 acres a mile; while 7,400 acres have been given for military and naval services, but in no single case more than 1,200 acres. That is not out of the way, for the Government of Canada gave 500 acres of land to each officer who was on active service during the Riel rebellion in 1885. As Mr. Forrest has pointed out in his report, the accusations of land-grabbing made against West Australians must be rejected by all fair-thinking men. It is evident to any one who reads the records, that close and careful hands have dealt with the public lands since 1850. And it is not likely that, under responsible government, there would be more land-grabbing than with the present half-and-half constitution.

Before leaving this part of the subject one must note the fact that Sir Frederick N. Broome supported a proposal put forward at the Federal Council in 1885, that 50,000,000 acres of the Crown lands of Western Australia should be reserved for a Federal Defence Fund, on condition that a railway should be constructed from Perth to Adelaide out of a Federal loan of £5,000,000. There is nothing wild about such a scheme. It is only a bold anticipation of a policy which must embody the principle involved here. If the federation of the colonies comes, there would eventually be a transcontinental railway, and that railway must be built out of federal funds, towards which Western Australia should contribute by land or cash. And the principle is the same in either case. The land is the people's, but not to be held simply as land. If it is converted into the general development and the prosperity and advancement of the State, it is still the people's. The people are still the landlords, having received a *quid pro quo*.

The existence of what is called poisoned land is a serious matter,—more serious than West Australians themselves are willing to admit to strangers,—but there are always those who will tell evil tales, and I did not find them wanting in the land of the Swan River. I was told that poisoned lands cut up large areas of good land, in such fashion as to destroy their value as squattages, and discouraged investors so much, that those who came to spy out the country returned disappointed. On the other hand, I was assured by the Commissioner for Lands, and prominent squatters, that the poisoned land was neither impossible nor so general as I had been informed. Two of these squatters from the Champion Bay district had themselves taken up large areas of poisoned land, on the terms laid down by the Government, and had converted large plains of waste soil into grazing lands that supported a sheep to every four or five acres. The terms offered are the following : "Any person desirous of obtaining a lease of poisoned land shall apply to the Commissioner, defining the boundaries and paying one year's rent at the rate of £1 per 1,000 acres. Within twelve months a proper survey of the land must be furnished at the expense of the applicant, and sufficient proof be given that the land is poisoned land. If the application is approved, a lease is granted for twenty-one years at £1 per 1,000 acres, on condition that the land is fenced in within three years ; and if the poison-plant is completely eradicated before the lease expires, the lessee will be entitled to a Crown grant." Not many squatters have taken advantage of this privilege, but a few have worked hard, have eradicated the poison, fulfilled the conditions, and received the grant. A huge effort is being made by the Land Corporation of Western Australia, Limited, to convert an immense area of poisoned land into good pasturage. Its holdings amount to 1,236,460 acres. Under any circumstances the colony cannot lose by the bargain. The land is waste, unoccupied, and valueless as poisoned areas ; and the company will pay enough for it in the end. The plant can only be destroyed, as Mr. Grant, a squatter who had coped with it, assured me, by grubbing it out persistently. It cannot be conjured away. For every acre of this land converted into stocked area, the Government might indeed pay a bonus, not merely give the land away. Beggars cannot be choosers, and the West Australian Government is an unhappy and helpless beggar in this case.

The lands of Western Australia are not, as I said before, encumbered by a mass of regulations overlapped and interlaced by oft-changed legislation. The coast is comparatively clear, and we can see to the end of things, as it were, without too frequently altering the focus and consulting the chart. All town and suburban lands in the colony are sold by public auction at an upset price to be determined by Government. Any person may apply to the Commissioner to put up for sale any town or suburban lands already surveyed, on depositing 10 per cent. of the upset price, which is returned if he does not become the purchaser. Should the purchaser not be the applicant, he must pay 10 per cent. on the fall of the hammer, and complete his purchase within thirty days. There are four methods of obtaining land by conditional purchase in the South-West division :—

1. By deferred payment with residence within agricultural area.

2. By deferred payment with residence outside agricultural area.

3. By deferred payment without residence.

4. By direct payment with residence.

Agricultural areas of not less than 2,000 acres may be set apart by the Governor-in-Council, the maximum area to be held by any one person being 1,000 acres, and the minimum area 100 acres, the price being fixed at not less than 10*s*. an acre, payable in 20 yearly instalments of 6*d*. an acre. Where the purchaser does not reside, as under the third condition, he must pay double price, or £1 per acre. The fourth condition is made to meet the case of *bonâ-fide* settlers who may have property, and who may reside elsewhere in the colony, and who, because of the uneven quality of the land of the colony, may not be able to secure all needed agricultural land where they reside. The Government may set apart, in any of the divisions, special areas for purchase, of not less than 5,000 acres. Any lessee in the Kimberley or Eucla Divisions may have a reduction of one-half the rental due under the regulations for the first fourteen years of his lease, if in the Kimberley Division he have in his possession, within five years, 10 sheep or one head of large stock for every 1,000 acres leased ; or, in the Eucla Division, if he have expended £8 per 1,000 acres in tanks, wells, dams, or in boring for water. In all divisions except the South-West, twelve months' notice is given in the *Government Gazette*, that it is the intention to throw open land for conditional purchase, and, after the expiration of this time, the pastoral lessee shall cease to have any claim to the land so declared. If, however, the area is not sold or taken up, the Commissioner may grant the lessee right to depasture his stock upon the whole, or any portion, of this proclaimed area, or the land may be restored to the lessee, if, after a fair period, the land be not taken up.

As in New South Wales, the rent of pastoral land is paid in advance. A pastoral lessee has no right to the timber on the land, although a clause may be inserted in the lease, permitting the lessee to cut timber for building, domestic uses, and improvements. Licenses may be issued also for the cutting and carting away of timber. Under these licenses has sprung up the sandal-wood industry.

In the South-West area the minimum rent is £1 per acre ; in the Gascoyne Division there is a progressive rental of from 10s. to 15s. ; in the Eucla Division from 10s. to 15s. per acre, progressive ; in the North-West Division from 10s. to £1, progressive ; and in the Kimberley Division from 10s. to a £1, progressive. The leases are for twenty-one years, and in all but the South-West and Eastern Divisions, if the land is so shut in by other holdings as not to contain 20,000 acres (the regulation block), a lease may be granted for a lesser quantity ; but in no case may a lease be granted for less than £5 per annum. In the Eastern Division the rental is progressive, running from 2*s.* per 1,000 acres, to 7*s.* 6*d.* for the last seven years in the twenty-one years' lease.

I have thus briefly set down the land regulations, knowing that there are many people in the other colonies and in England, who are interested in conditions of land rentals in Western Australia.

CHAPTER XXI.

WESTERN AUSTRALIA IN 1889-90 (*Continued*).

RESPONSIBLE GOVERNMENT.

RESPONSIBLE Government for Western Australia may be accepted as a foregone conclusion. The English Government is pledged to the new constitution, and it is now only a question of debate and voting. I had a long talk with Sir James Corry, member for Belfast, as we sailed the Indian Ocean, and he spoke confidently of the intention of the House to pass the Enabling Bill with little opposition. There will be the usual attack on a Government measure, a review of the whole West Australian case, and then the bill will be put through with a sigh of relief by the House. That is not only the opinion of Sir James Corry, but I find it confidently expressed in English journals. So far, good. It might appear, if that is beyond peradventure, that comment now is unnecessary, since there is apparently no need to bring fresh evidence to bear upon the matter. But the public will, perhaps, be none the worse for a look at the subject through the eyes of one who is on the ground, and has caught the feeling of the place, of the people, and of the conditions under which they work. It was to get the feeling of the place, I take it, that Sir Samuel Griffith visited Western Australia the other day.

I do not know that, by my visit, my views are altered about this great question, on which so much depends in Western Australia, but I can see old arguments in a clearer light; I can better understand on what basis of experience and prospect the inhabitants of this Western province ask for an expanded constitution.

The chief argument against Responsible Government is, handing over such an immense tract of land as 1,000,000 square miles to "a handful of people" to govern, and of which to make disposition. Now I may be very much alone in my opinion, but I cannot see this anticipated danger. Immense tracts of land do not necessarily mean immense treasures. Victoria is more valuable with its little area than is vast Western Australia, so far as we know it. What is known as the Eastern Division of Western Australia is large enough for four colonies, but what kind of a colony could be fashioned out of it? The Kimberley district would make a colony, but I much doubt if, for a quarter of a century yet, it could with advantage stand alone. It has resources, but they do not show, and they never have shown, such indications of value as Northern Queensland, for instance, exhibited long ago. People, I fear, talk somewhat wildly, when they emphasise the danger of giving immense tracts of land to 45,000 people to govern. There would be much less danger of land-grabbing in a colony having Responsible Government than in a Crown colony, as experience has shown in every dependency of England. The people must be trusted, their representatives must be trusted, and one doubts that Downing Street is more careful for the conservation of the rights of the people than St. George's Terrace or Macquarie Street. Allowing for the leakage that occurs in the administration of the most pious governments, it should be evident that, nowadays, little corruption can occur in the disposition of lands, especially under Responsible Government. There is always a suspicious opposition to every Government, and jealousy keeps even the corrupt moderately virtuous. Western Australia, as is known, has made no objection to the intention of the English Government to make the boundary of the new colony at latitude 28°, if it chooses to do so; and that is not to be wondered at, because then there will be a reduction of responsibility, and enough of the best of the colony left to make a fairly prosperous territory.

There seems, however, much reason in Mr. Forrest's proposal to make the division at 126° of longitude, which would take in the Kimberley and the Eastern Divisions. I incline to this the more because space must not be reckoned with in Western Australia as elsewhere. The North-West Division, the Gascoyne Division, and the South-West Division would make a compact colony, having a variety of resources sufficient unto itself, as is the case with Queensland. It appears to me better that the Eastern Division, which is, on the best authority, an impossible country, and the Kimberley Division, which must develop very slowly, should stand alone if any of Western Australia must do so. It will take all these three Divisions that I have mentioned to make a colony of real strength. I venture to say, had the members of the New South Wales and Queensland Parliaments, who spoke on this Western Australian question last August, read and studied the records of the colony thoroughly, there would have been sounder views on the question uttered. The speech that Sir Henry Parkes made on August 7th, 1889, was the most valuable contribution to the national side of the question that has been delivered. It had only the principle of the thing under consideration, and it fulfilled its mission with a dignified and constitutional comprehensiveness. In that speech Sir Henry Parkes said : " Now, the very fact of the enormous territory embraced by Western Australia, as it exists to-day, is sufficient, when we try intimately to survey the ground, to awaken the most serious speculations as to the future. We know the marvellous powers of a free Government in developing the energies of a people. We have seen it here in this colony; we have seen it in a marvellous degree in the great colony on our north. . . . It is supposed that there are persons of great influence, parties of great influence in the mother-country, who seek to hold that portion of the country now known as Western Australia, which probably would be about half of the whole, as a ground on which the more troublesome portions of the redundant population of the United Kingdom shall be shunted, as it were, with no object but to get rid of them." There are two things in connection with these utterances which excite one's attention—the power of free government to develop the energies of the people, and the danger of a disreputable immigration. I think most men in Western Australia will bear me out in the statement that the colony cannot be measured with the same measure applied to New South Wales and Queensland. I do not think we should look for that splendid advance in settlement and wealth which occurred in Queensland. I do not think we can confidently hint at any such advance. Does any one imagine that the advance in Western Australia will be either along the same lines, or in the same ratio? The signs are not yet born in the heavens of her progress that point to such an end.

Responsible Government does not make grassy plains and watered lands, nor destroy the poison plant, nor eradicate spinifex desert. The principle that Sir Henry Parkes laid down is sound, but it works according to its environment. It does not create capital ; it does not make markets. We must dream of it no Patmœan dreams.

What it does do is to create confidence. That is its chief office. The people like to know that they are ruling, and capitalists like to know that the Government is a set of politicians over whom, by their votes or influence, they can have some power. That is a potent thing. To have an administration and a party sent in to make laws for you, and responsible to you for the way they fulfil their promises, is a matter that begets confidence in the capitalist. To have a voice in the disposal of one's own taxes, and in shaping the conditions under which one labours, every citizen desires. But, after all that is acknowledged, there remains the great thing needful, and that is, the resources which give an invitation to capital. Under Responsible Government, with all its dangers, the fullest development takes place, and, under it also, men rise to a sense of greater freedom and more responsible citizenship ; but it is no magician's wand that " converts the dry rock into standing water," and makes " the desert to blossom as the rose." It tends towards an extension of natural and personal courage ; it reduces a sense of distrust or uncertainty which is so common in Crown colonies, and which is as often unjust as just. Queensland would never have sprung like a young giant to the place it holds, had it not had marvellous strength of soil, and great stores of mineral wealth. Responsible Government only gave her greater freedom to exercise her power. And I am sure that is what Sir Henry Parkes wishes to be understood to mean. He points to Queensland merely as an example of what is possible under Responsible Government. Western Australia is not Queensland, and her best friends know well that she has more frame than muscle. They have no fantastic visions. They know that they have a share of good pastoral land and a share of good agricultural land, and perhaps a goodly share of mineral wealth. But they know also that their colony must walk with modest step behind her sisters, unless the unexpected occurs, and she wakes up some fine morning to find she has a great mineral heart within her. We must reckon by what we know, and Western Australia is, as has been said before, no longer a young colony; she is as old as Victoria, or South Australia.

As for England making the reserved part of the colony a refuge for her social outcasts and beggar population, no one seriously believes there could be any such intention. She has had the chance to do so, and she has not done so. Besides, is it reasonable to suppose that the Home Government could be so foolish as to set immigrants down in the Kimberley or the north-west district, as they would in an agricultural colony? Both these districts of the north are pastoral and mineral, and, to do anything in either, money is necessary. They are regions where the capitalist will go, taking after him the miner and the labourer; but as for settling immigrants in this boiling north, why, none who understand can help but ridicule it. What the English newspapers say, what a few English politicians say, is of little account, because the Colonial Office does not in these days act upon the suggestions of irresponsible and ill-informed persons. I do not think there need have been any fear that the English Government would attempt to do more in the way of immigration, outcast or otherwise, than she has done in the past. The English working man, when he cries out for the retention of some land that he may go freely to, and without restriction, as an emigrant, says what he does not mean. He has not gone to Western Australia when he has had the chance. Under Responsible Government he will have as great encouragement, and greater, to settlement as he ever had from the Crown.

I heard the speech delivered by Mr. Morehead, the Queensland Premier, on the subject of Responsible Government for Western Australia, and I confess to a keen sense of disappointment. He went to as great an extreme in his contention of "Australia for the Australians" as the British politician does when he claims Australia as a heritage of the British race. Between the two extremes there is a point of union and justice. By encouraging immigration, Australia, on her part, does her duty; and England, on her part, does hers, when she gives to each portion of the continent, that has population enough to warrant it, Responsible Government. In this connection I quote Mr. Forrest:—

"This latter definition is surely the correct one; and this being so, those persons in England who have recently been speaking and writing so much with regard to the lands of Western Australia, and of their great rights and privileges in connection with those lands, would do well, I think, to remember that there is a ' Greater Britain beyond the sea, whose founders have at least equal rights and equal privileges with those who have remained at home.' To all such, however, the best reply is in the enlightened language of Lord Norton, ' In what does such patrimony consist? Only in the right of the Crown to dispose of such lands for the local use of the community. The right is just as Imperial exercised through the local Government as by the Crown from home; indeed, much more so, as the local use is best understood by those on the spot, and our constitutional theory is national responsibility.'"

There are objections raised against Responsible Government by citizens of Western Australia, which have weight. Mr. George Leake, now Acting-Puisne Judge, was one of the strongest opponents to the bill; and his case was not so weak as some would have it to appear. He held that the convict element was a dangerous factor in a country possessing Responsible Government, and declared that the people, as a whole, were not yet qualified to exercise all the functions of a more expanded Constitution. He pointed out the freedom there is from office-seeking under the present system, the independent discharge of public function that obtains, and the evils that are likely to ensue from the assumption of the franchise and the exercise of wide political privileges by the present population. These objections are met by the overwhelming evidence given regarding the smallness and the unimportance of the convict population. Besides this, it will be provided in the new constitution that no one who has been a convict may hold a public office. This was not done in the other colonies, as most people know. The convict population will, it is contended, not exercise the franchise to any extent, for they are in very many cases not householders, nor, by the fulfilment of any other condition, entitled to vote. As for the other objections, they are to be met by the testimony of experience. Faults, dangers there have always been in Responsible Government, but the judgment and the rule of the people are to be trusted in the long run. They have confidence in themselves, and the faults that arise are overbalanced by the general progress. This is felt by the wisest of the advocates for the new constitution in Western Australia, and they look forward with confidence to a movement of emigration and capital towards the colony from the other colonies and from England, as soon as the House of Commons passes the Enabling Bill. There will, of course, come in at the same time adventurers, political and otherwise ; but that, while to be deplored, is not to be feared, for other countries and colonies have gone through the same experience, and have not suffered beyond what is good for them.

Western Australia's claims for self-government are as strong as were those of the other colonies, though her resources are not so great. The principle was recognised long ago when she was given a half-and-half constitution, which Sir William C. F. Robinson described as neither "fish, fowl, nor good red-herring." Because she has not such great resources as the other colonies, she needs the enlarged privileges more, in order to use to their best advantage such strength and latent wealth as she possesses.

The time seems ripe for the exploit. The question is closely connected with that of federation, which is, while I am writing, under discussion in the Conference at Melbourne. There could be federation without Western Australia coming in, but one of the great uses of the union would be fettered. Canada's federation was a most incomplete thing until British Columbia entered. She could better do without Nova Scotia or Prince Edward Island than without that western province, for with it was connected her defence. So with Australia. There could be no great scheme of defence until Western Australia entered the union, and she could not enter until she became a self-governing colony. The other colonies demand what she demands, because it affects the whole continent. This is thoroughly recognised by such men as Sir Malcolm Fraser, the present Administrator of the colony, and other old and trusted politicians such as Sir James Lee Steere.

I think the public men of Western Australia are to be trusted. They impressed me with the loyalty of their motives and their intelligent conception of government and legislation. I read carefully through the speeches delivered by members of their Legislative Council on this great question, and talked with a number of the most responsible men of the colony; and I would stake their thoroughness against the more showy qualities of many well-known politicians in other colonies. The people generally are not acute or broadly perceptive, but they struck me as being free from political soddenness and the tendency to view political misdemeanours lightly —a thing not unknown in some of the other colonies. One cannot anticipate any sudden or extraordinary commercial growth in Western Australia, even though self-government should come. The indications point to a quick palpitation, and then a steady pulse-beat, stronger, however, than it ever was before.

I am aware that I have not been enthusiastic about Western Australia. I have tried not to let a most warm hospitality interfere with my judgment; and it may be that, setting feeling aside, I have been too critical, and on too slight a basis of knowledge. I can but plead, in such a case, that there is less to be feared from underestimation than from over-valuation. I have felt it my duty to set down such conclusions as would serve to convey to the mind of the inquiring an idea of what the country is like, and of what it is capable. There will be renewed attention given to Western Australia in the next few years, and these notes may act as hints to the curious. They may serve here and there to check wild investment, and to dissipate dreams of a new Tarshish or Ophir. One cannot but have hope for the colony; in fact, a larger hope than its past would warrant. Now that the first rushes to the other colonies are over, now that communication is constant with the eastern centres and with England, people who are on the lookout for quiet investment will think of this slightly-settled land,—its minerals, its timbers, its pearls, its grains, and its fruits, and will do as I saw several doing when I was there—make little journeys to the colony, if haply they may find interest-producing investments.

Of the timber one can speak with no uncertainty. Between 31° and 35° south latitude there are splendid areas of jarrah, one of the finest woods in the world; the renowned kauri, white-gum, red-gum, York-gum, and sandal-wood. This timber is thickly set over 30,000 square miles of territory, and from it will come a great amount of wealth. But the timber trade must be carried on in connection with other industries. No country ever became rich by cutting down timber. There was £33,525 worth of sandal-wood exported in 1888. Baron von Mueller, whose researches in Australia have been of such value, speaks in the most glowing terms of the woods of this colony. Mr. W. H. Knight, twenty years ago, gave evidence as to the value of the jarrah, and Mr. Ernest Favenc quotes some of this testimony in his book on the colony. It is found that piles driven down in the Swan River were, after being exposed to the action of the wind, water, and weather for forty years, as sound and firm as when put into the water. Mr. Favenc presents a table which shows that the wood is practically indestructible. It completely resists the attacks of the white ants, where stringy-bark, blue-gum, white-gum, and black-wood are eaten through, or rendered useless, in from six to twelve years. The karri timber grows to an enormous height, rivalling the Gippsland and the Huon gums, while at the same time it is sound and durable.

The following figures will give an idea of what the pearl-fisheries promise: In 1871 the value of the shells exported was £12,895 ; in 1888 it was £80,311. In 1879, however, it was £96,525. This is not the most valuable industry to the colony, but it is one that, if carried on in connection with other industries, should be a source of great wealth. It and the sandal-wood cutting, however, take away the selectors and small farmers from the land, and lessen to some extent more desirable settlement. Mr. Favenc cites instances in which pearls were found worth £1,000 each. The fisheries generally show little development. All the best varieties of the Australian fishes are found in Western Australian waters—the schnapper, the king, the jewfish, the bream, the taylor, the whiting, the skipjack, the mullet, and the herring. There is, however, only one fish-preserving factory in operation in the colony.

There is much good to be said of this colony, and others who see it may speak of it more glowingly and more wisely than myself. What I have written has been in the thought of the best interests of the colony and of Australia as a whole. It all may be summed up in this: Western Australia has fields for investment ; she has good pastoral and agricultural land to be taken up ; she has fisheries to be developed ; she has fine fruit areas ; she has mineral possibilities ; but she and her resources must be approached with temperate desire and prudent outlook. As she is, she offers favourable, but not brilliant, opportunities. I take my leave of her with gratitude for much courtesy, and with a hope that what I have written may not be considered unfair, whatever else may be thought of it.*

---

* Since the above was written the Enabling Bill has been passed, and the whole of the colony has been handed over to the Government at Perth. Mr. John Forrest has been made Sir John Forrest, Responsible Government is in full swing, and the revenue of the colony is not only higher than it ever was before, but there is a surplus over expenditure.

CHAPTER XXII.

CONFEDERATION IN 1890 *AND* 1891.

MAKERS OF CONFEDERATION: SIR JOHN A.
MACDONALD AND SIR HENRY PARKES.

IN writing a few lines on these two distinguished Colonial statesmen, one finds a good starting-point in the fact that they were both born in Waterloo Year ; the one in Sutherlandshire, Scotland, the other in Warwickshire, England. And it might almost seem that they were both born under the same star of political fortune. But the one, at five years of age, was carried to Canada, and the other did not seek the hospitable shores of Australia till 1839. Young Macdonald developed quickly, and was called to the Bar at Kingston, Ontario, in 1836. Even then he was a striking figure, with his clean-shaven face, always to remain so, and his debonair manner. I have heard one of his friends and contemporaries of that period tell how popular the young barrister was, and how quick and biting was his wit. It was not, however, until 1840 that his practice as a lawyer became large. He defended Von Schoultz, one of the rebels of 1837, and though he did not get him acquitted, he established a reputation as a criminal advocate. Seven years after this he was elected to Parliament. Sir Henry Parkes was not elected to the

Legislature of New South Wales until 1854. Sir John A. Macdonald has been in Parliament continuously for forty-seven years, and Sir Henry Parkes for thirty-seven years,—but not quite continuously. There have been one or two slight breaks in the record. Far apart as are the spheres of action of these great politicians, they have met. I think it was at Ottawa in 1881. A year and a half ago Sir Henry Parkes said, in his high-pitched, deliberate voice, in answer to a question regarding his meeting with the Canadian Premier, "Sir John Macdonald gave me the impression of being a shrewd leader, a master of the craft of politics, and a man of wide knowledge. He has wonderful shrewdness, wonderful shrewdness."

No two men were ever more unlike in personal appearance: the one slightly fashioned, of nervous action and kindliness of countenance; the other heavily built, with a leonine head, and a face of marked reserve and power. Yet both have similar political characteristics. That shrewdness with which Sir Henry Parkes correctly credited Sir John A. Macdonald, he possesses himself to a marked degree. They both have the faculty for seizing without apology the thunder of their opponents. They both are keen to see the drift of public opinion, and then to suddenly spring a policy in consonance with that drift; they both have the ability to turn attention from a coming danger to some more congenial topic and popular movement. Honest as Sir Henry Parkes undoubtedly is in his advocacy of Australian Confederation, there are those who say, with reason, that he would not have sprung it upon the country when he did if he had not feared the growing power of Protection in New South Wales. He could not consistently give up the policy of Free Trade of which he had been an advocate so many years; he could not tarnish his Cobden Medal by going boldly over to Protection. But he said: "The Free Traders are willing to leave the question of Free Trade and Protection to the judgment of united Australia." Then, as basis for the growing necessity of Confederation, he pointed to the Defence Question and the Chinese scare. Sir John A. Macdonald * has done the same thing lately in forcing his opponents to show their full hand, and driving them to declare for Commercial Union, while he chose the safer middle ground of Reciprocity. He saw the Grits give up the safe plank of Free Trade, and he is about to take it for his party.

But more than that: Sir Henry Parkes is not the father of Australian Confederation. The real leader of Confederation thought was originally the Hon. James Service of Victoria. Yet Sir Henry Parkes is called, and will be called, the chief maker of Australian Union. Sir George Cartier in Canada was as weighty an advocate and maker of Confederation as Sir John A. Macdonald; yet, so far as popular opinion goes, the Canadian Premier is held to be the maker of Confederation. He was the most outstanding figure in the Convention; he did most to reconcile conflicting factions; he became the first Premier of the Dominion, and history will give him, if not more praise than his due, at least more praise than others. Confederation in Canada was the only possible solution to a political dead-lock caused by the jealous conflict of Ontario and Quebec. In Australia, Confederation has its origin in a fast-growing conviction that large national concerns could be better dealt with by a Dominion Parliament.

Sir John Macdonald is the most convincing man in

---

* Sir John A. Macdonald is since dead.

Canada, and he is personally the most popular. He has great forensic ability; he has great private bonhomie; he is a master of repartee. The lances of hate break on his shield, and the disappointment that he is forced to give to his office-seeking friends, as "Old To-morrow," is robbed of its sting by his tact. He has been familiarly known for a generation as "John A." Everybody calls him that. As an instance of his warm-heartedness and good memory this anecdote is worth telling. He had not visited a certain town for many years. When he arrived quietly at the station, a score of cabmen politely pressed their claims. "Where's Bill?" Sir John said. Dilapidated and ragged, Bill came forward. "Is it me you're wantin', Sir John?" and he pointed despairingly to his wretched vehicle. "I never change a good servant, Bill. On the box with you." And, amid the cheers of the other cabmen, Bill drove the Premier to the town. As an example of his dramatic manner of speaking, his defence of himself on the occasion of the Pacific Scandal, in the early Seventies, may be taken. Among many other sayings of like character, this occurs: raising his hands above his head he said, "Before Heaven these hands are clean!" Sir Henry Parkes is slow of utterance, and in the form of his speeches belongs to a past generation. He has little gift of humour, and is, as he said to me one day before I left Australia, "a lonely man." "I belong to no club," he said, "and never did. I belong to no secret society. I have no insurance on my life. I often come to this great building (the office of the Colonial Secretary), after a stormy and important night in the House, and read myself to sleep with Kingsley, Carlyle, or Lowell, with no one else here but the caretaker. I never had a close friend. My recreations are books and animals." At his home he makes pets of a kangaroo,

kangaroo rats, dormice, robins, pheasants, and opossums. Without much artistic judgment he has great artistic inclination. He is also something of a poet. I believe he would rather be remembered as a poet than as a statesman. And while, like Sir John A. Macdonald, he always, in times of crisis or expected crisis, works upon the loyalty of the people, in his poetry he is socialistic, anarchical, anything that is "advanced." Sir John A. Macdonald has been a politician, and that alone, for at least thirty years; he has had no other tastes or ambitions. Sir Henry Parkes has sought the literary and artistic companionship of great Englishmen. He has numbered among his acquaintances Thomas Carlyle, Lord Tennyson, Robert Browning, Thomas Woolner, George Holyoake, Richard Cobden, John Bright, and Florence Nightingale. From a long letter written to him by Carlyle in 1867 I make the following extract: "You owed me nothing for 1862; it is rather I that owe you. There are traits about those innocent evenings you spent with me which I shall not forget. Your face is still brought to me as if I saw it, and beautiful wise things said of you by one whom I shall now behold no more!"

The last words Sir Henry Parkes said to me were, "If you ever write anything about me don't forget the dumb things."

* * * * * *

Notable Men in the Australian Convention.

To those who know the delegates, the Federation Convention sitting in the dull chamber of the New South Wales Assembly has elements of personal, as well as political, picturesqueness. The face of one of the most distinguished, if not the most distinguished, of Australians, looks down in peaceful silence on the beginning of a consummation which he, William Charles Wentworth, had dreamed and prophesied. And the man who is leading the movement is one who fought Wentworth tooth and nail in 1853-54 on the proposed Constitution Act, and fought him successfully; so successfully that the veteran legislator was obliged to give up a cherished part of his scheme—a colonial nobility with hereditary privileges. It was plain Henry Parkes then, once keeper of a toy-shop in Sydney, afterwards journalist, and a poor one, pecuniarily, at that. Now it is Sir Henry Parkes, K.C.M.G., and Knight Commander of the Crown of Italy, the most venerable figure in all Australasia, save one. That one more venerable is Sir George Grey, of New Zealand, of noble life and high service, of rare attainments and personal popularity, and possessed of many fads. Sir George Grey has always been more statesman than politician. Sir Henry Parkes has of necessity ever been more politician than statesman. Sir George Grey began his Australian public career as the Governor of South Australia in the early Forties. He was then Captain Grey, and as such became also Governor of New Zealand, and brought the first Maori war to a close in 1846. It was under the second administration of Sir George Grey, between 1861 and 1868, that the ten years' Maori war began, developed, and was, to use Harry of Monmouth's words, "broken all to pieces." Sir George Grey's life has been one of singular excitement and experiences. He was Governor at the Cape in difficult times, and he wooed hardship and adventure in the rudest forms as an explorer in Western Australia. In New Zealand he is the figure to which all creeds and politics turn with respect;

though in politics, at least, he holds a by no means popular creed. He is a Republican pure and simple. In the Confederated Australia that he would like, everything must be elective—Legislative Councils, Royal Commissions, and Governors. It is not strange to see a man like Mr. George R. Dibbs, of Sydney, the leader of the Opposition, advocating an Australian Republic, as he did the other day at the Convention. He is a big, bluff, good-natured man, a regular "Cornstalk," and a "gosh-almighty" Australian, whom his party the public find hard to take seriously, but who still tenaciously fights for office, and gets it occasionally. But Sir George Grey is sedate, refined, and scholarly. He has always taken deep and effective interest in all Australasian affairs, and his conclusions command at least respect; they may even do more. Now, at eighty years of age, he is the Nestor of the Federation Convention.

Yet Sir Henry Parkes is the more remarkable man. He has always been in manner of life more or less humble, because poverty has always dogged his steps. His paper, the *Empire*, failed; everything that he ever touched in a business way went by the board. But his political life has been free from stain. No man ever accused him, and sustained his accusation, of using office for the commercial advancement of himself or his friends. As a leader he is strong, as a departmental administrator he is weak. He is the broadest and most powerful thinker in the political arena; but he stumbles at details. He is an autocrat in his Cabinet; he is impatient of criticism. He has held his place by sheer force of will, by his political skill and his adroit parliamentary methods. In his dealings with the other colonies he has demanded always that he, and his colony, shall be considered first; and he has succeeded in securing what he demanded. Sir Henry's strongest hour in this Convention was when he made his great opening speech on the general scheme. His weakest one will be when the details come up;—details such as the disposition of the railways of the colonies, the appropriation of the public debts, the adjustment of the tariff, the apportionment of dominion and provincial rights, and the thousand-and-one knotty questions that must be settled; and he will not speak till the hour is come; but when he speaks the Convention will listen attentively. Sir Thomas McIlwraith, of Queensland, is of all political men in Australia the most downright, the most uncompromising, the most thorough, and, in appearance, perhaps the most distinguished. His personal bearing has gone far to encourage a greater dignity in the Queensland Parliament, both in speech and legislative manner, than is noticeable in any other Parliament of the colonies. His mind is cast in a large mould, his ideas are large, his conclusions are carefully worked out : and he is likewise dominating and quick-tempered. Born in Scotland, in 1835, Sir Thomas is a graduate of Glasgow University, and holds from his Alma Mater the degree of LL.D. conferred in 1881. He has done more to foster Federation, or " National " sentiment, as he called it, than any man in Australia, excepting the Hon. James Service; and hence it is that Queensland sends, in the person of three of its delegates at least (Sir Thomas McIlwraith, Sir Samuel Griffith, and the Hon. J. M. Macrossan), a group of the strongest men in the Convention. Sir Thomas McIlwraith has been in Parliament twenty-one years. He has twice been Premier, and several times Minister, and would be Premier to-day did his health permit. His most notable act was the annexation of New Guinea in

1883. He is at present a member of the Ministry of which Sir Samuel Griffith is chief. Sir Samuel Griffith is totally unlike his colleague in physique, habit of mind, and political practice. He is a Welshman, of fifty-five years of age, who went to Australia with his father in 1854. He is a university graduate, and a successful barrister and Q.C. ; has been in Parliament since 1873, and has twice been Premier. He has no personal magnetism of manner ; he holds his place by virtue of great ability and political skill. Like his colleague, Sir Thomas McIlwraith, he will have weight with the Convention ; but the weight of learned political counsel rather than immediate personal influence.

For several reasons the Hon. John Forrest is one of the most interesting figures at the Convention, if he is not one of the most prominent. It is but a few weeks since he was made the first Premier of Western Australia under the new Constitution. He was born in Western Australia, and is known best, perhaps, to Englishmen as an explorer. In 1870 he made the journey from Perth to Adelaide by way of the Australian Bight—a journey beset by many and great dangers, as Eyre's sad record bears witness ; and in 1874 he undertook the still vaster and more dangerous task of crossing the heart of the country, from Perth to the telegraph line that runs north and south between Adelaide and Port Darwin. The young explorer—not then thirty years of age—made the journey successfully, and one of the greatest achievements in Australian exploration had been accomplished. Such men should make trusted politicians. As Commissioner for Lands under the old Crown Colony system, Mr. Forrest established himself in the confidence of the people. He was a delegate to the Imperial Conference in 1886. He has always held strong opinions on Federation, and has proclaimed against the arbitrary lines dividing the colonies and defying every natural and geographical law. He is possessed of broad views, and has the power of expressing them simply and directly.

Mr. Forrest belongs to a group of young men whose influence will not be without effect in the Convention. It includes the Hon. Alfred Deakin, of Melbourne, the Hon. Edmund Barton, of Sydney, and the Hon. Andrew Clark, of Hobart, Tasmania. The most distinguished of these three is Mr. Deakin, who was Chief Secretary in the late Victorian Ministry, and held the office for nearly five years. Scarcely thirty-three years of age now, Mr. Deakin almost stepped from the university into Parliament, and came at once to the front. It was he who held the Gillies Ministry in power—his adroitness, his alertness, his nerve, his resources. Not inclined to hide his light under a bushel, he will do at the Convention what he did at the Imperial Conference in London: speak as for the general good and work all the time for Victoria. He refused knighthood, but, like most Victorian politicians, he is outwardly devout in his loyalty to the throne. This is the more singular, because Victoria is, in growth and habit, the most democratic of the colonies, Queensland excepted. The Hon. Edmund Barton is considered a coming man in New South Wales. He was one of the most successful speakers that ever presided over the New South Wales Assembly. Two years ago he became converted to Protection, and is virtually the leader of the Protectionist party; but he has a seat in the Legislative Council, and Mr. Dibbs is the nominal leader. He also is an Australian by birth, and holds a seat in the senate of his university. Mr. Clark is Attorney-General of Tasmania, and, if not a man of very considerable calibre, has the faculty of presenting a case strongly and concisely. He is a better speaker, if not as able a politician, as his chief in the Tasmanian Cabinet,—the Hon. P. O. Fysh.

The Hon. Duncan Gillies, of Victoria, is a man of great astuteness without having any claims to remarkable ability. He had the wit, however, to form a coalition Ministry, and to surround himself with men who could carry much of the burden of leadership for him. He only lost his place at last by a lack of judgment in appointments to office, and not through any policy of his opponents; though the fiscal question was afterwards made a cause of attack. Mr. Gillies can be trusted to lend his influence in keeping the scheme of the new Constitution as near to that of the British model as possible. He will have little sympathy with Sir George Grey's aspirations. In this he will be supported by such men as Sir Harry Atkinson, so long Premier of New Zealand; of Sir Patrick Jennings, who was Premier of New South Wales during the Jubilee year; of the Hon. Thomas Playford, the Hon. Dr. Cockburn, and Sir John Downer—all of whom have led the Government in South Australia. But there is a troublesome figure in the group. The Hon. Thomas Playford is of burly make, burly temper, and sturdy thought; and so fearful is he that South Australia may suffer fiscally in the proposed Confederation, that he may be expected, as he did last year, to make a speech breathing criticism and threatening.

CHAPTER XXIII.

STRAY PAPERS: ART NOTES—FRONTIER LIFE IN AUSTRALIA AND CANADA.

ART is alive in Australia. It has passed a time of travail. More than is the case with other young countries, the Australian Governments are paternal. Though this fact is sometimes perilous to courage and self-dependence, painting and sculpture are not likely to suffer from too much administrative care. Others of the fine arts are practised in an area of wider understanding and patronage. People will dance, and they must therefore pay them that pipe; they will sing and play—especially in Australia—and they in consequence demand songs and music and some one to teach. Churches require organists, musical societies need conductors, theatres must have orchestras; and so the musician can at least make a living. He calculates upon a demand that he has not himself created, but which has been the outcome of a general instinct and predisposition. Not so the artist in the pioneer times. An illustrated journal employs him occasionally, a theatrical manager requires work now and then; but, freely speaking, he stands alone. He must educate taste, outlive neglect, secure patronage and respect, and be modest therewithal, as the true artist is. It takes a long time for real art feeling to possess the population of a young land. It is taking less time in Australia than elsewhere. Art is there cultivated by Government, served by artists' societies duly recognized as national, sought by students, and patronised by the people. Australians have the money to buy with, the land is rich ; and when once the fashion sets in, as it must, of buying Australian pictures—then, to native artists, a good time will come. The people of Australia are practically unconscious of their progress in the love of the fine arts. They are in the movement, and therefore have not perspective ; they do not inquire or define. In politics they are ardent students, but they are also partisans, and the division gives them perspective. They quarrel with every item on the estimates save those that concern education and art ; those they pass in silence, and that silence means either ignorance or reverence. The instincts of the Australian people are right, they only need direction ; there will come, and now is coming, discrimination.

An inquiry here may contribute to a clearer understanding of these things in England. England can as little afford to disregard Australia in the matter of the fine arts, as she can afford to be indifferent to Australian commerce, to its gold, and wool, and coal. English musicians sell their music in the southern continent, and they have their operas produced at the large theatres of the capitals ; sculptors send out their statues for the public squares, parks, and gardens ; dramatists sell their plays to managers in Sydney and Melbourne ; actors from the London theatres reap goodly harvests there, and painters find liberal customers for their works in Australian governments and Australian citizens.

It may be said, without exaggeration, that New South Wales has one of the best water-colour collections in the world. The collection has not its value from the presence of the work of such masters as Turner, but because in its 130 examples it represents most of the water-colour painters of the more modern British School. When, nineteen years ago, the New South Wales Government gave its first £500 towards the purchase of pictures for a National Gallery, the trustees of "The Academy of Art," as it was then called, decided to begin with water-colour drawings. This was wise. The trustees thought thus: water-colour drawing is the peculiar achievement of the British School, it is a medium well adapted to a young country and to young artists, and the effect of spending money in this way would probably be greater in proportion to the amount than if the small grants were spent in oils. This was in 1871. In 1881 the Government of New South Wales gave not £500 but £5,000 for the purchase of pictures for the National Gallery, which had taken the place of the Academy of Art. The grant has been continued till to-day. The art treasures in the Sydney National Gallery at the present time represent in money about £50,000. In Melbourne they have spent as much. Sydney has as spacious a room for its water-colours as for its oils. It is notable, however, that the younger colony, Victoria, led the way in the art movement, and had an endowed National Academy before one was inaugurated in New South Wales. In Melbourne the trustees of the National Gallery are also trustees of the National Libraries and Museums. The Art Gallery, however, is under the immediate supervision of Mr. George Folingsby,[*] the master of the School of Painting. In Adelaide the Melbourne system is followed. The two eastern colonies have committees of selection in London, and it is through these bodies that the colonies have

---

[*] Mr. Folingsby is since dead.

secured some of the famous pictures which adorn their galleries. Old frequenters of the Royal Academy, the Grosvenor, and other exhibitions, and art lovers generally, on visiting these new institutions will find themselves face to face with old friends. In the Melbourne Gallery may be seen Alma Tadema's *The Vintage Festival*, Watts's *Love and Death*, Elizabeth Thompson's *Quatre Bras*, Cope's *Pilgrim Fathers, Moses Bringing Down the Tables of the Law*, by John Herbert, Edwin Long's *Esther, Josephine Signing the Act of her Divorce*, by E. M. Ward, Clarkson Stanfield's *The Morning after Trafalgar*, Turner's *Dunstanborough Castle* (presented by the Duke of Westminster), Briton Rivière's *A Roman Holiday*, Thomas Faed's *Mitherless Bairn*, John Linnell's *Wheat*, and Keeley Halswelle's *Heart of the Coolins*. These are but a few of a large number of pictures by men of mark and note—dead and living. Sydney in its oil-paintings is as fortunate as Melbourne, and in its water-colours even more so. There hang upon the walls of the National Gallery of the parent colony works of Sir Frederick Leighton, Sir John Millais, Peter Graham, Edwin Long, Luke Fildes, Vicat Cole, Seymour Lucas, and of many more good men.

Not the least satisfactory thing in connection with the Australian galleries is the comprehensiveness of the collections. In the Sydney gallery, for instance, there are works from the French, the Belgian, the German, the Italian, the Spanish, the Austrian, the Bavarian, and the Swedish schools. It was quite impossible, of course, that the colonies should secure a collection of even the old English masters. For their present uses it was better that the work of modern men should be secured. But while acting under this conviction, the mistake has been made of securing several pictures of one artist, instead of endeavouring, at every step in this first stage of development, to broaden the area of style by increasing the collection of modern artists. As for the great masters, it must ever be that the citizen and student of Australia will be obliged to come to the Old World to see them. If the expenditure of money is of any value in estimation —and in this case it is—it may be mentioned here that the collections in the three galleries existing in the colonies represent about £130,000, South Australia, with its annual grant of £1,000, being credited with about one-tenth of this amount in its sixty-five pictures.

The efforts of the Governments and the trustees of the different galleries in the purchase of statuary have not been without merit, but the measure of that merit is not great. There are to be seen statues from the hands of the late Sir J. E. Boehm—who has contributed more than any other sculptor to art treasures in this department—Marshall Wood, C. B. Birch, G. Fontana, Christian Rauch, Henry Woolner, and Percival Ball. Yet despite the levy that has been made upon the talent of good men, more mistakes have been made in the purchase of statuary than in any other direction in the region of art. There are statues in bronze in Sydney and Melbourne towards which no eyes are turned in admiration. But thanks to one or two sculptors who are giving their life-work to Australia, there is improvement. Mr. Ball's statue of William Wallace, which stands in the public square of Ballarat, teaches a daily lesson of the dignity and beauty of the art. It should be mentioned that the Victorian Government is establishing what may be called branch galleries in the provincial towns. At Ballarat the Fine Arts Gallery contains a dozen paintings lent by the metropolitan gallery. If sculpture and painting are gaining from the efforts of Mr. Ball in Melbourne, New

South Wales has certainly lost nothing by the appointment of Mr. Julian Ashton, President of the Artists' Society, to a seat on the Board of Trustees of the National Gallery.

One must write with considerable reserve on the question of art instruction in Australia. Five thousand pounds a year may purchase a masterpiece from the Academy or the Salon, but it cannot make a master off-hand. However, Governments think most and first about the masterpieces. The New South Wales Government has been induced at last to give a yearly endowment of £500 to the Art Society of the colony for the institution and conduct of art classes, under the direction of Mr. A. J. Daplyn. In 1890 over ninety students entered themselves for the privilege of studying in the gallery. With feeble private teaching here and there, with limited guidance in design in the Technical College, or with conventional industry in the public schools, elementary art instruction has moved on its purposeless way, until at last the New South Wales Art Society has aroused the Government to action. But the long inanition has left its lethargy, and art teaching, even with this responsible body, has not aroused enthusiasm. Still it grows, and there is life and individuality in the work of Australian artists. In Melbourne good has been done. For sixteen years there has existed in connection with the Victorian National Gallery a School of Painting, and a School of Design, the director of the National Gallery governing one, and an accomplished artist directing the other. In connection with this School of Design there is a collection of casts from the antique, of rare excellence and value. This is a thing in which the National Gallery of Sydney is entirely deficient, and with which the Art Society is badly provided. In 1889 there were in attendance on the art classes in the School of Design, one hundred and forty students. The exhibitions held in connection with the schools make one hopeful. As might be expected, the drawing is not remarkable, but there is some perception of colour and some faculty for composition. Too much must not be expected of a land to which Art is new.

The growing earnestness of the Victorian Government may be judged from the fact that it provides a liberal scholarship to the most successful student of each year in the School of Painting, who has completed his course, to enable him to study three years in some art centre of Europe. The effect of such action has been not only to send to Europe the fortunate possessor of the scholarship, but also to influence many other students to go to Munich or Paris to study. It may be seen from this that the art feeling is stronger in Victoria than in New South Wales, whilst instruction is more comprehensive and developed. In Adelaide also a commendable work is being attempted. The Government, as in Victoria, has required that students shall pass through a thorough course in the School of Drawing or Design before they enter the School of Painting. Acceptable as this is, it does not commend itself to the young student; and last year there were but twenty-one students in the Adelaide School of Art. Behind this, as a cause, lies the wage-earning factor. It is felt in all the colonies. Rising communities do not learn easily the secret of patience, and the eager young, urged on by ambitious parents, desire to rise quickly from the shackles of drawing, and to revel in the region of colour and composition. As soon as some pretty tricks of colour and sentiment are mastered, and that is not hard, the student can begin to sell. There lies the rub. In Melbourne and Adelaide the authorities are learning that the lines must not be made too rigid at first; conditions must be reckoned with in making regulations. There is no conscript service in art; there can be no state prison discipline in new communities; the element of compromise with necessity and circumstances must exist. Yet good has been done. The South Kensington examinations are being held in the colonies with excellent results.

Of the work accomplished by the artists of Australia no final estimate can be made. With early days—that is, a quarter of a century ago—the names of Conrad Martens, Brierly, Chevalier, Prout, Terry, and Louis Buvelôt are associated, and how little appreciated Australia knows. Like the poems of Kendall and Gordon, their pictures were without honour until the grass was growing over their graves, or until they had passed into a larger area of recognition, in which Australian praise or blame was of small account. In later days came George Folingsby, S. Glover, of Tasmania, John Gully, of New Zealand, Alex. Johnstone, W. C. Piguenit, an Australian by birth and in feeling, and the Collingridge brothers; and still more recently, a large number of such earnest men as Charles Hern, Ford Patterson, C. Roberts, George Walton, George Ashton, L. Hopkins, A. Fulwood, and others. In Sydney and Melbourne there are now two exhibitions of the Art Societies held in the year, and where once a handful of people, chiefly personal friends of artists, attended, thousands pay their shillings to see the couple of hundred pictures that represent the half-year's work. It cannot be said that the artists have always been patient in their struggling life. Criticism and reproach have been levelled at Government, people, and trustees of the National Gallery because of lack of support and patronage. Why did the Governments not aid the societies? Why did the trustees not purchase the pictures of Australian artists? Why had the Art Society of Sydney no representative on the Board of Trustees, of which not one member was an artist? These questions have been answered so far as Sydney is concerned with much satisfaction to all. The Art Society has received a grant, the trustees have bought several good pictures of Australian artists, and the President of the Art Society, and a member of it also, sit with the trustees of the National Gallery.

It was not the protests alone that did it. Artists have done better work during the past five years; the societies have therefore advanced in importance, and the newspapers of the colonies have loyally advocated the interests of local painters, and often have given extraordinary prominence to the work done by their organisations. The public are tempted yearly by Art Unions, which, if not a very dignified kind of business on the part of the artists, serves at least to give them advertisement and to enlarge their constituency. And the happier order of things will come in time. With such of the public as have become art patrons, there is a demand for subjects having local colour and feeling. This is perhaps the best thing that could happen to the artists. It tends to make them more observant of home life and to humanise their work. A special room has been set apart in the Sydney gallery for the work of Australian artists. The light of larger appreciation rises but slowly in this land of little leisure and much money-hunger; but it rises. A token of this is the presentations of pictures to the National Galleries during the last few years. One gift has brought forth another. During 1889 pictures by Edwin Long, David Cox, and A. W. Holden were presented to the Sydney Gallery. In the growth of the art feeling of the past half decade there are special influences to be considered. The Grosvenor Collection which came to Melbourne in 1888, the Loan Collection that drew vast crowds to the Centennial Exhibition in 1889, and the Exhibition by the Royal Anglo-Australian Society of Artists that was held in the colonies in 1890, did good work for both students and people. They refreshed and inspired the former, and interested and excited the latter. And the healthiest sign of that interest and excitement is the improving character of the work of the last four years. The pictures exhibited now are of the life around ; they are honest in that at least.

A distinguished literary man said, not so long ago, that there was nothing to paint in Australia. There is nothing anywhere that may not be painted if the eye that looks upon the world, and all that therein is, really sees, and if the mind to which it reflects its impressions has the power of selection. A bullock-team on the Darling Downs is as worthy a thing to paint as an English wheatfield ; Govett's Leap lends itself to stately power as much as the Highlands of Scotland ; and there are tints in the skies of the South, and colours on the shores of Australian seas, as full of beauty as any that ever rose before the eyes of a master. There is something more than a long monotony in Australian scenery. The man who really lives the life knows that. The true Australian knows it, and he is beginning to see what the office of the artist is. During the year 1890 the Trustees of the National Art Gallery at Sydney expended £6,530 in acquiring works of art. Among the artists from whom oil paintings were purchased are E. Waterlow, Marcus Stone, David Roberts, and John Brett. The London Committee of the Melbourne

Gallery have purchased this year Mr. F. Dicksee's *The Crisis*, one of the most notable (though not of the best) of the Academy pictures, and J. W. Waterhouse's *Ulysses and the Sirens*.

Frontier Life in Canada and Australia.

Here are two countries under the same flag, peopled by the same race, governed after the same fashion, and engaged in a large number of similar pursuits; yet the one lies in the far North and the other glows in the languid South. Wheat-growing, cattle-ranching, mining, fishing, and law-making are common to both; but developed under what different conditions! There is in Australia no gathering into barns, no housing of cattle, no constriction of freedom in labour or pleasure. In Canada expansion gets a check every year; not a permanent check, but one that gives gravity to progress and prevents exuberance. In December, the Canadian frontier-man is keeping himself snugly in doors, or wood-chopping, getting his grain ready for the sowing, taking his grain to market—when he can—and "choring-round" generally, with the thermometer at anything from $10°$ to $40°$ below zero. Australia in the time of sparkling yule-logs, the holly and the frost of the Northern lands, is sitting under heat that varies from $85°$ to $120°$ in the shade. And doors and windows throughout the land are wide open; as they are in the more northern parts of the country the year round. The days in the year are few when an Australian frontier-man cannot sleep outside with or without a blanket. This makes all the difference in the habits and character of the bushmen of the two countries. The frontier-man in Australia is careless, drawling, opulent in manner, and has a fervid tendency to tea and "swizzles." The former he takes at every meal when in the scrub, and on the plains at work; the latter he absorbs when he is in the vicinity of a bush pub, or in the township.

A few words of comparison here. A pub of Australia is a tavern or hotel in Canada; a township is a village; a stock-rider is a cow-boy; a humpy is a shanty; a warrigal or brombie is a broncho or cayuse; a sundowner is a tramp; a squatter is a rancher; and so on through an abundant list.

Canadian frontier-men have not had the luxury of hunting black-fellows as buffaloes were hunted on the great plains; they have not had the unwritten privilege granted to them by Government to "disperse" the blacks by fair means or foul. They have not as much sport as their Australian cousins. Then, again, they have not had to meet the same dangers and vicissitudes. Settlers in Canada are safe enough with Blackfoot, Cree, and Piegan. But a razed homestead or murdered family has too often met the eyes of the Australian frontier-man. It is then that he avails himself of the privilege of dispersion. The shepherd has been found speared beside his fire; the stock-rider nullah-nullahed in his blanket; or the boundary-rider brought down in his tracks; and that makes justice free of hand and short of shrift when it goes on a dispersion tour.

The Canadian has none of that. The Indian gives him little or no trouble, and his chief enemy is the cold. This cold makes him hardy, firm, and decisive in action. He is more alert, more temperate, and more subdued than the man of the back-blocks, as the up-country of Australia is called. Apart from murder, the worst thing that can happen to a Canadian is to be caught in a cold "snap," or a blizzard on the prairies. The worst thing that can chance to an Australian is to be caught in a salt-bush plain without water. I have counted scores of graves of "station-hunters"—lonely rail-girt graves—on the Tibbooburra track and in the Warrego country; poor wayfarers that crawled across an arid, furnace-like plain in search of water and a station. Perhaps the horse had died or became knocked-up, and its rider had drunk its blood to quench his thirst. The Canadian has an easier time than that, if he keeps his head level, and knows where he is going, and evades the storms and blizzards. But so few Canadian frontier-men do anything in winter that the peril is minimised. There is nothing to be feared, of course, in the woods, where wood-chopping is the occupation, and little in the hunt for moose, elk or caribou, or whatever may yet be left of Canadian wild animals since the buffalo departed. With some pine or spruce branches, a cellar-like hole in the snow, and a fire and blankets, he can fare well enough. He can even get along without a fire if he has plenty of evergreen trees near, and can tunnel a hole in the side of his snow-grave to be further protected. But what can protect the Australian from heat and thirst? The cold climate of Canada has really less of peril to the settler than that of Australia. And in the summer there is nothing more delightful than the prairies and mountains of the Dominion. At its worst, the prairies are less depressing than the grey and deathly salt-bush and quartz plains of Australia; at its best, Australia is never, except in some of the tropical parts, and in the Blue Mountains and Gipps-land Valleys, more beautiful than Canada. The Canadian rancher in districts such as Alberta turns his cattle and horses out to forage and grub for their winter living, and worries himself no more about them until they come back in the spring. Then, of course, begins the same "business" which occupies the mind of the Australian squatter the year round—hunting and dispersing, or bringing in wild cattle—called in Australia "clean-skins," because of having no branding mark—rounding-up, branding, driving, marketing, and selling.

There is much less of wild frontier life in Canada than Australia. The Canadian north-west is given up to agriculture and cattle ; and since the cattle-ranching is not nearly so developed as it is in the United States or Australia, the frontier population is smaller. In Australia there is added wool-growing and sugar-planting; and, since this is the staple production, bush life is on a much larger scale. Every little township in the heart of Australia is a rendezvous for the shepherd, the drover, the stock-rider, the sugar-cane worker, the squatter, and the planter. The shepherds and drovers are not always picturesque. A felt hat, wide in the brim, a shirt of blue or some neutral tint, a belt with a case-knife in it for killing sheep and cutting a meal, a loose jacket, and top boots, is the modest costume. As often as not laced boots and shoes are worn, the reason being that top boots, if they get wet, are difficult of use. The shepherd or drover is most picturesque when he is out on the plains, on, as it were, his native heath, among the myall, the mulga, the quondong, the stay-a-while, and the wattle trees ; where he sits by his little fire on the banks of some creek, and with his billy of tea and his dog muses and drones and philosophises with a deal of pessimism. The shepherd and boundary-rider of Australia is reserved almost to taciturnity. He knows a verse or two, or perhaps a couple of dozen of verses, of Adam Lindsay Gordon, the horseman poet of Australia, and he speaks by the card of that ill-fated philosopher. One will hear in the depths of the Australian wilds quotations from Gordon's "Roll of the Kettle-drum," or "The Sick Stock-rider," or " The Romance of Britomart." And stock-rider, and shepherd, and squatter, and planter are alike in this. It sorts with the sombre note of Australian scenery, and the melancholy effect it has upon the minds of those who are under its influence. I recall a ride over the waste plains of Australia in drought time. My companion had little to say till he was asked if Gordon hadn't lived in that part of the country at one time. Yes, was the reply; and then Jim the stock-rider told of a week he had with Gordon knocking down a cheque—not Gordon's cheque, for he, poor chap, had seldom one to treat so. And Jim, shaking his head, mournfully said, " He was a goer, my word! Saw him take a run with his horse across a split in the country, twelve feet wide, and he cleared it, so help me!" And then, as if talking to himself, Jim quoted from Gordon,—

> "I've had my share of pastime, and I've done my share of toil;
> And life is short, the longest life a span;
> I care not now to tarry for the corn or for the oil;
> Or the wine that maketh glad the heart of man."

Now that is the key-note to the character of the frontier-man of Australia: a sense of irresponsibility, a cavalier-like hopelessness, a riding the track of life for all that it is worth. And if not altogether so, still the pessimism remains with the best of them. The Canadian has not that. He does not go in for knocking down his cheque. The land he lives in may be severe in climate, but it is robust, invigorating, clear, and hope-giving. Cheeriness and courage are the things begotten by the climate of Canada and of the Western States of the American Union.

There is another feature of the frontier life in the two countries which is singular. It is the Mounted Police. In Canada this body is more like a military service than anything else, and has in it some of England's and Canada's best blood. In Australia the aboriginal is engaged in the service, and of course a place in it has not the savour which attaches to a position in the Canadian North-West Mounted Police, or the N.W.M.P., as it is called. But the work of both is much the same, with harder times for the Canadians. The winter duty is more than trying ; often it is cruel, solitary, and dangerous. There is no day in which the Australian cannot camp comfortably beneath the stars ; but the members of the N.W.M.P., with the thermometer at 40° below zero, have to forego the luxury of sleeping, many a night together. The Canadian police-soldier is more smartly dressed than the Australian of the same class. He is gay in scarlet and blue, and at drills looks quite like a Lancer. These sister-countries are both well protected by their police-soldiery, and the frontier-man takes justice in his own hands no longer. Hunting down cattle-stealers and marauders, and securing criminals, is now the work of " The Force." This is relieved along the border by interchange of courtesies with the Marshals of the United States, who reciprocate in the matter of capturing criminals, and in restoring lost cattle to that side of the line which they ought never to have left. The tokens are many that the days of frontier excitement on the two great continents, America and Australia, are numbered. The buffalo-hunt is no more, and the kangaroo-battues are growing less. Those endless narrow trails upon the prairie tell of the one ; but there will soon be nothing at all to tell of the other—neither trail nor tail. And with the going of wild game goes the wild life ; and the frontier-man in both these lands will, in another twenty years, be robbed of his picturesqueness and of much of his distinctive character. But he is still a figure for the romancist, the poet, and the historian.

And my pleasant task is done.

GLOSSARY.

baal . . . an aboriginal expression of disapproval.
back-blocks . . the far interior of the country.
banksia . . a vine and flower.
billy . . . a small tin pail for boiling tea.
bingey . . . belly.
black-birder . a kidnapper of natives.
black-fellow . aboriginal.
black-tracker . aboriginal employed in tracking criminals.
boundary-rider . a mounted station-hand who watches the boundaries of a station property, fences, etc.
brigalow . . a rough scrub-tree.
brogmanshia . a flowering vine.
brombie . . a wild horse that has been tamed.
brownie . . a kind of currant loaf.
buck-board . . a buggy without springs.
bunya-bunya . a tropical tree.

chinkie . . . Chinaman.
cockatoo-farmer . a settler with a very small farm.
coil . . . sleep.
coo-ĕ-ĕ . . . the "halloo" call of the back-blocks.
cornstalk . . a name for the rural Australian.
corrobboree . . the dance of the black-fellows.
country-rock . the ordinary stone of the country.

damper . a large scone of flour and water baked in hot ashes.
dead-finish . . a rough scrub-tree.
dingo . . . the wild dog of Australia.

GLOSSARY.

flame-tree . . a tree with a bright coral-like flower.

gidja . . . a tree of the scrub species.
goin' bung . . becoming bankrupt.
gunyah . . a black-fellow's hut of twigs and bark.

"*humpin' their bluey*" . . carrying their swag or chattels.
humpy . . . a black fellow's hut; gunyah.

Jackeroo . . a new chum working on a station.
jarrah . . . a hard-wood tree.

"*knocking down his cheque*" . spending the cheque got for shearing.

larrikin . . the young rough of the country. Owes its origin to a sergeant of police who described some youthful prisoners as being guilty of "larrikin round," *i.e.* larking round.
laughing-jackass a bird (the mopoke) with a shrill call or cackle.
lubra . . . an aboriginal woman; a gin.

mallee . . . a hard-wood tree.
mulga . .. . a hard-wood tree.
myall . . . a sweet-smelling hard-wood tree.

new chum . . one who is new to the country.
nulla-nulla . . a battle club.

picking out the eyes of land . to pick out the best spots.
puntie . . . a scrub plant.

quart-pot . . a small tin pail or billy.
quondong . . a wild bush with a small red or yellow apple.

rounding-up . getting the cattle gathered together.
rouseabout . . the lowest of the station hands; a Jack-of-all-work.

GLOSSARY. 447

salt-bush	the wild alkaline bush of the plains on which horses and sheep feed when the grass is gone.
selector	one who takes small portions of land for farming or settlement, and who may select land for this purpose on a squatter's station leased from the Government.
Shearers' Joy	a name given to colonial beer.
shirallee	a swag; or bundle of blankets, etc.
shot me dead	discharged me.
station	the squatter's homestead.
stay-a-while	a tangled bush, sometimes called wait-a-while.
sundowner	a tramp; given the name because he generally appeared at stations at nightfall.
swag	bundle of blankets, etc., to be carried on the back.
swizzle	a drink of liquor.
to dummy	to take advantage of the land-law by paying another to occupy land.
to shout	to treat or stand liquor.
tucker	food.
wait-a-while	see *stay-a-while*.
wallaby	a young kangaroo.
wallaby track	on the tramp.
warrigal	a wild dog, wild horse; anything aboriginal.
wurley	a black-fellow's house; humpy; gunyah.

Printed by Hazell, Watson, & Viney, Ld., London and Aylesbury.

MESSRS. HUTCHINSON & CO.'S
New Works on
AUSTRALIA & NEW ZEALAND.

HUTCHINSON'S
Australasian Encyclopædia
(Including NEW ZEALAND),
COMPRISING
AN ALPHABETICAL DESCRIPTION OF ALL PLACES IN THE AUSTRALASIAN COLONIES, AN ACCOUNT OF THE EVENTS WHICH HAVE TAKEN PLACE IN AUSTRALASIA FROM ITS DISCOVERY TO THE PRESENT DATE, ITS NATURAL HISTORY, SCENERY, RESOURCES, LAWS, CONSTITUTION, AND STATISTICS, AND BIOGRAPHIES OF DISCOVERERS, EXPLORERS, OFFICIALS, AND COLONISTS, FROM THE EARLIEST DATES TO 1855.

By GEORGE COLLINS LEVEY,
Companion of St. Michael and George; Commander of the Crown of Italy; Chevalier of the Legion of Honour, etc., etc.
Author of the "Handy Guides to Australasia and the River Plate," etc

In Crown 8vo, half leather, gilt, 7s. 6d. net.

The student, politician, or man of letters who desires to obtain information about Australasia, has to consult a large number of works of reference, if indeed he can by any means obtain what he seeks. The articles in the existing Encyclopædias are generally incomplete, and are all more or less out of date; while the contributions to Australogy by Blair, Henniker Heaton, and others, although extremely valuable, usually touch upon only one branch of the subject, are to a considerable extent out of date, and are not generally available.

The AUSTRALASIAN ENCYCLOPÆDIA will give all necessary knowledge about Australia and New Zealand in a complete, although succinct form, and it is hoped and believed that the book will supply a want which has been long felt in Great Britain and the Australasian Colonies.

LONDON: 25, PATERNOSTER SQUARE, E.C.

HUTCHINSON & CO., PUBLISHERS.

New Works on Australia and New Zealand—*continued.*

EDITED BY PHILIP MENNELL, F.R.G.S.

The Australasian Dictionary of Biography.

(Including NEW ZEALAND and FIJI.)

COMPRISING NOTICES OF EMINENT COLONISTS FROM THE INAUGURATION OF RESPONSIBLE GOVERNMENT DOWN TO THE PRESENT TIME (1855-1892).

By PHILIP MENNELL, F.R.G.S.,

Assisted by Eminent Colonists.

In crown 8vo, half leather and cloth gilt, 10s. 6d. *net.*

It is proposed to afford in handy form information respecting Australasian men and women of mark. The AUSTRALASIAN DICTIONARY OF BIOGRAPHY will discharge the twofold purpose of perpetuating the memory of deceased notabilities and of recording the careers of the living. It is intended to re-issue the work periodically; and the price will, it is hoped, secure for it a wide circulation and a permanent place as a work of general reference.

BY G. COLLINS LEVEY, C.M.G.

A Handy Guide to Australasia.

(Including NEW ZEALAND and FIJI.)

Its Resources, Finances, and Physical Features; together with a Complete List of the Mercantile Houses of Great Britain doing Business with Australasia, the Tariffs of the various Colonies, etc., etc. With Maps.

Crown 8vo, cloth, 2s. 6d.

LONDON: 25, PATERNOSTER SQUARE, E.C.

HUTCHINSON & CO., PUBLISHERS.

New Works on Australia and New Zealand—*continued.*

The Web of the Spider.
A Story of New Zealand Adventure.
By H. B. MARRIOTT WATSON,
Author of "Marahuna," "Lady Faintheart," etc.
Crown 8vo, in cloth gilt, 6s.

AN AUSTRALIAN "UNCLE TOM'S CABIN."
SEVENTH THOUSAND.

The Black Police: A Story of Modern Australia.
By A. J. VOGAN.
With Map and Illustrations by the Author.
Crown 8vo, cloth gilt, 5s.; or in paper boards, 2s.

BY HELEN MATHERS.   POPULAR EDITION.

Sam's Sweetheart: An Australian Novel.
By HELEN MATHERS (Mrs. HENRY REEVES),
Author of "Comin' Thro' the Rye," "Cherry Ripe," etc.
In crown 8vo, cloth gilt, gilt top, 2s. 6d.; or in picture boards, 2s.

BY SIR JULIUS VOGEL, K.C.M.G.
FOURTH EDITION OF

Anno Domini 2000; or, Woman's Destiny.
By SIR JULIUS VOGEL, K.C.M.G..
Crown 8vo, cloth gilt, gilt top, 2s. 6d.; paper boards, 2s.

The *Daily News*, in a leading article, says: "Everybody wants to know something about the year 2000, or something about the destiny of woman, and most persons would be glad to know a little about both. The volume is interesting from its cover onwards. 'A.D. 2000' is a dream, but a dream with a purpose. It is one of those fascinating forecasts of the perfectibility of man which are apt to beguile the leisure of the sluggard of intelligence."

LONDON: 25, PATERNOSTER SQUARE, E.C.

HUTCHINSON & CO., PUBLISHERS.

The Fate of Fenella.

The Most Extraordinary Novel of Modern Times. Every chapter has been written by a Well-known Writer of Fiction, without consulting his or her collaborateurs, the result being a remarkable and intensely interesting novel and literary curiosity. The Authors are:—

Helen Mathers.	Mrs. Lovett Cameron.	Adeline Sergeant.
Justin H. M'Carthy.	Bram Stoker.	G. Manville Fenn.
Mrs. Trollope.	Florence Marryat.	Jean Middlemass.
A. Conan Doyle.	Frank Danby.	H. W. Lucy.
May Crommelin.	Mrs. Edward Kennard.	Clement Scott.
F. C. Phillips.	Richard Dowling.	"Tasma."
"Rita."	Mrs. Hungerford.	F. Anstey.
Joseph Hatton.	Arthur A'Beckett.	

By the Australian Artist, MISS MARGARET THOMAS.

A Scamper through Spain and Tangier.

With numerous Illustrations by the Author.
Demy 8vo, 12s.

BY PROFESSOR CHURCH.

Pictures from Roman Life and Story.

Crown 8vo, cloth gilt, 5s. With Illustrations.

DEDICATED TO HER MAJESTY THE QUEEN.

A Memoir of Admiral of the Fleet Sir Provo Wallis, G.C.B.

With Letters, Photogravure Portraits, Illustrations, and Charts.
By J. G. BRIGHTON, M.D.,
Author of "Life of Admiral Sir P. Broke," etc.
Demy 8vo, cloth gilt, 16s.

"One of the most delightful books of literary and artistic gossip ever printed."
—*Liverpool Mercury.*

Cigarette Papers: an After-Dinner Chat.

By JOSEPH HATTON,
Author of "By Order of the Czar," "Clytie," etc. With 80 Illustrations by C. Raven Hill, A. J. Finberg, J. L. Sclanders, and John Wallace.
Crown 8vo, cloth gilt, 6s.

CHEAP EDITION.

The Princess Mazaroff.

By JOSEPH HATTON,
Author of "By Order of the Czar," etc.
Crown 8vo, cloth, 3s. 6d.

LONDON: 25, PATERNOSTER SQUARE, E.C.

www.ingramcontent.com/pod-product-compliance
Lightning Source LLC
Chambersburg PA
CBHW032001300426
44117CB00008B/862